The Lost Cities of Africa

The Lost Cities of Africa

BASIL DAVIDSON

With photographs, maps, and line drawings

an atlantic monthly press book

little, brown and company

boston/toronto

For copies of rock engravings at Tondia I am indebted to
M. Raymond Mauny, Director of Archaeology at the Institut de
L'Afrique Noire, Dakar, who made them and has generously
allowed me to reproduce them.

I am indebted to Dr. Gertrude Caton-Thompson and the Clar-
endon Press for permission to reproduce the drawing of stone
steps at Great Zimbabwe.

ATLANTIC–LITTLE, BROWN BOOKS
ARE PUBLISHED BY
LITTLE, BROWN AND COMPANY
IN ASSOCIATION WITH
THE ATLANTIC MONTHLY PRESS

to
Gervase Mathew
and
Thomas Hodgkin

And when some thoughtful spirit in the future shall wish to write this history as it should be written, may this work in some fashion serve him, rough and disordered though it be.

GIOVANNI-BATTISTA RAMUSIO IN 1563

If a man will begin with certainties he shall end in doubts: but if he will be content to begin with doubts he shall end in certainties.

FRANCIS BACON

Introduction

The Rediscovery of Africa

A LITTLE OVER A HUNDRED AND FIFTY YEARS AGO A YOUNG SCOTS surgeon named Mungo Park, more dead than alive from months of quenching travel, rode through Saharan sand and thorn into the remote city of Segu on the upper reaches of the river Niger.

"Looking forwards," he would write, "I saw with infinite pleasure the great object of my mission — the long sought-for majestic Niger, glittering to the morning sun, as broad as the Thames at Westminster, and flowing slowly *to the eastward.*"

The italics were his own, and they were understandably triumphant. Ever since Ptolemy, sixteen centuries before, men had written on maps that the Niger flowed to the westward. Arabs of the Middle Ages, true enough, had known the middle course of the Niger for what it really was; but Europe, newly considering Africa in times of mercantile expansion, could be sure of nothing of its geography but the outline of the coast, and a little, here and there, of the obscure lands beyond.

"The course of the Niger, the places of its rise and termination, and even its existence as a separate stream are still undetermined," declared the prospectus of the African Association, founded in London in 1790 for "Promoting the Discovery of the Interior Parts of Africa," and it resolved that one of its explorers "should ascertain the course, and if possible, the rise and termination of that river."

Mungo Park perished on the Niger before he could plot its course to the sea, but others followed. Within seventy years or so the main geographical facts were fixed and clear upon the continental map, and one misconception after another was corrected, one zone of ignorance after another filled with detail. African discovery took its place among the triumphs of the nineteenth century. The geographical myths and legends disappeared; in place of these, mapmakers could record the knowledge of sand and swamp, forest and savannah, snow-capped mountain range and bracing highland that the discoverers had won.

A similar process of discovery is now occurring, about a hundred years later, in the field of African history. Historians and archeologists — British, French, African, Italian, Belgian, American — have embarked on journeys of historical discovery that parallel the geographical ventures of Park and Clapperton, Caillié and Barth, Livingstone, Stanley, and so many more. What the nineteenth century achieved for the geography of Africa the twentieth is well towards achieving for its history; and once again the truth these pioneers are finding has proved, often enough, the reverse of what the outside world had generally believed.

Thus the chart of African history, so lately bare and empty and misleading as the maps once were, begins to glow with illuminating detail. Bearded monsters and "men whose heads do grow beneath their shoulders" begin to disappear; and humanity, in all its smallness and its greatness, begins to emerge. And it begins to be seen, if fleetingly and partially as yet, that the writing of African history is not only possible and useful, but will be as well a work of rediscovery — the rediscovery of African humanity.

The Negro, many have believed, is a man without a past. Black Africa — Africa south of the Sahara desert — is on this view a continent where men by their own efforts have never raised themselves much above the level of the beasts. "No ingenious manufactures among them, no arts, no sciences," commented David Hume. "No approach to the civilisation of his white fellow creatures whom he imitates as a monkey does a man," added Trollope. Even within the last ten years a former Governor of Nigeria could write that "for countless centuries, while all the pageant of history swept by, the African remained unmoved — in primitive savagery." Even in 1958 Sir Arthur Kirby, Commissioner for British East Africa in London, could tell the Torquay Branch of the Overseas League that "in the last sixty years — little more than the lifetime of some people in this room — East Africa has developed from a completely primitive country, in many ways more backward than the Stone Age . . ."

Africans, on this view, had never evolved civilizations of their own; if they possessed a history, it could be scarcely worth the telling. And this belief that Africans had lived in universal chaos or stagnation until the coming of Europeans seemed not only to find its justification in a thousand tales of savage misery and benighted ignorance; it was also, of course, exceedingly convenient in high imperial times. For it could be argued (and it was; indeed, it still is) that these peoples, history-less, were naturally inferior or else they were "children who had still to grow up"; in either case they were manifestly in need of government by others who had grown up.

This view of African achievement, or lack of achievement, is now with increasing knowledge seen to rest on no more solid a foundation in truth than that earlier belief about the Niger's flowing to the westward. Geographical discovery has proved that the Niger really flows to the eastward. Historical discovery is now proving that the development and growth of society and civilization in Africa really contradict this stereotype of "centuries-long stagnation." The world is changing its mind about the past of Africa.

What can be said about this past — about the formative fifteen or twenty centuries, that is, before European discovery and conquest? What can be said and what, where present knowledge fails, is it reasonable to believe? This book is an attempt — necessarily tentative, summarized, and selective — to answer these questions against a background of the whole of Africa south of the Sahara.

It relies, of course, on the work of many specialists in many fields; and those who are curious to pursue the subject further, or to check its references, will find a list of principal sources at the end. Though I have tried to be faithful to the evidence, the ambiguous nature of some of this evidence may have involved, here and there, mistakes of fact and emphasis. My belief is that these are few enough to leave the general picture both clear and reasonable.

The outline of African growth over the past fifteen hundred years or so is still unsure at many points. Much remains unknown; much may yet prove unknowable. Neat generalizations about a continent so wide and various will usually be wrong. Yet the central fact which stands forth from the work of many historians and archeologists over the past ten or twenty years is that much more is known, and much more can be said with a fair assurance of being right, than was generally suspected or thought possible. These last few years, in short, have uncovered much African history; and this book may be regarded, I hope, as a useful "situation report" on many and exciting finds.

I have tried to steer between the rock of prejudice and the whirlpool of romance. Inquiries into the African past have suffered from both; and of many writers who have tried to go safely between them, discouragingly few have managed to succeed. Those who have gone down in the whirlpool of romance are of two kinds. Some have thought it wise and necessary to fill their charts of the African past with tales of Sheba and Ophir, of strange Phoenicians building cities in Rhodesia, and mysterious peoples "from the north" who came and stayed but altogether vanished. These are the modern versions of bearded monsters and of men "whose heads do grow beneath their shoulders"; and a better understanding of the subject is gently but firmly erasing them from the map.

Other romantics, moved by a sentiment that may be more

generous but is no more scientific, have come to grief through writing "high civilizations" into the continental African past where evidence for them is entirely lacking. Africa south of the Sahara contributed in no small measure to the great civilizations of the Nile Valley; but south of the Nile Valley it no more enjoyed in antiquity what modern convention has agreed to call a high civilization than did northern Europe or northern America, and for reasons, perhaps, which may not be altogether different from one another. To say this is not to diminish the human achievement in continental Africa, but to place it in its true perspective; for that achievement, when seen against its formative background and measured by its civilizing growth, was great and noble in its own right, and needs no romanticizing gilt to make it seem so.

On the opposite side there are those who have shipwrecked themselves on the rock of prejudice: the rock, in this case, of an unremitting skepticism. It is an old and hoary rock, mute and menacing, and covered with the debris of sad reputations. Exactly a hundred years ago, on returning from long travels in northern and western Africa, Heinrich Barth, who was surely the most intelligent of all the nineteenth century travelers in Africa, and sailed these historical narrows with a mastery and brilliance that none has yet repeated, gave it a passing word.

"Any writer," he warily remarked, "who attempts to recall from obscurity and oblivion the past ages of an illiterate nation, and to lay before the public even the most elementary sketch of its history, will probably have to contend against the strong prejudice of numerous critics, who are accustomed to refuse belief to whatever is incapable of strictest enquiry." Sensible and farseeing when they were written, these words retain their application to the writing of African history in our own day, although skeptics are less numerous and self-assured than they were a hundred years ago.

Let me carefully assert, therefore, that much has still to be learned of the African past. No definitive outline will be possible for a long time. "We are discovering new things," Mathew could tell the second London conference on African history and archeology in 1957, "every six months." Wide gaps persist. Whole territories remain to be explored. Many findings are in hot debate. The word "probably" should be read into these pages more often than it is actually written there.

Yet when all such reservations are made — and they ought to be made, even when for readability's sake I have omitted to repeat them — there remains the stuff and substance of a solid and reliable beginning. Though not definitive, the outline is tolerably firm and clear. And what this new outline suggests is something neither "inferior" nor "mysterious" but a story of success and failure, disaster and resurgence and fulfillment, which is no different in its essence from the story of any of the major families of man. This rediscovery of Africa goes indeed toward the recognition of the essential unity of the peoples of Africa with the peoples of the rest of the world. The "lost islands" of African humanity are joined to the main.

To the grandchildren of the skeptics whom Heinrich Barth had in mind this may seem a fragile claim. So I have set my course by a conservative estimate of the archeological record and refrained from speculation except here and there, where the text will make it plain. Wherever authorities have differed or still greatly differ among themselves I have stated differences so that the reader may have both views — or several views — before him. This is therefore the right place to acknowledge my debt to many authorities: to those who have gone out of their way to help me, by conversation or correspondence, with advice and criticism and information not yet published — none of which, of course, makes them responsible for what I have written; and to those, as well, who have allowed me to borrow their photographs. I hope they will bear with my failings and believe that I have done the best I could with the patient help they have given me. Should any of them chance to read this book and find some virtue in it, they may safely regard this virtue as a tribute to their pioneering labors.

The Lost Cities of Africa

This book is about Africa and Africans south of the Sahara Desert, during the fifteen hundred years or so before the colonial period began.

Its aim is to present in outline what is now known and what it now seems reasonable to believe about some leading aspects and achievements of African life and civilization during that time, and thus to contribute to an understanding of the origins and background of Africa today.

It is founded on the work of scholars and specialists over many years, but mainly over the last ten or twenty years — especially fruitful as these have been for the archeology and history of Africa.

Contents

Illustrations

one

The Peopling of Ancient Africa

. . . the land shadowing with wings which is beyond the rivers of Ethiopia. . . .

Isaiah 18:1

1 The Possibility of African History

SOME FIFTY YEARS AGO, IN A CLEARING OF the Congo forest, a Belgian sat making notes. For the time and place this Belgian, whose name was Emil Torday, was an unusual sort of man, an unusual sort of European. What he wanted was neither rubber nor ivory nor conscript labor, but information about the past.

And he had come far in search of it. After traveling for many hundred miles up the Congo River from its Atlantic mouth he had continued on his way into the heart of Africa. He had traveled up the Kasai River and then along the banks of the Sankuru, and now, somewhere in the dense green middle of an Africa that was almost completely unknown to the outside world, he had reached the Bushongo people, and sat listening to their chiefs and making notes.

For the benefit of this European, one of the first they had ever set eyes on, the elders of the Bushongo recalled the legend and tradition of their past. That was not in the least difficult for them, since remembering the past was one of their duties. They unrolled their story in measured phrases. They went on and on. They were not to be hurried. They traversed the list of their kings, a list of one hundred and twenty names, right back to the god-king whose marvels had founded their nation.

It was splendid, but was it history? Could any of these kings be given a date, be linked — at least in time — to the history of the rest of the world? Torday was an enthusiast and went on making notes, but he longed for a date. And quite suddenly they gave it to him.

"As the elders were talking of the great events of various reigns," he remembered afterwards, "and we came to the ninety-eighth chief, Bo Kama Bomanchala, they said that nothing remarkable had happened during his reign, except that one day at noon the sun went out, and there was absolute darkness for a short time.

"When I heard this I lost all self-control. I jumped up and wanted to do something desperate. The elders thought that I had been stung by a scorpion.

"It was only months later that the date of the eclipse became known to me . . . the thirtieth of March, 1680, when there was a total eclipse of the sun, passing exactly over Bushongo . . .

"There was no possibility of confusion with another eclipse, because this was the only one visible in the region during the seventeenth and eighteenth centuries."

Torday's achievement was to reveal the *possibility* of African history in the centuries — the protohistoric centuries — before written documents occur. It is with these centuries that this book is largely concerned, and it will be seen that much has been learned since Torday's pioneering fifty years ago.

But the scene demands a little setting in the further past. What can be said, if anything, about the remote beginnings of mankind in Africa — about the earliest men or manlike creatures of the dawn of prehistory?

Manlike apes lived in Africa a million years ago. More and more of their fossils have turned up over the last forty years or so. Were they manlike apes or apelike men? It is still an open question, for the "missing link" between the common ancestors of apes and men, and the creature which prepared the way for Homo sapiens, has yet to be identified.

There are several strong contenders in the field, represented by fossils which have come, mainly, from South Africa and East Africa. Of several different types, these ancient animals — whether nearer to apes or nearer to men in terms of evolution — were undoubtedly proto-men of one kind or another. In Professor Raymond Dart's illuminating phrase, they "trembled on the brink of humanity."

They stood "in respect of brain size, manufacture of tools and knowledge of fire," says Dart, "on the very threshold of humanity. Whether they crossed that threshold is the enigma for future anthropology; but it is a puzzle in the human story to which Africa doubtless holds the answer."

That Africa may hold the answer to the earliest development of man himself is also suggested by evidence from East Africa. Finds in East Africa, mainly in Uganda and Kenya, not only include the earliest evidence yet available of Homo sapiens, thus leading to a claim by some anthropologists, so far not denied, that Africa was the cradle of humanity: these finds suggest as well that Homo sapiens developed not only from less successful and since vanished types of humanity, such as Neanderthal Man, but also from his own specific and as yet unrevealed line of evolution.

What dates can one hope to apply? There is no point in trying to divide prehistoric time into years, for the years stretch out to thousands and to millions until they evade the liveliest imagination. All that can be done is to try and define some of the milestones on that remotely echoing trail; but even this, considering the difficulties, makes a remarkable and as yet uncertain feat of prehistoric detection.

Prehistorians have lately reached tentative agreement on a probable sequence of climatic changes in East Africa, and such is the richness of the evidence they have even tried to establish a correlation between this sequence and climatic changes in other parts of Africa, as well as in Europe. They distinguish four main pluvials or rainy periods in East Africa over the last half-million years or so; and these, they believe, were probably coincidental with the four main Ice Ages, or glaciations, of Europe. Their principal reason for thinking that Homo sapiens occurred first of all in Africa is that stone tools have been recovered from deposits laid down during the earliest of these pluvials, whereas stone tools in Europe turn up only much later in the long sequence of "glacials" and "interglacials." Thus tools found in Uganda are the oldest tools ever found anywhere.

These four pluvials of East Africa are called — after the sites from which their tools or fossilized evidence was taken — Kageran, Kamasian, Kanjeran, and Gamblian. But it is only in Gamblian times — beginning, perhaps, some twelve or fourteen thousand years ago — that the story begins to make much sense. By Gamblian times, however, Homo sapiens was not only well established as an inhabitant of East Africa (and of other parts of Africa), he was well into the Old Stone Age and was practically, by pluvial standards, a modern man. He had, as it were, long since ceased to worry about his rivals, whom he had survived; or even about his enemies, whom he had learned to kill or trap or even domesticate. Sometime during this last pluvial there disappeared from Africa the last manlike rivals of man as we know him — Neanderthal Man, Rhodesian Man, and others caught in evolutionary stagnation. From now onward, though often with tremendous gaps, the story of Stone Age humanity takes on coherent shape. The foundations were securely laid, the successfully adaptable human type was firmly fixed.

Thereafter it has remained for humanity to develop the potentialities within itself, to migrate and multiply and populate the earth.

2 *Lines of Migration*

IN TERMS OF GEOLOGICAL TIME, MAN'S MULTIPLICATION IN AFRICA — as elsewhere — began only yesterday. Yet in terms of decades and millennia it began so long ago that the routes it took and the conditions that promoted it belong only to the realm of intelligent guesswork.

What were they like, those men and women of Gamblian times? They were probably unlike any people now surviving in Africa, with the possible and partial exception of the Bushmen of the Kalahari and the Pygmies of the Congo. Perhaps they were the lineal ancestors of those lithe hunters of small stature and, to us, strange physiognomy; perhaps they belonged to a racial type which anthropologists call Bush-Boskop, or, nicely evading any suggestion of certainty, boskopoid. However that may be, they spread and multiplied and held their ground, and traces of them have been found in many regions of the continent.

Some time around 5000 B.C. new types of humanity appeared in Africa. The Negro, or Negroid, type was prominent among these. His earliest remains have come, so far, from much the same African latitude: a fossilized skull and some other fragments from a Middle Stone Age site near Khartoum in the Sudan, and another skull and some bones from beneath thick clay at Asselar, some two hundred miles northeast of Timbuktu in the western Sudan.

These people, these "Negroes" (for neat racial pigeonholes have little application here), undoubtedly multiplied in the years after about 5000 B.C. An analysis of some eight hundred skulls from pre-dynastic Egypt — that is, from the lower valley of the Nile before about 3000 B.C. — shows that at least a third of them were Negroes or ancestors of the Negroes whom we know; and this may well support the view to which a study of language also brings some confirmation, that remote ancestors of the Africans of today were an important and perhaps dominant element among populations which fathered the civilization of ancient Egypt.

The year 1958, as it happens, brought vivid illumination to an otherwise meager record. A French explorer of the Sahara, Henri Lhote, returned to Paris with a wonderful collection of copies of rock paintings and engravings. His exhibition of these was a memorable affair.

For here was human history on the grand style, tier after tier of Saharan styles that told of a bewildering succession of different peoples through uncounted millennia, ranging from marvelously sensitive pictures of animals to no less sensitive portraits — the word is not too strong — of men and women; from scenes of wheeled warfare to scenes of pastoral peace; from gods and goddesses that surely came from ancient Egypt to masks and figures that just as surely did not. Many of them were the work of Negro peoples in a time that was probably not long before, or not long after, 4000 B.C.

From such evidence as this the empty centuries enlarge and echo with forgotten peoples. It had earlier been thought — and the opinion is useful to an understanding of the complexity which accompanied this peopling of ancient Africa — that the Sahara had known four main periods of habitation during its time of fertility. The earliest of these had been a hunting people, who were eventually followed by a cattle-keeping people, and these last, or their successors, had acquired horses around 1200 B.C. Into this bare outline Lhote has now poured a wealth of new evidence which brings it suddenly and wonderfully to life. Basing himself on recognizable variations of painting and engraving style, he suggests no fewer than sixteen different phases of occupation between the time of the hunting people and the time of the cattle-keeping people — "a fact," he says, "that is astonishing and revolutionary, since it was unthinkable until now that the Sahara could have known so many different populations."

This reminder of exceeding complication in the peopling of the old Sahara — and, of course, not only of the old Sahara — is useful when one looks at the difficulty of tracing where the lines of African migration really went, and what kinds of humanity really followed them. Bushmen, very rare in modern Africa, may represent the only close link with the "boskopoid" populations of remote antiquity. Negroes are undoubtedly another ancient African stock. But the story does not end with these and their permutations. There has long been present in Africa another human type, lumped together today mainly on a linguistic basis but originally possessing characteristics that were neither boskopoid nor Negro. These are called Hamites.

These Hamites have a "white" morphology. They go back, it seems, to the "Caucasian" stocks which also produced most Europeans, although so long ago that any reading of modern "white and black" into ancient Hamite and Negro would be singularly meaningless; and in Africa they are customarily divided by anthropologists into two great branches, eastern Hamites and northern Hamites. Their beginnings in Africa are as unknown as the beginnings of the Negroes. Like the Negroes, they may have occurred first in Africa or they may have occurred first in Asia and come to Africa by migration. It is anybody's guess. In a recent letter to the writer Dr. L. S. B. Leakey, whose great authority as an anthropologist in Africa gives special weight to his uncertainty on this point, suggests that Negroes followed Hamites into East Africa. "My own guess, but it is only a guess, and has no better foundation than other speculations, is that a Hamitic people were developing in East Africa from about 5000 B.C. onwards, and that at a much later date a Negro invasion resulted in the half-Hamite and, just possibly, also in the Bantu."

Whatever may have been the true precedence of migration, there is little doubt that the mingling of Bushman (or "boskopoid") and Negro and Hamite produced, at some more or less distant time in the past, the ancestors of a majority of modern Africans. Thus the Hottentots of southern Africa appear to have come from a mingling of Bushman and Hamite. The numerous and multiplying peoples of Bantu language group appear to be a mingling of Negro and Hamite and now and then of Bushman too. And there are plenty of other possible or probable combinations. If later types of Hamite today occupy much of the northeast of continental Africa, and peoples of the Bantu language group predominate in the southern half of the continent, while "pure Negroes" appear most often in western Africa, the distinctions are largely those of language and anthropological convention. They imply little as to precedence of ancient migration and settlement, and nothing at all as to "inferiority" or "superiority."

The point is worth emphasizing if only because an imagined superiority of Hamite over Negro — read white over black — has often been, and sometimes still is, what Mr. Justice Holmes* in quite another connection once called "the inarticulate major premise." This premise has no foundation in the facts, neither for ancient Africa nor for relatively modern Africa. Evolution and development in Africa, as elsewhere, have their major key not in racial but environmental circumstance; and there is nothing in the world to show or suggest that Negroes, had they lived in North Africa instead of Central Africa, would not have "done as well" — or as "ill" — as the largely Hamitic Egyptians and Berbers of the Nile Valley and the Mediterranean shore. Later on in history, as it happens, Hamitic cattle-keepers would invade an East Africa that was largely agricultural and largely Negroid or boskopoid or a mixture of both; and would impose a more backward system of society on a more advanced one.

Yet the myth of "Hamitic superiority," veiling as it generally has an "inarticulate major premise" that Negroes are a naturally

* In his dissenting judgment on Lochner v. New York, U.S. Supreme Court, 1905.

inferior people, dies hard. Only the other day an otherwise serious anthropological student of East Africa, when describing remains of a primitive people found in Kenya, recorded that they might be Hamitic except that it was "difficult to see why a civilized people such as the Hamites should have lived at this altitude," which was about as sensible as saying that a civilized people like the Irish should not have lived in bogs. It was not their race which enabled the Irish — or this or that people in Africa — to civilize themselves, but the varying conditions of environment.

There is another reason for insisting on this point. Time and again the achievements of men in Africa — men *of* Africa — have been laid at the door of some mysterious but otherwise unexplained "people from outside Africa." It is not only the Hamites who have given scope for the "inarticulate major premise" of an inherent African (or Negro) inferiority. Over the past fifty years or so, whenever anything remarkable or inexplicable has turned up in Africa, a whole galaxy of non-African (or at any rate non-Negro) peoples are dragged in to explain it. The Phoenicians are brought in to explain Zimbabwe in Rhodesia. The Egyptians are produced as the painters of the "white lady" of the Brandberg in southwest Africa. Greeks or Portuguese are paraded as the inspirers and teachers of those who worked in terra cotta and in bronze in medieval West Africa. Even the Hittites have had their day. Yet every one of these achievements and phenomena is now generally agreed to have had a purely African origin.

The problems of backwardness and progress — even when and where these really exist, and are more than the illusion of Euro-pocentric frames of thought — cannot be explained along these simple lines. They cannot be explained along any racial lines. Environment, not race, provides the key. And that is why it will be found that even when African peoples have taken much from outside, at different times and places, their process of borrowing — whether of techniques or beliefs — has always undergone an adaptation, through environment and circumstance, into societies and cultures and civilizations which became specifically and uniquely African. Achievement and failure can alike be traced to the same complex and endlessly interesting source: the interplay of men and their environment.

3 *The Desert Barrier*

SOME TIME BEFORE THE FOURTH MILLENNIUM B.C. THE SAHARA began to lose its green fertility. Its great rivers, running southward to the Niger and eastward to the Nile — their arid beds may still be traced in fruitless outline — began to dwindle and perish. Its lakes began to disappear. Its peoples began to migrate elsewhere.

There is plenty of evidence for this long, disastrous change. Those earliest Stone Age Negroes of Khartoum — they who laid foundations for much of the civilization of the Nile and manufactured pots even before pots were made in Jericho, earliest of the world's known cities — lived beside a river which rose in flood between twelve and thirty feet higher than it does today.

They used barbed spearheads of bone that were later supplanted by beautifully precise harpoons with three or more barbs and a perforation through the butt; and the nearest parallels to these harpoons of the Nile Valley occur at sites in the Wadi Azaouak, two thousand miles to the westward across the grim Sahara that we know today. Even as late as the third millennium large numbers of cattle are known to have found grazing in lower Nubia where, as Arkell says, "desert conditions are so severe today that the owner of an ox-driven water-wheel has difficulty in keeping one or two beasts alive throughout the year." And anyone who has traveled in these dusty latitudes will have noticed how the wilderness of sand and rock that lies to the west of the Nile, far out upon the empty plains, is scored with ancient wadi beds which must once have carried a steady seasonal flow of water, but are now as dry as the desert air.

The immediate reasons for this long and ruthless desiccation, which is still going on, are unknown; they belong, clearly enough, to the same grand order of events which pushed the equator southward through the ages, governed the advancing and retreating ice, and set the course of storm and cyclone in prehistoric times. The important point, at any event, is that the Sahara began to offer a major barrier to human passage some five or six thousand years ago — at about the same time, that is, as Negro peoples began to move and multiply, and North Africa began to develop settled agriculture. In thus stretching a barrier to human contact between the lands to the north and the lands to the south, this Saharan wilderness would deeply influence the course of human development in Africa.

North of this worsening desert there was intense and seldom interrupted contact between all the developing societies and civilizations of North Africa, the Middle East, and the Mediterranean. South of the desert there was more or less unrestricted movement throughout the continental mainland, so that Negro or Negroid people are found today in almost every part of it. But the south and the north were increasingly divided from one another. They developed apart. They developed differently.

This broad truth is subject to reservations. Contact between north and south was never completely severed. Raiding and trading and migration routes led southward from the Fezzan to the Niger, or coastwise down the Red Sea and round the eastern horn of Africa. Carthage traded down the western coast, though Phoenician secrecy has stopped posterity from knowing how much or how far. Horses and chariots were common in the Sahara for several centuries after about 1200 B.C., and later on there was the camel. Yet the trails across the desert were forbiddingly hard to follow, and long and hazardous. Even medieval Arabs, riding across the Sahara from established well to well, would need two months for the journey, and many who set forth would never reach their goal.

This is not to say, of course, that without the desiccation of the Sahara the growth of human society in continental Africa would have followed a Mediterranean pattern. This vast and various continent must always and in any case have developed irregularly, unequally, some peoples being ahead of others, for the nature of the country, its forests and its plains, healthy uplands and malarial swamps, abundance of some forms of vegetation and complete lack of others, would always have imposed irregular and unique patterns of development.

Yet desiccation of the Sahara is none the less important in the record. North of the desert the civilizations of the Fertile Crescent were free to act and react upon one another, piling invention upon invention, exerting ever-renewed pressures of rivalry upon themselves and their neighbors until, in the course of centuries, they moved from primitive beginnings to the hierarchical splendors of an age of bronze. South of the desert there penetrated even to the peripheral peoples of that time no more than the faint and puzzling echo of this northern ferment: the echo was lost, the effect was vain.

To ask why early civilization should have appeared in the Nile Valley, the Near East, Mesopotamia — and not in northern Europe or in southern Africa — may be an interesting exercise in speculation. At this stage in knowledge, it can be little more. River-valley cultivation seems to be the clue. Early civilizations all took their rise in great river valleys; and these, no matter how much they otherwise differed, all had the peculiar characteristic of natural irrigation and soil renewal. Annually these rivers offered new soil, exceptionally rich soil, for cultivation. They enabled nomadic man, then discovering the possibility of growing food rather than merely collecting or hunting it, to turn from his no-madic life. In so doing — in settling in one place for several years at a stretch — he was faced with the technical problems of regular cultivation. And in solving these problems — precisely where river irrigation annually offered new soil — he also solved the problem of growing a surplus of food.

And with the emergence of this hitherto unknown phenomenon of surplus food, there emerged the foundations of commerce. But trade was the foundation, in turn, for permanent settlement; and permanent settlement meant specialization, the division of labor, the growth of cities. And the growth of cities meant civilization, the development of central government — of the autocratic and often divine rule that was peculiar to Bronze Age Egypt and other ancient civilizations. And with that the conditions were present when calculation was required, if only to count the goods that priests of the Pharaoh piled in his granaries and storehouses; and it was early means of calculation which led in turn to means of writing. Much of this complex and anything but automatic machinery of growth has been charted by archeologists over the past fifty years of revolutionary discovery. If the exact procedures are still in question, the general nature of the process is accepted.

South of the desert, largely severed from communication with the civilizations of the ancient world, things went differently. Conditions of river valley settlement that were decisive in the Middle East, India, and China appear to have failed in continental Africa. Not only that, so vast was the land that need for a surplus of food at any one place was absent too. Early peoples, running short of game, simply moved elsewhere. And whenever agriculture and, later on, metal age technique produced a greater density of population than any given area of land would support, the same thing happened again: sub-tribe hived off from parent tribe and marched away to new land.

Often enough it would move to virgin land. Sometimes it

would collide with earlier migrants or earlier nomads, and then the shunting process would begin once more, until waves and tremors of new migration would slowly ripple out across the forests and the plains. To this simple picture there were large and obvious exceptions. Yet it is a picture that is worth holding in mind because it helps to explain both means and motive in the peopling of historic Africa. Many tribal histories are known by now; invariably they include the story of migration and new settlement. Often enough they tell of movement from the northward or eastward, and the *general* trend of migration was very probably from north to south. Thus the picture south of the desert is one of restless ever-quickened movement across a continent where no great mountain ranges or unflankable deserts ever interposed a lasting check. Even dense forests that wall the Congo basin witnessed this onward penetration of nameless tribes in times beyond memory. They moved like the unseen armies of the stars, southward, westward; then, as time passed, returning on their tracks, eastward, northward, in hidden orbits that we do not know.

4 Giants and Heroes

This peopling of continental Africa over the past fifteen hundred years or so was seldom or never with the peoples who are known today. For the most part they were peoples who have slipped from memory, or remain there only in the guise of legendary ancestors, marvelous men with shining eyes and unbreakable courage who opened unknown country long ago for those who should follow and come after. Their heroes were the Feinn and Beowulf of the modern peoples of Africa; and even now the echoes of their pioneering still wonderfully linger.

"They wandered without let or hindrance to places where no man had ever been before," an old man of Bunyoro in Uganda told Gray of the "Bachwezi" forerunners of medieval times. "One could not look them in the face," the legend adds, "because their eyes were so bright that it hurt one's own eyes to look at them. It was like looking at the sun."

The ancient Sao of Lake Chad, says Lebeuf, "appear in legend as giants of prodigious force, and surprising feats are celebrated in their name. With one hand they dammed the rivers; their voices were so great that they could call from one town to another, and birds took flight in panic whenever one of them should cough. Their hunting expeditions drew them far from their dwellings; in a single day they would go hundreds of miles, and the animals they killed, hippopotamus and elephant, were carried easily on the shoulders of these fortunate hunters . . . Their weapons were bows from the trunk of a palm tree . . . Even the earth bore their weight with difficulty . . ."

Yet tribal legend, needless to say, never gives us the first inhabitants. It is overlay on overlay. All one can do is peel off layer after layer until the information altogether fails. For the many peoples of the Bantu language group — those who now predominate in central and southern Africa — this peeling off is possible for three or four hundred years into the past, and here and there — as for example with Torday's Bushongo — for a somewhat longer period. Many of the peoples now living in the central and southern continent appear to have reached their present habitat within the past few hundred years, but some of them reached it — shouldering aside the closely related peoples whom they found or merging with them — much more recently than that.

The Bushongo are a case of long establishment. They seem to have lived in the region of the Sankuru river for seven or eight hundred years; and in the course of this time they evolved a highly distinctive culture that was eminent alike in social order and artistic production. The Sala, one of the Ila-Tongo peoples of north-western Rhodesia, represent the opposite case. They are one of many peoples whose establishment is relatively new. "Sala history," says Jaspan, "is said to start from about 1820, when a chieftainess, Namumbe, appeared from a district to the northwest of Lusaka, and founded a village . . . Namumbe died in about 1835. Her sister, Maninga, inherited the chieftaincy, but was later ousted by Chongo, Namumbe's son . . . He exacted a tax of all elephant ivory and all skins of game killed by his dependents."

What motives inspired this forming and re-forming of tribes and tribal groups — sometimes of disparate elements, of men and women from other tribes — may be seen from many of these tribal histories. A good example is that of the southern Lunda and their related neighbors of the lower Congo. "The first large-scale emigration from the Lunda kingdom," says McCulloch, "was that of Chinguli and Chiniama, the brothers of Lueji"— Lueji was high chieftainess of the Lunda between 1590 and 1610 —"and their followers, between 1590 and 1625. Among the reasons for their departure suggested by the various traditions are displeasure at their sister's succession to power . . . Chinguli went westwards and ultimately founded the Bangala people of northern Angola and the western Belgian Congo. Chiniama went southwards and then westwards, and he and his followers founded the Luena, Chokwe, and Luchazi peoples."

The process was complex and long enduring. Of the Bechuanaland peoples, wrote Ellenberger in 1912, "Napo, the younger brother of Mochuli, being unwilling, as he said, to live like a reed overshadowed by a tree, left his elder brother and migrated south about the end of the fifteenth century . . ." To which Schapera, writing a few years ago, adds that "All that can be said with some confidence is that the Tswana" — of Bechuanaland today — "were already in the eastern half of their present habitat by about 1600 A.D." During the next two centuries "each of the existing clusters became increasingly subdivided. It was a constantly recurring feature in Tswana history for a tribe to secede under a discontented member of the ruling family and move away to a new locality. There it would set up as an independent tribe under the chieftainship of its leader, by whose name it generally came to be known."

The dates are approximate, but there is little doubt that they are approximately right. Like these random samples of migration history they would greatly mislead, however, if they led to an impression of mere repetitive movement within a social framework that was stagnant or incapable of change and growth. Developing along their own lines of growth, these vigorous and multiplying peoples were inventive and successful in surviving and settling where few or none had ever lived before. Some of them — and the Bushongo are a notable case, yet only one of many of this kind — achieved great stability and cultural distinction. They conquered their environment and learned how to live at peace with it; and the word "primitive" can be applied to them, with any degree of justification, only in a strictly narrow and technological sense.

On this, Emil Torday's comment will stand. He was writing of King Shamba Bolongongo, whose rule over the Bushongo began around A.D. 1600 and who is said to have abolished his standing army and forbidden the use of the throwing knife in warfare. "A central African king of the early days of the seventeenth century," says Torday, "whose only conquests were on the field of thought, public prosperity, and social progress, and who is still remembered in our day by every person in the country . . . must have been a remarkable man indeed." Torday, it is true, was an enthusiast; yet his thoughts on the past of central Africa, even if they stray a little to the side of a romantic idealism, are none the less nearer to the truth than the miseries of savage chaos that others have presented as a description of that past.

Against the background of this interweaving process of migration and stability, there are several important points to be made. If the present peoples of continental Africa began to multiply from rarity some four or five thousand years ago or less, it appears that only in comparatively recent times — perhaps within the last thousand or fifteen hundred years — have they become really numerous and spread across the continent and acquired the strength they have today.

And it is this probable fact of their major movement and migration and settlement in the fifteen centuries or so before the coming of European trade and penetration that gives this proto-historic period its great significance. This is why the definitive history of African peoples, when finally it gets itself beyond the hesitations of the learned and the speculations of the unlearned — when finally it gets itself written — will have to explain the course of the discovery and growth of agriculture in continental Africa, and even more, the course of the discovery and growth of the use of metals, but principally of iron. And this is why — returning to the necessarily modest limits of this present outline — these questions will be treated as of crucial value and importance. For it was the extension of agriculture and the use of iron, with all the added mastery of environment which these imply, that accompanied and governed both the need and the possibility of successful migration into new and unknown lands.

The achievement was not a small one. Across this inhospitable continent — difficult, intemperate, lacking many of the stable vegetables that sustained mankind elsewhere — these peoples spread themselves thinly, and survived. It is a large point, for example, that this migratory process certainly discouraged social growth from one form of society to another. Always able to move further on, since the land was so wide and its inhabitants so few, these moving peoples were seldom or never faced with the social and economic crises which helped to promote change in narrower and more densely populated lands. Hunting and fishing and the tilling of a little land for bare needs had given them an adequate means of survival. So long as this means continued to be adequate they would not seek to improve it. They would move elsewhere, follow the teeming antelope, look for new pastures, clear new ground.

Yet the record is very far from one of stagnation. These were pioneering peoples. They tilled where none had tilled before. They mined where there was none to show them how. They discovered a valuable pharmacopoeia. They were skillful in terraced irrigation and the conservation of soil on steep hillsides. They built new and complex social systems. They transformed whatever they could borrow from other and technologically more advanced social systems to the north, added and adapted and experienced and invented, until in the course of time they acquired a range of technique and a mastery of art, a philosophy and attitude and temperament and religion, that were unique to themselves and make the "Negro-ness," the *négritude*, they have today.

This African metal age of the last fifteen or twenty centuries, in short, is the formative period of modern Africa. It possessed its own dynamic of growth and change. It produced its own cultures and civilizations, uniquely African. It is the central theme of this book.

But before embarking on this central theme it will be useful to cast back into high antiquity. How much did this pre-medieval and medieval achievement in continental Africa owe to the ancient civilizations of the north? Where did the lines of influence run, and how important were they?

The Mystery of Meroë

. . . Very heavily with marvels of the land of Punt: all goodly fragrant woods of God's Land, heaps of myrrh resin, and fresh myrrh trees, with ebony and pure ivory, with green gold of Emu, with cinnamon wood and incenses and eye cosmetic, with apes and monkeys and dogs and skins of the southern panther, with natives and their children.

The loading of the
ships of Queen Hatshepsut: about 1460 B.C.

1 Lords of the Southern Frontier

SOME FOUR HUNDRED YEARS BEFORE JULius Caesar crossed the English Channel a group of young adventurers — "wild young fellows," Herodotus calls them, "sons of the chieftains of their country" — wagered with their friends that they would cross the Sahara from north to south. Leaving Cyrenaica, where they lived, these Nasamonians traveled for a long way southward and westward. After passing "the region of wild beasts" and going for many days over the sand — and the Sahara then was not much kinder to travelers than it is today — they at last saw trees growing on a level spot and began to pick their fruit.

"While they were doing so they were attacked by some little men — of less than middle height — who seized them and carried them off. The speech of these dwarfs was unintelligible, nor could they understand the Nasamonians. They took their captives through a vast tract of marshy country, and beyond it came to a town, all the inhabitants of which were of the same small stature, and all black. A great river with crocodiles in it flowed past the town from west to east."

This earliest account of the Niger — or was it perhaps the Komadugu which flows eastward into Lake Chad? — reached the ears of Etearchus, an Ammonian king who lived in the neighborhood of modern Derna. He in turn told it to some people of Cyrene, who happened "to get on to the subject of the Nile and the riddle of its source" while in conversation with him; and they in turn told it to Herodotus. It is almost the only fragment that survives of what must once have been a vivid narrative of travel and communication across the desert.

Several of the high civilizations of antiquity that were fathered in the valley of the Nile and the Near East were important for continental Africa; but it is not easy to say how important. The state of modern knowledge, very imperfect in this matter, suggests that they were much more important than was previously thought; and that their contact with peoples to the south and southwest of them was frequent, though not continuous, over a long period. Those bold young Nasamonians may have traveled where none of their own people had gone before; it seems probable, though, that they followed a route which had long been known and used by other Libyan peoples, and most of all by the Garamantes who lived to the west of them, south of the gulf of Tripoli, in what is now the Fezzan. Archeology in this field of north-south contact is only at the beginning of its work.

The foundation for it, however, lies in the scientific dating of ancient Egypt, and is reasonably firm. Digging at Jericho during these past few years has shown that settled agriculture in the valley of the Jordan goes back at least eight thousand years. City life began in that earliest of all the cities of the world as long ago as the sixth or seventh millennium before Christ. But agriculture in the well-watered valley of the Nile, not far away, seems to have begun much later. The earliest dating so far achieved — by radio-carbon tests which may be taken as broadly reliable — shows that Neolithic people camped and cultivated beside the broad waters of the Fayum Lake, mapped nowadays simply as a "depression," in the centuries between 4500 and 4000 B.C. Through these years, and the years that followed, cultivation became strongly established for several hundred miles along the banks of the lower Nile. These agricultural people of the Neolithic — of the age of agriculture before the use of metals — were settled groups. They and their kind achieved what no one there before them had achieved:

they discovered how to overcome nomadism, always the accompaniment of dry cultivation, by a "shifting" agriculture which relied on the regular use of water. By 3000 B.C. they had yoked oxen to ploughs and were cultivating fields instead of hoeing plots.

These were the origins of dynastic Egypt, of the centralized state over which divine Pharaohs would rule for nearly three thousand years. Its beginnings were obscure and slow; we cannot see them clearly. But what became known, much later, as the first dynasty of Pharaohs is thought to have begun soon after 3000 B.C. — some fifteen hundred years, perhaps, after the Neolithic peasants of the Fayum had embarked on their long experiment in settled agriculture and primitive irrigation.

By the beginning of the fourth dynasty, perhaps three hundred years later (the exact dates are still in question), Egypt had emerged as a flourishing monarchy with a strong government and a firm grip on new means of wealth. Several centuries of uniform government, imposing a centralized control of the annual floods of the Nile, constructing a vast system of dykes and irrigation channels, had raised Egypt far above the Neolithic level. Great annual harvests of barley and wheat — descendants of those wild grasses domesticated by Asian peasants and brought to the valley of the Nile many years before — supported a growing population, provided the central government with a regular surplus of food, enabled and stimulated commerce, and paid for the pyramids and other monuments that Cheops and his successors would begin to build around 2500 B.C. The great years of Egypt had begun. The crucial transformations had been made.

How far southward and westward did this river-valley civilization send its influence? There is a fairly good answer to the first part of this question, though somewhat blurred at the edges, since we are now in the period of pictorial and written records. The records, unfortunately, refer only to the south, perhaps because it was only towards the south that new power along the Nile could be securely established, and new sources of wealth regularly tapped. The banks of the middle Nile and its surrounding country were temperate and fertile then — even in the time of the Middle Kingdom, after 2000 B.C., the people of lower Nubia (the so-called "C Group" peoples who lived in what is now the northern Sudan) could graze large herds of cattle in country that is now so dry, to recall Arkell's words, "that the owner of an ox-driven water-wheel has difficulty in keeping one or two beasts alive throughout the year." The early Egyptian Pharaohs, accordingly, looked southward and aspired after conquest. The story of their southern expeditions accompanies the whole of their history and that of their successors. Interwoven product of Africa and Asia, dynastic Egypt was almost always in contact with neighbors to the south.

It was also in long-enduring contact with Libyan peoples of the cattle-grazing savannahs to the west of the Nile — in what is now the grim Sahara — but this contact was never one of stable conquest; and the records of it, or the few that were made and have survived, are fleeting and purely warlike. What little can be learned of it comes from archeological inquiry into Libyan and Carthaginian settlements along the North African coast and, increasingly now, into other Libyan settlements of the Sahara itself. One of Lhote's most interesting discoveries, among the rocks and fluted canyons of the Tassili mountains of the central Sahara, is the evidence of Egyptian influence in this remote and long deserted place. During their sixteen months of labor in those hills of heat and cold, he and his team found many rock paintings which clearly echo an Egyptian model. They even found, in this place without water, five pictures of Nile boats.

These contacts in the west, unlike those in the south, provide records of conquest and not of settlement. More probably, they are fragments of what Libyan peoples, warring with Egypt, had seen and heard of life on the Nile. There is nothing to show that Egyptian expeditions ever reached the Tassili mountains, though there is equally nothing to show that they did not. Little is certain in this vague and distant field. Only a few years ago it was generally denied that the old Sahara had ever known wheeled transport. Today it is firmly established that rock pictures of horses and two-wheeled chariots exist right across the desert from the Fezzan in the north to hills in the southwest which lead down to the Niger. Moreover, these horsed chariots are sometimes drawn not with an Egyptian style but with the "flying gallop" that was pictured in ancient Crete; and Lhote suggests that those same Peoples of the Sea who assailed Egypt around 1200 B.C., coming from Crete and neighboring islands, passed on their chariot practice to the Libyans whom they knew. (See page 68.)

But there is plenty to show that Egyptian expeditions went far southward up the Nile and along the southern coasts of the Red Sea. Here their records are many and remarkable, and made in various and helpful detail. Their traders and soldiers often reached the land of Punt and the land of Kush — Ethiopia and Somaliland and the Sudan of today. Perhaps they went still further; perhaps they reached the shores of Lake Chad and the forests of the Congo and the uplands of Uganda. If so, they have left no word or sign of it. For all its enterprise, direct Egyptian influence was never to penetrate beyond the lower and the middle valleys of the Nile. The great transmitters of Egyptian beliefs, ideas, and material inventions would not be the Egyptians themselves, but the peoples of Kush and the peoples of North Africa.

Yet these southern expeditions provide a vivid chapter in the story. With an astonishing persistence, drive, initiative, and skill, they departed for the south and did their trade and made their wars and took their slaves, returning long months afterward with more or less amazing things to tell. Userkaf, founder of the fifth dynasty (c. 2560 B.C.), inscribed his conquering name on the rocks of the first cataract of what is now Aswan, four hundred miles south of the delta. Sahure, who followed him, sent a fleet of ships down the Red Sea to the land of Punt, and made the earliest known record of direct communication with that distant land, although a son of Cheops had already owned a Puntite slave. These ships of Sahure's brought back quantities of myrrh and ebony, and metal that was probably electrum, a natural alloy of gold and silver. Another fifth dynasty expedition to Punt was commanded by Burded, "treasurer" of the Pharaoh, and among the items that returned with him there was a "dwarf," perhaps an ancestor of the Pygmies of Central Africa, who lived then, as it would seem, much further north than they do now.

The Pharaohs of the sixth dynasty (c. 2423-2242 B.C.) strengthened these trading contacts by outright conquest. Pepi I had such control of Nubia, the land beyond the first cataract, south of Aswan, that his powerful southern nobles were able to impress large numbers of Negroes into the royal army. They were generally used not in the land of their birth, needless to say, but in northern Egypt: a lesson which many other conquerers would accept, down the centuries, with levies of the conquered. Commercial interest by now had devised a way of getting ships through the rocks of the first cataract; and contact multiplied. Mernere, last Pharaoh but one of the sixth dynasty, thought it worth while going to see for himself; and a relief on the rocks of the cataract shows him leaning on his staff, while Nubian (or presumably Nubian) chiefs bow down in homage.

These sixth dynasty Pharaohs were strong enough to control their southern barons. Mernere used them to push his power southwards. He made Harkhuf, already lord of the region of the first cataract, into governor of the south as well; and Harkhuf and his fellow lords of the south are the earliest known precursors of all that long line of imperial pioneers who have penetrated continental Africa from the outside. Their exploits ring vividly across the years. Four times Harkhuf "went down" into the far land of Yam, taking seven or eight months to go there and return, leading strong caravans of asses to bear the loot, and soldiers to guard them.

Harkhuf may have reached the swamps of the upper Nile or even the hills of Darfur. In any case he must have gone far beyond the southern fringe of what is now the desert. He returned with ebony, ivory, frankincense "and every good product." Returning the fourth time, he brought a "dwarf" from this "land of spirits"— this "God's land" which the old Egyptians believed to lie west of the Nile and which had, for them, a mystical significance linked to their own remote ancestry. The Pharaoh's letter of thanks for this dwarf is preserved, nearly intact, on the face of the tomb that Harkhuf had prepared for himself. It is the only complete letter of the Old Kingdom that is known.

"Come northward to the court immediately," commands the grateful Pharaoh. "Thou shalt bring this dwarf with thee, which thou bringest living, prosperous and healthy from the land of spirits, for the dances of the god, to rejoice and gladden the heart of the king of upper and lower Egypt, Neferkere, who lives forever.

"When he goes down with thee into the vessel"— back to Egypt down the Nile — "appoint excellent people who shall be beside him on each side of the vessel. Take care lest he fall into the water. When he sleeps at night appoint excellent people who shall sleep beside him in the tent. Inspect ten times a night. My majesty desires to see this dwarf more than the gifts of Sinai and of Punt."

These were infrequent expeditions, expensive and difficult. Not until the beginning of the Middle Kingdom, after about 2000 B.C., would Egyptian power permanently establish itself in the lands beyond the first cataract. Southward conquest began again after a long period of disintegration that ended with the eleventh dynasty; and the powerful Pharaohs of the twelfth dynasty, founded about 2000 B.C., carried on the work. Traffic with Punt began again with Amenemhat II, second Pharaoh of the twelfth dynasty, and continued under Sesostris II. Forts were built at the second cataract, near what is now Wadi Halfa; and the frontier was established at Semna, where three forts were placed.

There was then no reason why Egypt should not have pushed its power much further south. But the Hyksos invaders, coming from Asia, intervened in 1700 B.C. or thereabouts; and it was not until the rise of the eighteenth dynasty, founder of the great imperial period of ancient Egypt, that further conquests were made. Then Tutmosis I, third Pharaoh of that conquering dynasty, led an army southward in about 1525 B.C., and reached at last the long fruitful stretch of the Nile that flows from Dongola. He stood, as Breasted puts it, "at the northern gateway of the Dongola province, the great garden of the Upper Nile, through which there would have been over two hundred miles of unbroken river." His inscription at Tumbus, near the northern end of the Dongola reach, proves it.

Breasted wrote more than fifty years ago. Since then we know that Tutmosis went right up the Dongola reach to the fourth cataract and beyond it, until he came to Kurgus, where he set up a boundary inscription that is yet to be deciphered. And Kurgus was less than four hundred miles from what is now Khartoum, or less than three hundred miles from what was to be the Kushite capital of Meroë. He or his patrols may have gone still further. Arkell suggests that the later capital of Meroë may have started as a humble frontier post of the eighteenth dynasty, although certainty about this will have to wait upon a proper excavation of Meroë's widespread ruins.

After the death of Tutmosis I the Kushites of the Dongola reach revolted against Egyptian overlordship, as did also their "C Group" neighbors to the north of them; but these revolts were crushed, and a long period of more or less peaceful intercourse with Egypt appears to have followed. But then comes the most dramatic and instructive of all the reliefs and inscriptions that deal with Egyptian prowess in the far south: the great series at the temple of Deir el Bahri, opposite Luxor, where the story of Queen Hatshepsut's expedition to the land of Punt, to the "myrrh terraces" and all they meant, is offered in a grand pictorial narrative spread around three walls.

These reliefs are vivid and immediate in their effect. The opening scene shows five vessels making ready to depart on their journey down the Red Sea. Three of them are already under sail, and one of them carries over its stern the inscription of a pilot's order, *steer to port*. Then they are sailing in the sea, "journeying in peace to the land of Punt," where they safely arrive and are greeted by a chief of the Puntites, Perehu, followed by his wife, who is remarkable for dark-skinned generosity of girth and limb. Beyond the Puntite royal pair and their three children and three servants driving "the ass that bears his wife," Puntite houses set on poles appear among the trees. The chief of the Puntites is exceedingly respectful, according to the inscriptions, and all the chiefs of Punt, who appear a little further on, are made to say: "Lo, as for the King of Egypt, is there no way to his majesty, that we may live by the breath that he gives?"

Whatever the truth of Puntite respect — and Punt, after all, was dreadfully far away from the scribes and artists of Queen Hatshepsut — the expedition was acclaimed a brilliant success. Another relief shows the loading of its ships for their return "very heavily with marvels of the land of Punt: all goodly fragrant woods of God's Land, heaps of myrrh resin, with fresh myrrh trees, with ebony and pure ivory, with green gold of Emu, with cinnamon wood . . . incenses . . . eye cosmetic, with apes and monkeys and dogs and skins of the southern panther, with natives and their children."

Punt was never conquered by the Pharaohs, but often visited by their ships and traders. Tutmosis III, following Queen Hatshepsut in the fifteenth century B.C., records the goods that were brought from there, generally by sea but perhaps overland as well; and already the gold and slaves that were to sound a dismal knell through so many African centuries are well to the fore. In a single year one hundred thirty-four male and female slaves were brought to the Pharaoh from Punt, as well as ivory, ebony, gold and cattle; while the combined tribute of the lands of Nubia amounted to one hundred thirty-four pounds of gold, as well as the familiar ebony and ivory and cattle and slaves.

Trading with Punt and power over Kush continued at least until Rameses II (c. 1292-1225 B.C.), strongest of the Pharaohs of the nineteenth dynasty; but thereafter the long period of Egyptian decadence sets in. Others would trade with Punt. And five hundred years later the kings of Kush would turn the tables on their former conquerors, and briefly conquer them in turn. The civilization of Kush — of the kingdom of Napata and Meroë — would have begun. It would last a thousand years and send its civilizing influence far to the south and west.

2 Egypt, Libya, Kush

SUCH, IN BROAD OUTLINE, IS THE RECORD OF EGYPTIAN CONTACT with continental Africa. Long-enduring though it was, this contact remained within relatively narrow limits. It occurred through a period when the lands to the south and west were drying up, losing their great fertility, becoming ever more difficult to penetrate and cross. If the populations to the south were already multiplying then — and we cannot be sure that they were, for we do not know enough yet of the history of settled agriculture — their migratory pressure was not towards the civilized lands of the Nile, but southward and westward into the remote interior.

Others would carry into continental Africa the fruits of ancient civilization in the Nile and the Near East and the Mediterranean. By the twenty-second dynasty, beginning in 950 B.C. and well into the period of Egyptian decadence, three new growing points were in existence; and each of these would act as an important "culture carrier." The first of these was that southern land of Kush, briefly a world power in the eighth century B.C. but strong within itself for many centuries thereafter, and, in some respects, the most truly African of all the great civilizations of antiquity. The second ancient civilization whose ideas, beliefs, and techniques were intimately linked with continental Africa was that of Carthage and the Lybico-Berber states associated with Carthage and partly derived from Carthage. And the third point of civilizing growth and irradiation was that of the southern tip of Arabia, the "incense lands" of what are now the Yemen and the Hadhramaut. Thence, traveling northward in the beginning of the tenth century B.C., "with a very great train, with camels that bare spices, and very much gold and precious stones," the Queen of Sheba — of Sabaea — came to Solomon. And thence, traveling southward at about the same time, the armies of Sabaea would land and settle in the highlands of what is modern Ethiopia today.

Each of these civilizations would contribute to belief and action in the lands to the south of them — just as the lands to the south of them, it must be thought, would already have given them much that they had made specifically their own. Egypt after 3000 B.C., Carthage and Kush and southern Arabia after 1000 B.C., would each push their influence southward and southwestward; and the crucial transformations of continental Africa — the discovery and growth of agriculture, the use of metals, the ideas and beliefs by which men lived and governed themselves — are inseparable from their influence and contact and reaction.

Intricate and prolonged, their specific contributions are hard to distinguish from one another. Some authorities hold that the decisively important technique of ironworking went southward by way of the peoples of Libya, who had it in turn from Carthage and the shores of the Mediterranean. Others believe that it went southward by way of Kush and Meroë — from what Sayce, an archeologist of fifty years ago, called "the Birmingham of ancient Africa." Probably both are true. Just as it is probably true that peoples in the south made their own discoveries as well.

Thus civilization, parent of the modern world, had begun in the river valleys of Mesopotamia and Egypt; its origins, at least in Egypt, had been African as well as Asian. After some two thousand years or so these civilizations of high antiquity had taken their ideas and techniques to other lands and peoples. Through that long age of bronze the Minoans and Ionians and Hittites had in turn transmitted the essence of what they knew to southern Europe. Phoenicians had taken the same knowledge to North Africa. Egypt had taken it to Kush. Many peoples had taken it to southern Arabia. Others, elsewhere, had founded Bronze Age civilizations in India and in China.

The ripples were penetrating everywhere into new lands. What can be said of this penetration into continental Africa?

3 Meroë

THE RUINS OF THE ANCIENT CITY OF MEROË ARE AMONG THE GREAT monuments of the ancient world; and their history is an important part of the history of man. Yet in spite of these claims on the interest of posterity, not much more is known of the life that was lived at Meroë and its sister cities of Kush than was known when Herodotus asked the priests of Elephantine about it twenty-four centuries ago, and was told little or nothing for his pains.

These ruins lie about a hundred miles down the Nile from modern Khartoum, a little way beyond the riverside town of Shendi.

Royal pyramids mark it from the distance. Between these and the Nile, across a gravel plain some two miles broad, the surface of the ground is curved by long low mounds which show where Meroë once flourished. To the left, close by the river, are the partly cleared ruins of that Temple of the Sun of which Herodotus heard faint news. Nearby, the railway running northward goes straight through two thirty-foot mounds of pebblelike material that is glittering and black — the lavalike slag and "bloom" of smelters' ovens long since cold.

Archeologists have yet to find the opportunity — and this means, of course, the money — to investigate more than a tenth part of this wide ruin field of Kush. Here among the low dry hills of the sixth cataract there lies, practically untouched, the richest archeological site that yet remains in Africa; perhaps the richest that yet remains in any part of the world.

At Meroë and other points not far away there stand the solitary ruins of palaces and temples that were built for a civilization which flowered more than two thousand years ago, while all around, still undisturbed by any spade, lie the city mounds of those who built them and lived within their shadow. Even a few hours' observation in these ruins will yield interesting relics of that distant time — stelae in fine basalt that are deeply engraved with a writing which can be read but not yet understood, fragments of white plaster that once covered these shining forts and temples, scraps of painted pottery, stones that have not yet lost their vivid decoration. Abandoned here and there the granite rams of Amun-Re, god of the sun, crouch like small indignant sphinxes in the wind-blown ochreous sand.

Reisner, Griffith, Garstang and one or two others have excavated at Meroë. To Reisner and Griffith we owe a fairly complete knowledge of king and queen lists that reach back in scarcely broken succession for a thousand years before about A.D. 200. The site of the Temple of the Sun is cleared of debris, so that its basic structure

may be imagined without much difficulty; and several other buildings, among them a Roman-style bathhouse, are in like condition.
On their low hills beyond the city the pyramids have all been entered, long ago by grave robbers who knew or had found the way
into slanting corridors that lead down to the burial chambers deep
beneath the apex, and within the past half century by archeologists. But the rest is tantalizing silence.

In 1958 the Director of Antiquities of the Sudan Government,
Dr. Jean Vercoutter, who is a distinguished French Egyptologist,
was completing a preliminary list of important Meroitic sites, and
had reached, somewhat to the dismay of the financial authorities,
as many as two hundred; while a visiting team from the Humboldt
University of Berlin, under the leadership of Professor Hintze,
one of the world's few specialists in Meroitic hieroglyphs, was
searching for new sites so that the final list might be reasonably
complete. Even with a trowel Hintze and his colleagues were turning up new information. While I was at Naga, where he and his
expedition were encamped, he told me of a trial dig within a
hundred yards of the Lion Temple which had gone through sherds
and city rubbish for as much as seventy-five centimeters.

Some of these sites are large, and one or two may properly be
called gigantic. Temple buildings rear themselves from the sandy
floor of the Butana desert as though haphazardly put down there,
only yesterday, for the winds of the desert have kept them
strangely free of engulfing sand while covering the cities that lay
near them. Twenty miles into the desert from Meroë, along a
lost road from Wad ben Naga, ancient river port on the Nile above
present-day Shendi,* there is the sand-blurred ruin of Musawarat
es Safra, a palace or a temple or perhaps a combination of the two
— residence of a god-king or a goddess-queen — that lies in tumbled splendor across the floor of a flat arena in the hills. The old

* Excavating in 1959, the Sudan Antiquities Service under Dr. Vercoutter
has come upon important Meroitic finds at Wad ben Naga.

fertility, product of skillful irrigation, has long since gone; and Musawarat, like its companion sites, seems planted now in nothing but the sand. Yet in the day of its building, between the beginning of the first century B.C. and the end of the first century A.D., it need have feared comparison for size and dignity with few of the monuments of its time.

Little now remains of it but foundations and walls that are intact with skillful bonding to a height of five or six feet, and a score of headless columns. Its position lies within a wide amphitheater of hills. With irrigation and a little more rainfall than today, it must once have been a place of pleasure and romantic charm. Here one might have strolled upon smooth terraces and looked across green fields to hills that were clothed with trees. And to this place, however lost and forgotten now, the traders and ambassadors of the eastern and the Mediterranean world, and of the African world to the south and west, would have brought their goods and paid their interested homage.

Though not Egyptian, the god-kings and goddess-queens of Musawarat had learned Egyptian pomp and comfort. Theirs had been a Bronze Age polity — literate, hierarchical, replete with slaves and royal accumulation of wealth, given to the building of great monuments, and, one may suspect, rigid in its manners with the ingrained strength of a long tradition. Around the central palace are the ruins and occupation mounds of household retainers and priests of the royal cult, of stables and offices of commerce. Well-made ramps and girdle walls surround a lengthy complex of central buildings — colonnaded, sheltered from the sun in those old days, skillfully constructed, offering all the evidence of long and leisurely occupation through an age which had passed from immemorial stone and bronze to iron — the evening of an ancient world that must have felt within itself, even then, melancholy doubts of change and imminent upheaval. As many centuries had separated the queens who ruled at Musawarat —

Amanirenas, Amanishakhete, Naldamak, Amanitere — from the founders of their line as separated Queen Victoria from Saxon Harold. But the end of Kushite greatness, by the time that Musawarat was famous, would not be long delayed.

4 The Triumph of Kush

KUSH WAS AN AFRICAN CIVILIZATION WHICH HAD TAKEN MUCH from the outside world. Twenty miles beyond Musawarat stand the temples of Naga, best preserved of all these ruins and dating from the same period. Here at Naga, upon the rear wall of the Lion Temple, there is engraved a four-armed three-headed lion god whose remote inspiration was possibly Indian, possibly Carthaginian, possibly of that oldest Africa which "gave the gods to Egypt." Fifty paces away, and perhaps at much the same time, the citizens of Naga built another and smaller temple — the archeologists have called it, cautiously, a "kiosk" — that is hideous in its jumbled mixture of styles but undoubtedly recalls a Roman example.

Above these solitary temples, on the desert skyline, other buildings add to the record of a civilization that was manifestly an African synthesis of ideas then common throughout the civilized world. Anyone who passes through Khartoum, and cares to climb the stairs of the museum to the first floor, may see, for example, a small metal pot of an undoubtedly Chinese shape. For nearly a thousand years this Sudanese civilization of the middle and upper Nile — the Kushite civilization of Napata and Meroë — was a major African center for the exchange of ways of thought, belief, and manufacture.

The ancient world had had no doubt of the importance of Kush. It was a Kushite dignitary, after all, whom the apostle Philip encountered and baptized, while the Crucifixion was still

KUSH AND MEROË

yesterday's event, on "the road which goeth down from Jerusalem to Gaza," a conversion that was duly written with triumph into the Acts of the Apostles. "And behold, a man of Ethiopia, an eunuch of great authority under Candace, queen of the Ethiopians" — one of those goddess-queens, that is, who ruled Kush from the colonnaded peace of Musawarat es Safra — "who had the charge of all her treasure, and had come to Jerusalem for to worship, was returning, and sitting in his chariot, read Esaias the prophet." A Christian at the court of Musawarat es Safra? The records are silent. They are lost, or still lie hidden beneath the desert sand.

Some sixty years earlier, Kush had troubled the Roman peace in Egypt. Kushite troops had raided Philae and Elephantine on the southern frontier that Augustus had established, and overpowered three auxiliary cohorts planted there to defend it. Petronius, governor of Egypt, had brought down as many as ten thousand infantry and eight hundred cavalry to recover possession, had pursued the Kushites southward to their former capital of Napata, at the up-river end of the Dongola reach, and taken and destroyed that city. Though he failed to capture the Kushite ruler, he succeeded in releasing Roman troops fallen captive there, and in recovering statues of Augustus carried away by earlier Kushite raiders. Some 1940 years later, digging into the floor of one of the palaces at Meroë, Garstang found an effigy that Petronius had missed, a fine bronze head of Augustus which is now, by another of the accidents of history, in the British Museum.

Nobody can tell what other fine things and everyday things may await discovery beneath the untouched mounds and temple floors of Meroë and Musawarat and Naga and their like, for nobody has looked to see. As a field of archeological study, Kush has suffered from the overshadowing of Egypt, whose apparently inexhaustible graves and temples have yielded and continue to yield a wealth of information on the distant past and — weighty consideration with subsidized excavators — a wealth of objects desirable for exhibition in museums. That those who have financed excavation over the past half-century should have laid such stress on the finding of "objects" may not be much to their discredit, but the quest has tended to concentrate archeological attention on Egypt to the exclusion of less glittering territories. And even when other territories were investigated they have suffered from the same obsession. At least one of the rare excavators of Kushite civilization was so deeply interested in discovering "objects" that he failed to publish his excavation notes; for the most part, indeed, he does not seem to have made any.

This was true neither of Reisner nor of Griffith, to whom we owe the greater part of what is known of Kush. Between them they systematically excavated the royal tombs, both at Napata and Meroë; and although Reisner also failed to publish his excavation notes he kept them with care, and they are now being published for him by Professor Dows Dunham. Others have labored honorably in this field; and it says something for continued British interest in Kush, during the years of the Anglo-Egyptian Condominium, that the first article in the first issue of *Sudan Notes and Records*, published in 1918, was a discussion of the Kushite king-lists by Reisner himself; while Dr. A. J. Arkell, a former Commissioner of Antiquities under the Condominium Government, has lately written the best general account that has yet appeared.

But money was lacking. Little more than the surface could be scratched. Only the royal tombs — admittedly the most attractive and historically perhaps the most important of the sites — could be examined. All that is really clear, apart from a bare outline of Kushite rise and fall, is that this civilization was crucially important not only to the social evolution of the Sudan itself, but also to the growth and spread of civilizing ideas and technologies throughout much of continental Africa to the west and south. These coming years will open many ways to a better understanding of the African past; not a few of the keys are likely to be found at Meroë.

The bare historical outline is brief enough. Kush emerges from the decadence of imperial Egypt. Already by 800 B.C., or perhaps a little later, the hard-pressed Pharaohs of the twenty-second dynasty seem to have conceded a practical if not yet quite admitted independence to this rising power on their southern boundary. Governed from Napata, below the fourth cataract where the Don-

gola reach begins, this new Kushite power incorporated much that
was Egyptian. Tutmosis I had been here as early as 1525; Napata
by 800 had long become a famous center for the worship of Amun,
the sun god symbolized by a ram. Some authorities hold that the
hereditary ruling family of Kush was supported in its bid for independence by dissident Egyptian priests of that pervasive cult;
there had been plenty of precedents for "southern dissidence"
ever since Egypt's "lords of the south" had ruled from Aswan.
Then Kashta, first "great king" of Kush, embarked on the conquest of Egypt itself; and Piankhy, his son, completed this conquest in about 725 B.C. Ruling from the Mediterranean to the
borders of modern Ethiopia and, for all we know, Uganda too,
these kings gave Egypt its twenty-fifth or "Ethiopian" dynasty, and
made Kush briefly into a world power.

In 666 B.C. there came another dramatic change. The Assyrians
invaded lower Egypt. Soundly beaten by that ironshod army — for
the weapons of the Kushites, like those of the Egyptians, were of
stone and bronze — they retired southward but saved their independence. Sometime around 530 B.C. — the date is not fully
agreed upon, but the balance of contemporary opinion favors
something like this — and for reasons that were probably economic, they transferred their capital from Napata to Meroë, several hundred miles further south. The main evidence for this date,
oddly enough, turns upon the number of buried queens. Until the
end of the reign of Malenaquen (553-538 B.C.) the average number of Kushite queens buried in each reign — as determined by
excavation of royal pyramids and tombs at Kurru and Nuri, near
Napata — was four; thereafter the average drops to one and a half
for each reign. It is therefore supposed that Meroë, much further
up the Nile, had grown steadily in importance during the years before 538 B.C.; that the center of gravity of the Kushite kingdom
had shifted gradually southward, and that burials of queens began
to be made at Meroë as well as at Napata.

The reasons for this southward shift — for this increasingly African emphasis — cannot as yet be more than guessed at. Perhaps the reasons were climatic and economic — that the royal household, doubtless very numerous and hard to nourish, required more food than Napata any longer could provide — for the dry grip of the desert was already making itself felt. Perhaps they were geographical and economic, for Meroë lay closer to the caravan routes along the Atbara River leading to the Abyssinian highlands and thence to the western ports of the Indian Ocean, where Kush was also a great and long-established trader. Meroë, moreover, was now becoming a center for the smelting and manufacture of iron, and that too would have increased its attraction. Or perhaps the reasons for the southward shift were simply dynastic and socially convenient, since "it had become customary," in Arkell's words, "for the kings to take queens from the Meroitic aristocracy, and naturally those queens preferred burial in their homeland." In any event Meroë became the capital of Kush some five centuries before the birth of Christ and continued as its capital for some three centuries after that. Its cemeteries, royal and otherwise, are known to offer an unbroken history of more than a thousand years.

The bare record is soon completed. During the first millennium before Christ, peoples from the highly sophisticated and technically advanced southern tip of Arabia — they who had sent the Queen of Sheba to Solomon in the tenth century and monopolized the maritime trade of the African and Arabian shores of the Indian Ocean — established themselves strongly in what is now northern Ethiopia. A powerful kingdom there, with its capital at Axum, later cut the ancient caravan routes between Kush and the ocean ports. Wars followed; and Kush was vanquished, probably soon after A.D. 300.

Thenceforward the records dwindle and disappear. Deprived of independence and isolated between a hostile Egypt and a conquering Axum, the Meroitic kingdom falls into silence, and is soon forgotten. Its last rulers are buried ingloriously beneath paltry little pyramids which stand no higher than the stone houses that Reisner, when excavating, would build for himself nearby; and sometimes not so high. All that remains of Kush returns to the desert, changes into something entirely different — into the Christian kingdoms of Nubia — or lingers miserably in decay. Here and there an archeological hint, tantalizingly thin, suggests that the Kushite royal family may have fled or migrated to the westward; and the traces of what may have been their passing reach out across the wastes of Kordofan as far as Darfur.

Yet Kush would leave an imposing heritage. A few hundred years later, whether in consequence of this eclipse and dispersal or of earlier trade and migration and "cultural drift," the Sao people of Lake Chad, twelve hundred miles to the westward, would be casting in bronze by the "lost wax" process that the peoples of the Nile had known; and it may wonderfully stir the imagination to remember that Chad legends even now recall the early Sao as "giants of prodigious strength"— immigrants of tall stature, just as a people coming from the Nilotic Sudan might have been; and of prodigious knowledge, just as men from Meroë must surely have seemed. Further westward the Yoruba and other peoples of West Africa would be worshiping their "divine kings"; and the cult of the ram and the sun would have become a religion of wide African loyalty.

Whatever the true lines of diffusion of such ideas may have been — and indeed they may have come originally from West or Central Africa — there is no exaggeration in saying that the history of much of continental Africa is inseparable from the history of Kush. This is one large reason — quite apart from its significance to the history of the Sudan — why excavation of Meroë and related sites ought to be attempted with substantial funds. If Meroë was not the only parent of the Iron Age in continental Africa, it was undoubtedly one of them; and perhaps it was the most important.

5 An Athens in Africa?

IRON IS GENERALLY THOUGHT TO HAVE BEEN DISCOVERED, AS A usable metal, at some time before 1500 B.C. in the Middle Asian region between the Caucasus and what is now Asia Minor. By 1300 B.C. it had become an important industry of the Hittites, who ruled what is now Anatolia; and the Assyrians must also have known of it by then. The Syrian coast understood some of the possibilities of iron within another two hundred years or less; and from Syria, no doubt, ironworking made its way westward to Egypt and Carthage and other growing points of ancient civilization in the Mediterranean. The superiority of iron over bronze lay behind the overwhelming victories of the Assyrian kings of Nineveh. For if it is true, as the poet said, that the Assyrian cohorts which overwhelmed Israel "were gleaming in purple and gold," it was iron that gave them the victory over their enemies. Iron weapons enabled Sargon and Sennacherib to push their armies southwestward, gave Esarhaddon his triumph over the Egyptians, and afterwards permitted Ashurbanipal to capture Thebes and to end the Kushite rule of lower Egypt.

For iron had remained rare in Egypt. The years of Bronze Age decadence had discouraged new departures. Kush, taking its example from Egypt, suffered from this; for although Kush had plenty of accessible iron, as well as trees to burn for charcoal, the Kushites seem not to have worked it on any significant scale until the ultimate centuries of the pre-Christian era. Thus grave goods in the royal tombs of Napata, at Kurru and Nuri, include no iron objects until the burial of Harsiotef in about 362 B.C. Herodotus, who made his frontier report on Kush in about 430, says that "in Ethiopia the rarest and most precious metal is bronze"— to the point that prisoners "were bound in golden chains"— and mentions that the Kushites (whom he calls Ethiopians, as did all

Greek writers of antiquity) used weapons tipped with stone. So that although iron objects may have occurred in Kush some time before Harsiotef's reign, they must have been exceedingly rare.

Yet after the rise of Meroë, as Wainwright says, "the most astonishing change had come over the scene. Smelting works on a gigantic scale had already been initiated at Meroë by the middle of that century [the first century B.C.] or even earlier." And Sayce, who looked at Meroë some fifty years ago, could write that "mountains of iron slag enclose the city mounds on their northern and eastern sides, and excavation has brought to light the furnaces in which the iron was smelted and fashioned into tools and weapons." By the time of the building of Musawarat, in short, Meroë was the center of the largest iron-smelting industry in Africa south of the Mediterranean coast. It is reasonable to suppose that its products — and, after its products, its technology — went steadily and irresistibly into the lands to the west and south. In this vitally important diffusion of iron technology, Kush was therefore to southern Africa what the civilizations of the Mediterranean had been to northern Europe a few centuries earlier.

Those who followed on the Meroitic age, along the middle reaches of the Nile, lived fully in an Iron Age. These still mysterious people, perhaps Nuba or Beja though at present known to archeology under the safely anonymous title of "X Group," even made camp stools of iron. Their lavish and flamboyant jewelry, bold necklaces of black and white quartz and red cornelian, belong to a firm tradition of their own, although further excavation into the mysteries of Meroë may show that they followed Meroitic workmanship closely. After the "X Group," and overlapping with it, came the "Nubians" — one can almost say, by now, the Sudanese — of the pre-medieval and medieval Christian kingdoms of the Sudan. These remarkable islands of Christianity endured from the sixth to the fourteenth century, and achieved a high level of stability and material progress. Not until the sixteenth century would invading Islam fully overwhelm them. A few frescoes and mud-brick churches of this African Christianity — failing where Christian Ethiopia, thanks to its mountains, would survive — are their only monuments.

Meroë and its civilization remain a mystery behind these subsequent upheavals. What may justify the word "mystery" is not the doubt of a great civilization having lived here and flowered through long centuries, but the nature of that civilization — its everyday life, its links with the outside world, its peculiarly African synthesis of many ideas that were not African, its marriage of these ideas to other ideas that were African through and through, and, lastly, its undoubtedly great significance for the tropical and subtropical lands to the southwest and south.

Astonishingly little can be said of all this now.* The hieroglyphic script of Meroë can be read, but not understood. Its western and southern frontiers must be guessed at. The tone and texture of its daily life can be suggested by no more than a handful of goods — and most of these from royal graves, for no others have been systematically examined — although this tone and texture grew and changed and deepened across a thousand years of continuous settlement and material invention. What was the social nature of this "divine kingship"? How did the men and women of Meroë and its sister cities greet the coming of iron, of iron industry, of commerce over half the world? What did these citizens know of China, whose bronzes they copied and whose silks they bought; of India, whose cottons they wore; of Arabia, whose cargoes they purchased? Who traveled from the south and west, and went to the south and west, and what became of them?

Of the influence of this civilization, so potent for the rest of

* In a long poem of the early third century A.D., a Greek writer called Heliodorus tells of a Meroitic princess who fell in love with a handsome man of Thrace — the lady was no less Meroitic for being called Ethiopian. Does this poem illustrate Meroitic life? The *Cambridge Ancient History* gives it a paragraph without raising this question, much less answering it.

continental Africa, we have nothing but a slender and uncertain knowledge. Today, happily, the prospect of knowing more is brighter than it was. Fired by an interest that is particular to the Sudan but general to much of Africa, the government of the Sudanese Republic has decided that Kush, its remote ancestor, shall have more public honor. But the old difficulty remains: excavation is unreasonably expensive, and the Sudanese Republic, rightly eager to modernize and grow, cannot spare much money for the past; so that although there is plenty of Sudanese interest in Kush, it is probably true that the excavation of Kushite civilization will have to rely — as the excavation of Egypt has had to rely — on the generosity of foreign donors.

They will not be wasting their time and effort. For this vast city of Meroë — like other Kushite cities still to be explored — took its rise on the middle Nile in those same centuries when Periclean Greece was engraving its mark on the peoples of the Mediterranean; and the importance of Meroë, allowing for place and circumstance, may not have been much less. Like Athens, Meroë traded widely with many nations, developed its own traditions of art and literacy, implanted its seminal influence far beyond its frontiers, endured in the manners and beliefs it had used itself and had passed to others long after its own power had vanished, and deserved an honorable place among civilizations that have influenced the world. With Meroë, one may reasonably say, the history of modern Africa has begun.

three

Kingdoms of the
Old Sudan

The tales told by the heart are kept in the heart;
and the writing thereof is the understanding thereof.

The Alkali of N'Gaski
to Sir Richmond Palmer

1 Early West Africa: Discoveries at Nok

MEROË FELL TO THE ETHIOPIAN POWER
of Axum in the fourth century A.D., and
vanished from the scene. Within four hundred years of its eclipse
the written records of West Africa begin.

Unlike the hieroglyphs of Meroë, these records can be understood as well as read, for they survive in good Arabic. Pushing
westward from Egypt, the followers of Mohammed had taken
Tripoli within eleven years of the Prophet's death; by A.D. 681 they
had reached the Atlantic. Even fifteen years before that they had
pushed their first expedition southward into the Sahara, and
within the next hundred years they would send many pioneering
columns into the Sudan, the "country of the blacks." * Yet Arab
presence in the south was seldom to be more than spasmodic
or commercial. They and their kind would invade the Sudan but
they would not follow their armies by any large-scale settlement.
For in 710 they passed the northern straits and discovered Spain;
and the Mediterranean would claim their major effort and, in
the end, exhaust their medieval strength.

Their records of the south begin with Wahb ibn Munabbeh,
who wrote in 738. To begin with they are mainly the records of
migration, footnotes in Arabic to the ceaseless peopling of an
African interior whose presence was still obscured by myth and
legend. Here was the earliest statement of West Africa's great
"migration legend" that would echo and re-echo for long cen-

* By the Sudan — Bilad es Sudan — Arabs meant all the lands that lie
immediately beyond the Sahara. But *this* Sudan, in this chapter and the chapters that follow, means the Western Sudan — the savannah lands between the
Atlantic and the confines of the Nilotic Sudan.

turies thereafter. The descendants of the posterity of Kush, who was the son of Ham and the grandson of Noah, says Ibn Munabbeh, include the peoples of the Sudan; and these are the Qaran (perhaps the Goran, east of Lake Chad), the Zaghawa (who still inhabit Wadai and western Darfur), the Habesha (Abyssinians), the Qibt (the Copts), and the Barbar (the Berbers).

Two hundred years later the greatest of the medieval Arab geographers, El Mas'udi, would give fresh life to this migration legend. "When the descendants of Noah spread across the earth," he writes in his *Meadows of Gold and Mines of Gems*, finished in 947, "the sons of Kush, the son of Canaan, traveled toward the west and crossed the Nile. There they separated. Some of them, the Nubians and the Beja and the Zanj, turned to the rightward, between the east and the west; but the others, very numerous, marched toward the setting sun . . ."

Somewhere behind this legend of migration from the valley of the Nile there may lie a large core of historic truth. Coming from the eastward and northeastward, migratory peoples or groups of peoples, occasional clans or fragments of clans, racially mixed, partially civilized, would enter the Western Sudan in a long procession of invasion and settlement whose ordering and limits practically escape all knowledge. One may guess at the pressures that made them move: Assyrian and Persian raiding and conquest in the valley of the lower Nile, the eclipse and fall of Kush, the miseries of dynastic strife, the search for wealth. One may guess at the manner of their welcome in the lands to which they went: fear of their weapons and admiration of their strength, interest in their wider knowledge, enslavement sometimes to their greater discipline and power of combination — qualities without which no migrating people would survive. But the details of their movement cannot be clearly understood.

Whom did these incoming migrants — these "Judeo-Syrian" groups, for example, to whom tradition awards the foundation of

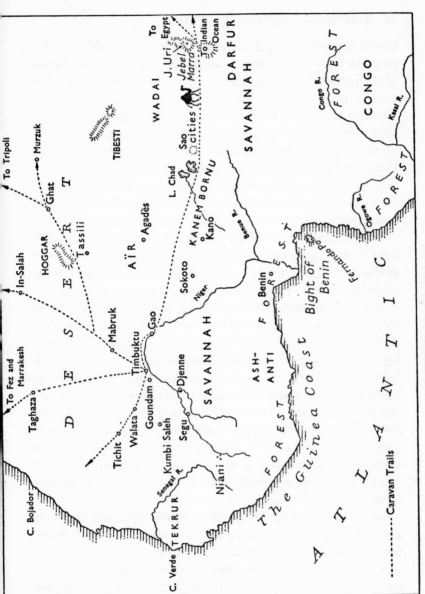

THE OLD SUDAN

Ghana in about A.D. 300 — find in the Western Sudan, whither they obscurely went? Lhote's pioneering work in the Sahara has lately suggested that Negroes had long occupied the land at least as far north as the mountains of Tassili, halfway to the Mediterranean coast. He reports from Tassili the painting of a mask that is strongly reminiscent, he says, of those still used by Senufu people of the Ivory Coast today. Writing fifty years ago, Delafosse thought that these Senufu were one of three indigenous peoples whom the migrants from east and northeast had found in possession of the land. Had they earlier lived much further north?

With the desiccation of the Sahara, migration would certainly have turned southward, but perhaps the point is somewhat academic. It is at least clear that by the time of Ibn Munabbeh, at the beginning of the eighth century, incoming migrants had mixed and mingled with Negro or Negroid peoples whom they found until the one had more or less completely absorbed the other. Some West African peoples have retained the characteristics of a "white" morphology. Notable among these, and perhaps most important among them, are the Peuls or Fulbe* who live today in many scattered fragments and appearances through the Western Sudan. Others, like the Songhay, have become (or always were) characteristically Negro. The "whiteness" or "blackness" of all or any of these peoples may be interesting from an anthropological and historical point of view; it must not, of course, be interpreted with any of the overtones of current racialism.

The earliest inhabitants of West Africa appeared there, in any case, many centuries earlier than these migrant groups whose wanderings would make the stuff of legend for Arab annalists. It is fruitless in the present state of knowledge to try and get much closer to the truth than that. Few investigators, for

* Fulani in English usage.

example, thought that Negroes had lived as far north as the Tassili, until Lhote's work became generally known — and Lhote's work became generally known no earlier than 1958.

But the last dozen years or so have brought several new fragments of evidence. Old Stone Age tools recovered from tin workings near Jos, on the plateau of central Nigeria, suggest that types of humanity may have lived there as long ago as the time of the Kanjeran Pluvial, the third of East Africa's generally accepted pluvials. Bernard Fagg reported in 1957 that tiny fragments of charcoal from one of these possibly Kanjeran levels gave an age, when submitted to radio-carbon test, that was "greater than 39,000 years." Thence through unexplored centuries the occupation levels of the Jos region appear to climb in more or less orderly procession through the Middle Stone Age to the New Stone Age.

In the New Stone Age, though, at levels that are tentatively awarded to the "Nakuran Wet" phase — the latest of the prehistorical East African phases, entering our own day — the story of this region takes an unexpected and exciting twist. A hint of this had come in 1931 from Nok, a village of the Jaba people of Zaria province, where a couple of human heads in pottery were recovered. They were smaller than life-size and appeared to have no connection with any culture that was known to have existed in the neighborhood. Three others were found in 1944, together with models of a human leg and foot, also in well-fashioned pottery, and a complete cooking pot. Then in the same year Bernard Fagg recovered a splendid pottery head at Jemaa, some twenty-four miles from Nok village.

Since then a great number of specimens of the "Nok figurine cult," as it soon came to be called, have turned up over a wide area reaching for some three hundred miles across the broad east-west valley that is made by the Niger and the Benue above the confluence of those great rivers; many life-size or near life-size "portrait heads," it should be noted, are among them. The likelihood now is that this interesting and advanced culture — modeling its thousands of portraits and stylistic figures — was spread widely across Nigeria and perhaps beyond; that it was the earliest iron-using culture in the region and therefore of revolutionary significance; and that it fathered many later developments in art, religion, and social organization. Further discoveries of its range and achievement may be expected.

Knowledge of its existence has already helped to revise many old notions of the African past. Europeans had often thought, for example, that Negro peoples possessed no native tradition of anthropomorphic art — of the more or less naturalistic portrayal of humanity. When the first astonishing heads and busts from Ife and Benin were brought to Europe sixty years ago and were seen to be portraits, or very like portraits, they were greeted with a chorus of disbelief: surely they were Greek or Egyptian or even Portuguese, for Negroes had never done anything like that?

Now Lhote's work in the Sahara has suggested that peoples of Negro type were painting men and women with a beautiful and sensitive realism before 3000 B.C. and were, perhaps, among the originators of naturalistic human portraiture. The Nok discoveries add their confirmation. These pottery heads and figures of central Nigeria stand much nearer to our own day, but they are nonetheless very old. Thus four scraps of carbonized wood from these "Nok levels" have yielded radio-carbon datings of about 3500, 2000, and 900 B.C., and A.D. 200.

"The first two dates," Bernard Fagg comments, "are almost certainly derived from earlier sediments, whereas 900 B.C. (approximating to the beginning of the Nakuran Moist Phase) and A.D. 200, probably mark the upper and the lower limits of the Nok Figurine Cult." It is about as much, at the moment, as may be said on the subject; except that its iron-using technique (of which plenty of evidence has appeared) suggests that "Nok society" was a transitional culture between stone and metals and reached its full development in the last two or three centuries B.C.

What peoples made such fine heads in terra cotta on the Nigerian plateau more than two thousand years ago and in such abundance can be anybody's guess; although some of the portrait heads suggest that Nok people were the direct ancestors of some of the peoples who live in central Nigeria today. One of the heads, for instance, shows a hair style in "buns" such as is still practiced by certain tribes of the Nigerian plateau. Any doubt of the authenticity of age of that particular pottery head (like other products of the Nok culture) is removed by the fact that it was found, during tin-mining operations, at a level whose approximate age is fixed by other evidence.

2 *From Kush and Carthage*

WAS THERE A CULTURAL AND LINGUISTIC UNITY AMONG THESE forest-dwelling peoples of a remote time? It seems possible. Yet we are now at a point where the lines of inward-coming migration start to merge — the arrival of those peoples from the northeast and east whose ceaseless movement would offer the material of legendary history for Ibn Munabbeh in A.D. 738. With El Mas'udi's restatement of the legend those sons of Kush, "very numerous, who marched toward the setting sun," have even acquired an historically attested direction: they "marched," that is, towards peoples of whom the Arabs had already heard. They "marched" "in the direction of Zaghawa, Kanem, Marka, Kawkaw, and Ghana, and other countries of the blacks and Demdemeh" (this last being a generic name, used by nearly all the old Arab writers, for peoples whom they believed were cannibals*).

The point is that they "marched" most precisely from the middle Nile to the middle Niger: along a trans-African route, that is, which migrating peoples had undoubtedly used from times that are exceedingly remote, and of whose existence the Arabs were well aware. There is nothing in the least improbable about this great route's having been regularly used in the remote past. Even today thousands of Nigerian pilgrims follow it to the Red Sea every year, and other thousands follow it back again; and two thousand years ago and more the climate and vegetation would have treated trans-African travelers in a gentler way than they do now. People came this way from the earliest times; and their beliefs and their inventions came with them. Lake Chad was not the source of the Nile, as some had guessed; yet their waters, in a cultural sense, none the less mingled from times of high antiquity.

There is practically no well-known people in West Africa without its legend of an eastern or a northern origin in the remote past. Sometimes these traditions are complete enough to allow an intelligent guess at their approximate date. Thus Biobaku has felt able to suggest that the founders of Yoruba civilization in southern Nigeria reached their country between the seventh and tenth centuries A.D., coming originally from the middle Nile. However that may be, the emphasis on eastern origin is clear and insistent with the Yoruba as with several neighboring peoples. But legend and tradition are only one source of evidence for eastern influence, if not for eastern origin.

The greatest of all the Egyptian temples of Nubia — of the southern land that would become the kingdom of Kush — was

---

* Which does not mean, needless to say, that the "Demdemeh," whoever they were, necessarily were cannibals. Even in the nineteenth century many Europeans believed that many Africans were cannibals, when they were not; just as many Africans believed the same of many Europeans.

built by an eighteenth dynasty Pharaoh, Amenophis III (1405-1370 B.C.), at Sulb on the west bank of the Nile. Its avenue of approach was guarded by rams and lions carved in granite. Both rams and lions were taken to their temples at Barkal, near Napata on the Nile, by the Kushite Pharaohs of the twenty-fifth dynasty — they who had conquered Egypt from the south. Thereafter the ram, symbol of Amun, became one of the great divine symbols of Kush. Even to this day you may find many granite rams at Meroë and Naga where they lie discarded in the lonely sand. But the ram, symbol of Amun, also made its god-like way along the North African coast, for the Lybico-Berber peoples of that region took it from the Egyptians just as the Kushites did, and probably at about the same time.

Wherever its earliest origins may have been — whether in North Africa or in Central Africa — the sacred ram was carried far across the continent. Many West African peoples have celebrated its divinity. The Mandingo of the Western Sudan consider that the god of storm and thunder takes earthly shape as a ram. The Yoruba national god, Shango, appears with a ram's mask and is equally the god of storm and thunder. The Baoulé of the Ivory Coast represent Niannié, the personalized sky, with the mask of a ram; and the god of lightning is also a ram for the Fon people of Dahomey. Divine rams in one guise or another, with one meaning or another, carry on right down through the Cameroons into the remote basin of the Congo. Carvers in wood are making them to this day.

These traces of cultural interpenetration can be many times multiplied, and are fresh proofs of that great unity in diversity which gives so much of African culture its characteristic quality of resonance, complexity, and age. Wainwright has shown how priestly breastplates, from Yorubaland in southern Nigeria of the medieval period, recall similar models dedicated to Amun in dynastic Egypt. Arkell has called attention to close likeness between Byzantine lamps found at Firka in Egypt (from a site of the post-Kushitic "X Group" people) and others taken from an old grave in the Gold Coast some years ago. The "divine kingship" of the Jukun of Benue river, in Nigeria, recalls the "divine kingship" of Kush and Egypt, and is far from being alone in that respect.

Other cultural borrowings may have come from the north. In her latest study of the beliefs and legends of the Akan people of Ghana, Mrs. Meyerowitz has suggested parallels between the old beliefs of North Africa and cults of the moon god and sun god and other divinities of the Akan of Ghana, so that the philosophy of human origins of the one comes to seem remarkably close to the same kind of ponderings of the other. Thus Melkart of Tyre, Phoenician "ancestor" of the royal house of Carthage which legendary Dido founded, was incarnate as a bull; the terra-cotta token of a bull's head, recovered from Carthage, is shown between the ideogram of Tanit — mother goddess of Carthage who gave birth to the universe without the aid of a male partner — and a figure of eight. And yet Bosummuru, "ancestor" of the Bono royal lineage of the Akan, is also incarnate as a bull. "A bull was sacrificed once a year," says Mrs. Meyerowitz, who has diligently gathered Akan tradition; this sacrifice symbolized "his divine death and rebirth." She adds that the figure of eight can also be found as a religious symbol among the Akan: "It suggests life, death and rebirth for ever repeating itself." Like Tanit of Carthage, the Akan god Nyame gave birth to the universe without the aid of a male partner. Like Dido, the "queen mothers" of the Akan have wielded power since times beyond memory. Whatever the true value of these parallels may be, they are undoubtedly useful in emphasizing the great complexity of social growth in ancient Africa.

There was certainly no automatic or mechanical transfer of ideas. This drift of peoples and their ideas about human origin, earthly and divine, may have wandered up and down the continent, or may have come steadily from the north and northeastward: it is in any case no more true that Egyptian or Kushite or Carthaginian or Lybian civilization was installed in pale reflection among the peoples of the south than it is true that the dominant ideas of the eastern Mediterranean, pushing northward into savage or barbarian Europe at about the same time or somewhat earlier, were reproduced in the same form or with the same consequences on the margins of the North Sea.

There is equally no case, one may emphasize, for supposing a one-way traffic in the diffusion of ideas and ideologies from the valley of the Nile into southern and central Africa. Dynastic Egypt was not born into a void; it emerged from a Neolithic womb, and this womb was African. The peasants of the Fayum Lake, those who laid the foundations of old Egyptian society, were not without their own ideas about life and the cosmos; the provenance of these ideas, or of most of them, was undoubtedly more African than Asian. "God's Land" with all its great ancestral spirits lay, for dynastic Egypt, neither in the east nor in the north, but far to the south and west. There is nothing to show that the earliest forms of ram and sun worship or of other cults made famous along the Nile did not take their rise in this obscure "God's Land" of "upper Africa," where, as we can clearly see today, they have flourished since. Indeed, it is reasonable to assume an interweaving and intershuttling process of elaboration and re-elaboration as ideas traveled back and forth, northward and southward; and suffered the molding pressure of different times and different peoples.

Those many populations of western Africa who claim an eastern or a northern origin may have essential truth in their legend. Yet this truth, after so many centuries of settlement and mingling, is always likely to mean influence rather than physical origin. It is well to bear all this in mind lest one fall into the error of imagining ancient peoples in Africa, two thousand years ago and more, as no more than a formless face whereon exotic features could be printed. Exotic features made their appearance, but were absorbed, and, through being absorbed, were inwardly transformed. They became as specifically West African as the religious customs of the Akan or the Yoruba; or as Christianity, springing from an Asian sect in Palestine, became European; or — long before that — as the purely African contribution to the civilization of the ancient Nile had become Egyptian.

Only in the last few years have anthropologists turned to a systematic study of the interwoven fabric of belief and thought that lies behind the apparently simple structure of tribal life in continental Africa. Much that seemed clear now becomes obscure; with new knowledge, much else becomes explicable. Increasingly one sees that the "stagnant centuries" of tribal Africa have been only a figment of the imagination.

3 The Coming of Iron

WHAT IS CAPE VERDE?" OBJECTED CHARLES II WHEN PRESSED TO found a new company of English venturers for the Guinea trade. "A stinking place." And the judgment, understandably as things were, would persist in Europe. Everything beyond Cape Verde that was known to discovering Europe — though for a long time little but the coast was known — seemed to approve this gloomy verdict: the swamps in their everlasting rain, the difficult slaving chieftains, the fevers and the heat, the ease of conquest and the bitter problem of maintaining conquest — surely everything here was primitive and hopeless? These peoples of the Guinea coast, twisted then by long decades of responding to the European demand for slaves, appeared all too easily as peoples without a history, without the means of progress, without the hope of salvation. Nothing with them, as many Europeans thought, could have changed since the age of apes and stone.

It was, as may now be seen, a figment of the imagination. Much had changed and grown: kingdoms and empires had risen and fallen and risen again, while civilizations of the Nile and Mediterranean, building on an African heritage of ideas, had long since made their large contribution. Ideas about the universe and the origins of life and government were important in this contribution. But for social growth in these lands to the south of the desert, ideas about the use of metal were probably more important; and ideas about the use of iron were almost certainly decisive.

How ancient is the use of metals south of the desert? Some judgments, even in these last few years, have reasserted an older European idea that Africans remained in the Stone Age until the colonial period began. Yet the broad facts are clear from an abundant documentation after the fifteenth century. The only African peoples who were still in the Stone Age at the time of fifteenth century discovery, it turns out, were Pygmies and Bushmen, peoples who lived in the Canary Islands and the island of Fernando Po, and perhaps one or two other communities on the mainland. Many African peoples, like their contemporaries in Europe, were still using stone and bone; but they were also using metal. They had used metal for a long time.

The first metals they used were gold and copper, for these occur in a natural state that is readily workable, and, even when smelted, are easier to smelt than iron. Thus in lower Egypt the transitional Amratian culture — a Neolithic culture that was acquiring the use of metal — knew of gold from Nubia before 4000 B.C., and *nub* in Old Egyptian was the word for gold. By the centuries that preceded the first dynasty — that is, before about 3000 B.C. — people in the Nile delta were making fine jewelry from gold. The peripheral peoples of Kush and Libya certainly had gold and copper and bronze long before they had iron.

In ancient West Africa, with plenty of gold but very little copper, early contacts across the Sahara no doubt included an exchange of West African gold against Libyan copper; and it seems likely that the charioteers of the Libyan Garamantes, if they really went across the Sahara to the Niger near Gao (as they now appear to have done), would have carried on this useful trade. Certainly this traffic was in course by early Arab times. El Husani, writing in about 950, says that gold was exchanged for copper in the Fezzan, where the Garamantes had lived; and no doubt the same was true elsewhere. Mauny, in a detailed study of the matter, concludes that the use of copper and of bronze came south across the Sahara after about 1200 B.C. — approximate date of the introduction of horses there — and that weapons of copper, though rare, continued to be made and used at least until 200 B.C.

But it is the date of the arrival of iron and iron working that is crucial. And this is so because a metal age cannot be said to have begun in continental Africa, as a distinct cultural period involving new forms of society and social organization, until the working of iron became common. Only with good iron tools would African peoples subdue the natural difficulties of living where they did, spread themselves across the land, flourish and multiply; and the copper and bronze ages of Asian and European antiquity are altogether lacking to the south of the Sahara. This is the reason, to repeat an earlier point, why study of Africa's Iron Age is of primary importance for an understanding of contemporary African origins. When did this Iron Age begin?

Iron tools and weapons may have reached Kush, as objects of rarity and wonder, as early as 600 B.C.; but iron smelting became intensive there only a good deal later. It became important as a cultural fact, perhaps, no more than two or three hundred years before the Christian era. Along the trans-African route between Nile and Niger, accordingly, knowledge of ironworking could scarcely have reached West or Central Africa much before the first century B.C. or even later. Transfer of this knowledge from Meroë would have been slowed down by those long-consuming semidesert miles, but also, probably, by a Kushite royal practice of keeping the craft of ironworking a closely guarded royal secret (or priestly secret, for the slag heaps of Meroë lie only a few hundred yards from the Temple of the Sun).

Of the strength and persistence of this monopolizing practice, indeed, there would be later echoes in the lands to the south. When Portuguese first reached the mouth of the Congo at the end of the fifteenth century, they would find that the *mani* or king of Congo was a member of an exclusive "blacksmiths' guild"; later knowledge has confirmed that the case was not a solitary one. "All over the Tawreg country [of the south Sahara]," Barth would report in the middle of the nineteenth century, "the *enhad* [smith] is in much respect, and the confraternity is most numerous. An *enhad* is generally the prime minister of every little chief."

Yet in spite of these delays, knowledge of ironworking may probably have reached West and Central Africa from Kush in the last years of the pre-Christian era. By this time, French scholars believe, Lybico-Berber peoples — whether the old Garamantes or the Tuareg of the desert or other intermediaries and traders — had already taken it southward. They base this belief on the fact that iron becomes general, in excavated North African graves, for the period beginning about 500 B.C.; and that iron had evidently displaced bronze for everyday objects in civilized North Africa by the third century B.C. This was at about the same time that iron became common in Kush. French authorities do not

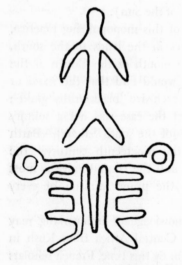

Chariot Rock Engravings

Charioteers regularly crossed the Sahara some two
and a half thousand years ago. Here are two rock
engravings of their horse-drawn chariots from Tondia,
near Goundam on the Middle Niger.

deny this — nor the solid evidence of those towering slag heaps
at Meroë — but they argue that Lybico-Berber peoples possessed
readier means of reaching West Africa than did the peoples of

Kush or the intermediary peoples who were commercially linked with Kush.

This French view has two strong arguments in its favor. The first, resting on firm evidence of rock engravings, is that at least two chariot routes crossed the Sahara between North Africa and the neighborhood of Gao, on the Niger, during the middle centuries of the first millennium B.C. Lhote has even felt able to suggest that the famous Libyan expedition of 19 B.C. by the Roman legate, Cornelius Balbus, conquered not only the Garamantes of the Fezzan — which is not in question — but went on southward until it reached the Niger. This may be claiming rather too much for Roman initiative. But at least two other Roman expeditions, those of Septimus Flaccus in A.D. 70 and Julius Maternus in A.D. 86, also penetrated far southward from the North African coast and probably reached the Sudan or its confines.

The second argument is one of dating. Mauny considers that peoples in the Western Sudan and its savannahs were smelting iron ore — plentiful there as in other parts of the continent — by as early as 300 B.C.; and this would support the view that they had the knowledge of how to do it from the north rather than from the east — unless, which is possible though not probable, they developed it independently for themselves. This knowledge they would subsequently pass on to forest peoples who lived, in turn, to the south of them.

But whether from Libya or Kush or from both, knowledge of ironworking was evidently common in the savannahs of the Sudan by the last centuries of the pre-Christian era. By the end of the first centuries of the Christian era it had extended to the southward far beyond the fringes of the forest. These dates are of central importance; they mark the beginnings of contemporary Africa.

If tentative and approximate, they are reasonable. All the evidence at present available supports them, while nothing contradicts them. They suppose an earlier period in which iron tools and weapons made their appearance south of the Sahara, and a subsequent period when mining and smelting industries were themselves installed in lands that were progressively to the south of one another.

Thus the appearance of iron in what is now Nigeria evidently coincided with the ending of the Nok "figurine cult," the last stages of which were probably transitional: new ideas and new techniques, that is to say, stimulated the growth of new societies. And by the twelfth century A.D., as we shall see, smelted iron from the far southeastern coast of Africa was going in large quantities to India — dramatic indicator of the change which had come about. The twelve or thirteen centuries between these two dates mark a period of great change and growth. They enclose the crucially formative period of pre-European and pre-industrial civilization in Negro Africa.

Not that other metals had failed to appear much earlier, whether as objects of veneration or of use. A statuette of the Egyptian god Osiris, made in bronze or copper and dating to about the seventh century B.C., has been found in the Belgian Congo; another statuette of Osiris, bearing the cartouche of Tutmosis III (before 1450 B.C.) has been reported from south of the Zambezi; Egyptian coins of the thirteenth dynasty (1780–1580 B.C.) are said to have been found in Madagascar. But these objects, or other gold and copper remnants of that early period, cannot be awarded much interest except as curios or as fresh proofs, if any were needed, of native ingenuity and the great mobility of man and goods across the ancient lands.

It was the smelting of iron that hammered on the doors of ancient Africa and broke them down. Through them there issued forth, in at least two wide regions of the central and southern continent, Iron Age civilizations which were pioneering for their time and place and which give pre-European history there its central interest and its main achievement. One of these regions was eastern and south-central Africa: the other was the Western Sudan and the lands that lay nearby.

4 *"Business with the King of Timbuktu"*

CLOSE UPON THE FENCE WERE SHEDS WHERE THE SOLDIERS LAY, the horses picqueted before them with their heads turned towards the sheds, and their food laid before them on the ground. Above each soldier's sleeping place, covered only on the top and open in the sides, were hung a lance, a small oval shield, and a large broadsword." Thus James Bruce, traveling up the Blue Nile in 1772, of the "black horse of Sennar." A Scots laird with a love of horsemanship, he found that this chain-mailed cavalry of the Sudan presented him with "one of the finest sights I ever saw."

Each warrior's quarters had hanging there a steel shirt of mail and, beside it, a soft antelope skin to cover it from the dew of the night. "A headpiece of copper, without crest or plumage, was suspended by a lance above the shirt of mail." The horses were "all above sixteen hands high, of the breed of the old Saracen horses, all finely made, and as strong as our coach horses, but exceedingly nimble in their motion." Of such were the horsemen of Adlan, lord of a kingdom whose frontiers reached, when Bruce was there, from the middle Nile to the borders of Ethiopia.

Bruce was not believed in Britain when at last he came home; and yet these might have been the cavalry of any of the kingdoms of the old Sudan, not only in 1772, when Bruce saw them, but at almost any time for many hundred years before. The din and glitter of such horsemen, quilt-mailed or chain-

mailed, accompany the pageantry and tale of all these states
and feudal empires which rose and flourished and disappeared
in the Sudanese savannah, three thousand miles long and perhaps five hundred broad: dividing the Sahara from the forests
of the tropical south, and joining the Atlantic to the Red Sea.

Europe was unaware of these states until the fourteenth
century, nearly a thousand years after the earliest of them began
its life. Norman merchants of twelfth-century Sicily, true enough,
had traded with the Muslim cities of North Africa: Pisans,
Genoese, Venetians, Provençals had followed them. Throughout
the Middle Ages commercial treaties linked the two shores of
the Mediterranean. Christian states established consuls in the
southern ports. But Christians were debarred from the interior.
For religious and commercial reasons the Muslim states insisted
on their absolute monopoly of intercourse with the continent
behind their Mediterranean seaboard.

But Jews could travel there. By the fourteenth century there
was founded in Majorca a famous school of Jewish cartographers.
The best-known of their atlases, made on royal commission from
one or other of the courts of Europe, was that of Abraham
Cresques. His "Catalan Map" of 1375 had something of the
same effect as the discoveries of Columbus over a century later.
It pushed back the frontiers of the known world. It gave a new
reality to the rumor of half-believed travelers' tales. It showed
the Atlas mountains of Morocco, for example, broken by a pass
that was used by merchants "going to the Land of the Negroes
of Guinea" — the great southward route by way of Sijilmassa,
in fact, that North Africans had used since time beyond memory. It marked Tenbuch (Timbuktu), Ciutat de Mali, Geugeu
(Gao), and Tagaza; and all these, amid a host of others, would
henceforth tease the interest and imagination of Europe until
the earliest European travelers, centuries after, could reach them
at last.

Yet information was hard to come by, and harder still to publish. Every maritime city collected its own geographical intelligence, but kept its own secrets. In those days of high risk and high trading profit, when Europe was beginning to venture on the seas and yet had scarcely learned to sail a ship against the wind or use the mariner's compass, men with such intelligence to sell could sell it dearly. They could sell it to Venice or the maritime cities of the west Italian coast. They could sell it to the court of Spain or to Prince Henry of Portugal — he whom history has called "the Navigator" not because he went to sea but because, more than any other prince of his time, he put order and system into the collection and collation of maritime news.

Many of the early maps were fantastic, and not a few were fakes. Yet little by little they gained in reality. One of the first to show a southern termination of Africa, for example, was that of Fra Mauro, made secretly in Venice in 1459 for the use of Prince Henry the Navigator. This early assertion that ships could sail round Africa if only they would go far enough to the southward was not proven until nearly thirty years later, when Bartolomeo Diaz actually doubled the Cape of Good Hope; but it rested, apparently, on the report of an Indian navigator who was said to have doubled the cape from the eastward as early as 1420. This will seem less surprising when it is remembered that Indian Ocean shipping was technically more efficient than European shipping until at least the close of the fifteenth century.

Since trading monopolies depended on a monopoly of information, Prince Henry kept Fra Mauro's map under cautious lock and key. Would Diaz and da Gama have seen it before they sailed on their long voyages to the south and east? It is hard to say how much those famous captains thought they knew. Had Magellan some idea that he could get from the Atlantic to the Pacific before he attempted the strait that would take his name?

"The sentiments of every person in the fleet," wrote Pigafetta, who sailed with him, while they rode in the waters east of Cape Horn before the attempt was made, "were, that it had no issue on the west; and nothing but the confidence they had in the superior information of the commander could have induced them to prosecute the research. But this great man, as skilful as he was courageous, knew that he was to seek for a passage through an obscure strait: this strait he had seen laid down on a chart of Martin de Bohème, a most excellent cosmographer, which was in the possession of the king of Portugal." And if Martin de Bohème was more than guessing, what unknown hero had brought that perilous fact to Europe?

If anyone, he might well have been a mariner of North Africa, and probably an Arab. Edrisi, an Arab nobleman of Andalusia who wrote for the Norman king of Sicily in the middle of the twelfth century, has a reference to Atlantic voyages which seem to have reached the Canaries; while Abulfeda (1273-1332) speaks of voyages round the world, which he describes as a sphere.

Then Omari, in the tenth chapter of his *Masalik al-absad,* reproduces a story which suggests that Atlantic voyages were made by mariners of West Africa in the times of the Emperor Kankan Musa of Mali; and which roundly states that the predecessor of Kankan Musa embarked on the Atlantic with "two thousand ships" and sailed westward and disappeared.

A tall story, perhaps; yet Mali had outlets on the Atlantic seaboard, while North African mariners evidently knew of the Azores several centuries before the voyage of Columbus.

"And I asked the Sultan Musa," writes Omari of the words of Ibn Amir Hajib, "how it was that power had come to his hands, and he replied: We come of a house where royalty is transferred by heritage. The monarch who preceded me would not believe that it was impossible to discover the limits of the neighboring sea. He wished to know. He persisted in his plan. He caused the equipping of two hundred ships and filled them with men, and of another such number that were filled with gold, water and food for two years. He said to the commanders: Do not return until you have reached the end of the ocean, or when you have exhausted your food and water.

"They went away, and their absence was long: none came back, and their absence continued. Then a single ship returned. We asked its captain of their adventures and their news. He replied: Sultan, we sailed for a long while until we met with what seemed to be a river with a strong current flowing in the open sea. My ship was last. The others sailed on, but as each of them came to that place they did not come back nor did they reappear; and I do not know what became of them. As for me, I turned where I was and did not enter that current . . ." * Is this all mere courtly embroidery? If Magellan ever saw a North African chart of the seas round Cape Horn it would detract nothing from his skill and courage. The point is that European sailors in the fifteenth and sixteenth centuries would have had extreme difficulty in obtaining such information even when it was known and often used by their non-European contemporaries. Yet here and there, wherever merchants had their say and royal monopolies were less respected, information began to go the rounds. By the sixteenth century it was beginning to be widely published.

Of these early publications of travelers' tales the most famous and most useful was edited at Venice, in 1563, by Giovanni-Battista Ramusio, secretary to the Most Illustrious Council of the Ten. Ramusio published a series of previously secret documents, among the most sensational (and the word is not too strong, given the general ignorance of the times) being a history and description of the Sudan by a captured Moor, Hassan ibn

* This is from a French translation made by M. Muhammad Habibullah. See Bibliography.

Mohammed el Wazzan el Zayyati — renamed, after baptism, Giovanni Leoni, or Leo Africanus — and the report of a voyage to the Guinea coast that a Venetian in Portuguese service, Ca' da Mosto, had made successfully in 1455, more than a hundred years earlier.

More than a hundred years earlier: yet to Ramusio and his readers the information seemed valuable and fresh. They took it in a practical way. Ramusio's comment on Ca' da Mosto's narrative gives strong advice to Italian merchants that they should go and try their luck upon the Guinea coast. They should *mandar a contrattar con il Re di Tombutto e di Melli* — go and do business with the King of Timbuktu and of Mali, send their cargoes and their agents to those kingdoms, where they would be well received and cared for, "those kingdoms being at present so much civilized and so desirous of the merchandise of Europe, as may be read in this book of Giovan Lioni."

Ramusio well knew the narrow limits of his knowledge, and offered his book as no more than a tentative beginning. Yet behind the locked doors of chanceries and royal map rooms the information was piling up; by Ramusio's time the Portuguese had been over half a century in India, had dispatched hundreds of ships down the west coast of Africa and round the Cape of Good Hope, and sent their agents inland wherever opportunity and profit offered. The service rendered by Ramusio — as by Hakluyt in England somewhat later — was to popularize a little of this knowledge; but it was no mean service.

Little by little Europe became aware of the Sudan. The names of Mali and Songhay were dutifully inserted on maps, even when little but that could be said of kingdoms generally believed to enjoy a more or less fabulous wealth and power. Exaggeration was excusable. Compared to the poverty of Europe then, the wealth of the Indies did seem infinite and wonderful; and if the Indies, then why not Africa as well? Later on, the reaction would be no less extreme in the other direction. Having begun by thinking them great, Europe would end by denying historical importance to these kingdoms of the old Sudan. The truth, as always, lay somewhere in between. Allowing for a disagreeable and difficult climate, medieval Timbuktu might reasonably have claimed as much of civilization as most of the university cities of medieval Europe. But nineteenth century Timbuktu — as its first European reporter, René Caillié, disappointedly found — seemed miserable indeed; compared with any of its European compeers of that time, it undoubtedly was.

Reassessment of the civilizations of the great bend of the Niger during the centuries between A.D. 500 and 1500 has rested partly on a fuller knowledge of the people and their traditions — knowledge that was first collected systematically and intelligently by Heinrich Barth in six great years of travel after 1848; and partly on a fuller knowledge of written records which had begun to appear in Arabic — or in Arabic script — from the eighth century onwards. From Wahb ibn Munabbeh in 738 to Leo Africanus in 1526 at least a score of notable Arab and Berber historians and geographers wrote of these Negro states; and to this documentation there must be added the writings of the scholars of the Western Sudan itself.

These last are important, for they provide much of what is known of the subject. The fullest is the *Tarikh es Sudan* of Abderrahman es Sadi, a learned citizen of Timbuktu who was born in 1596 and published his book — comprising a chronicle of Sudanese kingdoms, many short biographies of notabilities whom he knew, and an account of his own experiences as diplomatic intermediary between warring princes — around 1655. This book was known and used by Barth and other nineteenth century writers. Another Sudanese book, not much less useful, came to light only in 1911; like the *Tarikh es Sudan*, the *Tarikh el Fettach* was written in Arabic, literary language of the time (as

Latin had lately been in Europe), and is largely an account of Songhay. Its special interest comes from the fact that its author, Mahmoud Kati — also a learned citizen of Timbuktu, but a Negro where Abderrahman es Sadi seems to have been of Peul and Moorish descent — accompanied the great Songhay ruler Mohammed Askia on the Mecca pilgrimage and witnessed the Moroccan invasion which overwhelmed Songhay at the end of the sixteenth century. Though completed by a grandson of Kati's in about 1600, an anonymous hand has added an appendix which brings the story down to about 1660.

Both of these books abound in first-hand information and illuminating detail; they offer a convincing picture of the life of their day, but especially of its religious and intellectual aspects. "God has drawn to this fortunate city," wrote Sadi of the city of Djenné where he was employed as notary during the first part of his adult life, "a certain number of learned and of pious men, strangers to this country, who have come to live here. They are of different peoples and countries." In our own day the wheel comes full circle: as these lines were written the Grand Conseil or Federal Assembly of French West Africa had just elected as its president a citizen of that same proud city of Djenné.

These clerks and notaries, imams, teachers and historians of the Western Sudan — and some of their names are known, though their writings are lost or not yet found again — could look back on several centuries of enlightenment. With Timbuktu or Djenné as their intellectual centers, they had wide contacts with the outside world. Many learned men of Islam followed a tradition of voyaging up and down the world. Nearly three hundred years before the *Tarikh es Sudan* was finished, Ibn Battuta had come here after travels in Arabia and India and China, and written admiringly of the kingdom of Mali. The Negroes of this country, he says, "are seldom unjust, and have a greater abhorrence of injustice than any other people. Their sultan shows no mercy to anyone who is guilty of the least act of it. There is complete security in the country. Neither traveller nor inhabitant in it has anything to fear from robbers or men of violence. They do not confiscate the property of any white man" — that is, of any Arab — "who dies in their country, even if it be uncounted wealth. On the contrary, they give it into the charge of some trustworthy person among the whites, until the rightful heir takes possession of it." If the states of the old Sudan had no links with Europe they had plenty with North Africa, the valley of the Nile, and the Near East.

From an infinity of detail and dynastic strife across a thousand years three or four major states bulk large in the record, each related to one another and yet with distinctive features of its own. They are all civilizations of the savannah, of space-defying plains of grass and great seasonal heat; and they are all built on urban trade and a pastoral-agricultural economy. In all of them the great rivers of West Africa exercise a formative influence. The earliest is Ghana, already a centralized state when the Arabs first mention it in A.D. 800. The second is Mali, taking its rise in the thirteenth century but persisting until the seventeenth. A third is Kanem, which later became Bornu; and a fourth is Songhay, whose power and prestige would cover the fifteenth and sixteenth centuries.

Some of these states were the contemporaries of early medieval Europe, and may at times be accounted superior to it in civilization. "During these centuries," comments Palmer of the Kanem that was contemporary with the age of Saladin, "the Christian West had remained ignorant, rude, and barbarous, while Saracenic culture passed on the torch of civilisation to future ages. The nascent kingdom of Bornu" — growing out of Kanem — "drew its inspiration from Egypt and North Africa. Though its conduct towards the African peoples by which it was surrounded was callous and brutal, the degree of civilisation achieved by its early chiefs would appear to compare favourably with that of European monarchs of that day." While subsequent knowledge makes us think that Kanem and Bornu were entirely African states, ruled by African peoples who had long since absorbed and transformed such influences as had come from the north, there is no doubt that Palmer's comparison may stand. The medieval Sudan had little to fear from comparisons in civilization with medieval Europe.

It had its own strong character. Swinging tassels in the dust, harness brasses that glitter against quilted armor, long spears pennoned and pointed, brilliant cavaliers, all the creak and swing and clatter and pomp of an aristocratic army saddled for sack and loot; with the footsore plebs in goat skin, armed with clubs and spears and small hope, trailing out behind — such were the warrior columns of the old Sudan, the feudal fire and challenge that were thrown, times without number, against the easy marts and watered villages of one imperial region after another, now with one side winning, now with the other. The defenses might be poor enough and stratagems were seldom new: even the great Idris Alooma of Bornu could be celebrated for mounting an enclosure of thorns and stakes. "For all that," remarks Urvoy wisely, "do not let us smoothly despise these black warriors. This headstrong braggart cavalry and its rabble of infantry, these raidings and reivings or rare and brilliant battles that grew willy nilly from duel and skirmish — they were our own feudal army, they were Crécy and Agincourt."

Even in the time of their decay, when an age of industry and commerce up and down the world had long since eclipsed the trans-Saharan trade, these polities were not contemptible. "The view of this extensive city," wrote Mungo Park of Segu on the Niger at the end of the eighteenth century, "the numerous canoes upon the river; the crowded population; and the cultivated state

of the surrounding country, found altogether a prospect of civilization and magnificence, which I little expected to find in the
bosom of Africa." It is difficult now, looking back on these
pastoral kingdoms from what is practically another world, to re-
capture the effect they made on those who saw them. But the
effect was vivid and profound.

5 *Ghana*

EVERYWHERE IN THE ANCIENT WORLD, IRON PROVED A REVOLUTION-
ary equipment that enabled men to build new and more complex
societies; and it was no different in Africa. Once its metallurgy was
understood, iron was much more easily obtained than copper or
bronze, and was much more efficient. Those who had it could exercise, over those who did not have it, something of the same order
of superiority as musketeers would later exercise over spearmen.
Thus the peoples of Ghana, remarks El Zouhri some time before
A.D. 1150, make expeditions against neighbors "who know not iron
and fight with bars of ebony." The Ghanaians "can defeat them
because they fight with swords and lances."

The early kingdoms of the old Sudan were thus the product
of an iron-using superiority. This means that while the beginnings
of organized statehood in the Western Sudan cannot be traced
beyond the eighth century — though oral tradition takes them
vaguely some way further back — their earliest origins can be
safely attached to the period of installation of iron extractive
industries and of social changes associated with that development. This period begins around 300 B.C.

Both for work and warfare, the trans-Saharan trade had shown
by then the superiority of iron over other metals. Whether by
individual skill or native invention, by the capture of prisoners

or the purchase of secrets, by the migration of groups or of whole peoples from the north and northeast, iron was beginning to be mined and worked south of the Sahara. Thenceforth iron gave a new mastery over soil and forest, but also — as El Zouhri remarked in his illuminating comment — over stone and bone and wood-using neighbors. It gave, that is, an impulse to conquest and centralized government. It shook the foundations of Stone Age tribalism. It promoted new forms of social organization. It accompanied the creation of an African feudalism; and this feudalism, though always modified and molded by tribal law and custom, would have many parallels with feudalism in medieval Europe.

To this formative influence another, not much less disturbing and creative, was added. Emerging from the revolutionary growth of an ironworking industry and the changes it implied, these new states grew strong and prospered from their conquests but even more, as it would seem, from their international trade. Peoples of the Western Sudan might not control the sources of West African gold: for these lay mostly in the forest belt, and none of the states of the Sudan would succeed in any lasting penetration there. But they controlled the passage of this gold to the northward. Their cities flourished on its trade. They sold it to the intermediaries of the Sahara, who sold it again to the Mediterranean world and Europe; and they bought from these intermediaries the goods of Europe and the Mediterranean. In El Bekri's words, they or their agents carried gold "into every country." There is no exaggeration, Mauny argues, "in saying that the Sudan was one of the principal providers of gold to the Mediterranean world right through the Middle Ages, up to the discovery of America. It was this gold which had built the power of Ghana, and that of the Mandingo empire."

Behind the obscurities of early West African history, therefore, one may reasonably detect iron smelting and international trade as underlying factors which had decisive influence in the hands of men who practiced them. Political and military concentration became possible and, at least for those who could rule, desirable. Alliances of interest emerged, became fused into centers of power, acquired geographical identity, reappeared as territorial states; even when, as was surely the case, the people of the riverside villages and the nomads following their herds continued to live in much the same way as they had lived before.

Among these emergent states of the Western Sudan the earliest that rose to fame and fortune was Ghana. Its territory lay to the north and northwest of the upper Niger: significantly enough, on the gold routes to the north. El Fazari, soon after A.D. 800, named it "the land of gold." Shortly before 833 Kwarizmi marked it on a map that was otherwise a copy of one which Ptolemy had drawn long centuries before. But it was not for another two hundred years that a North African would write of Ghana in any detail. Then comes the vivid account of Abdallah ibn Abdel Aziz, known as Abu Ubaid, or better still as El Bekri. And although it is a work of compilation, written by a man who never visited Africa (or at any rate never visited the Sudan), this description of El Bekri's has the illuminating touch of full and good material. Writing at Córdoba in southern Spain, where he had at his disposal the official records of the Ummayad rulers and the gossip of contemporary pioneers, El Bekri sets forth in careful and discriminating detail what well-informed Mediterranean opinion, based on many firsthand reports and much military intelligence, believed to be the truth about Ghana and the lands beyond the desert. His work was finished in 1067, some thirteen years after Ibn Yasin, the Almoravid ruler of North Africa, had marched southward to invade those lands and had captured Aoudaghast, a tributary city of Ghana. This invasion had brought the Western Sudan much closer to the Mediterranean and Spain; and it was this that gave El Bekri his wide choice of material.

"The king of Ghana," El Bekri is writing in the year after William of Normandy crossed the English Channel, "can put two hundred thousand warriors in the field, more than forty thousand of them being armed with bow and arrow." It would be interesting to know what the Normans might have thought of Ghana. Anglo-Saxon England could easily have seemed a poor and lowly place beside it. "Ghana," says El Bekri in 1067, "is the title of the king of this people," and "the name of their country is Aoukar. The king who governs them at the moment . . . is called Tenkamenin, who came to the throne in 455 [that is, A.D. 1062] . . . Tenkamenin is master of a great empire and of a power which is formidable."

That this was more than travelers' embroidery may be seen from the fact that it took the Almoravid armies — rapidly victorious elsewhere — no fewer than fourteen years to subdue Ghana and seize its capital city. Ibn Yasin, fervent promoter of Islam, had marched southward from the Maghreb in 1054. In the following year he took Aoudaghast, a city that is entirely vanished today but was situated, according to El Bekri, two months' southward from Sijilmassa and fifteen days from the capital of Ghana. El Bekri says that Aoudaghast was "a very large city with several markets, many date palms and henna trees as big as olives," and "filled with fine houses and solid buildings." This city — a Sudanese city with many Moorish traders, for it lay at the southern terminal of the trans-Saharan caravan trail from Sijilmassa — the Almoravids "took by storm, violating women and carrying off all they found there, saying it was legal booty." But it was not until 1076 that another Almoravid leader, Abu Bakr, could take the capital of Ghana itself.

This capital had two cities six miles apart, while the space between was also covered with dwellings. In the first of these cities was the king's residence, "a fortress and several huts with rounded roofs, all being enclosed by a wall." The second, which also had a dozen mosques, was a merchant city of the Muslims: a city, that is, of those who had come southward to settle or tarry and trade — much, indeed, like the *sabun gari* outside the walls of modern Kano; although there in Kano it is from the south that men have come for trade and settlement. Of manners at the court of this pagan king, El Bekri provides a celebrated description.

"When he gives audience to his people, to listen to their complaints and set them to rights, he sits in a pavilion around which stand his horses caparisoned in cloth of gold; behind him stand ten pages holding shields and gold-mounted swords; and on his right hand are the sons of the princes of his empire, splendidly clad and with gold plaited into their hair. The governor of the city is seated on the ground in front of the king, and all around him are his vizirs in the same position. The gate of the chamber is guarded by dogs of an excellent breed, who never leave the king's seat, they wear collars of gold and silver. . . . The beginning of an audience is announced by the beating of a kind of drum which they call *deba*, made of a long piece of hollowed wood . . ."

Where was this capital city? As long ago as 1914 a French district officer, Bonnel de Mezières, dug into a site that was suggested by tradition (although not by any visible projection above the flat savannah) at a remote spot in the Sahel, a scrub and sand country north of the upper Niger. De Mezières found enough to make him believe that this had probably been the capital of Ghana in El Bekri's day; and later excavation has gone far to vindicate him.

Renewed work at this site of Kumbi Saleh, lying two hundred and five miles north of the modern city of Bamako on the Niger, began in 1939; only to be stopped, almost at once, by the war. Ten years later Thomassey and Mauny were at last able to undertake a systematic examination of these promising ruins in the light of a modern understanding of the matter. By 1951 they had tracked the remains of a large and elaborate Muslim city which had covered a square mile and may have had a population of about thirty thousand people, very numerous for the world of eight or nine hundred years ago when this city had evidently flourished.

Reasons for believing that this was the merchant city of Ghana reported by El Bekri, and that the king's city may yet be identified nearby — that Kumbi Saleh, in short, was Ghana's capital through the last period of its life as an organized state — are not yet conclusive, but they are strong. Thus the *Tarikh el Fettach* says that Kumbi had been the capital of the empire of the Kayamaga, while the *Tarikh es Sudan* explains that Kayamaga had been the name of the first king of Ghana (who had, according to tradition, no fewer than forty-three successors). And while there are other "Kumbis" in the region of Kumbi Saleh, there is none which offers archeological evidence of having once existed as a city of the first importance.

That Kumbi Saleh had been this, though, admits of no argument at all. Level with its dusty sub-Saharan plain though it is today, Kumbi Saleh had once been great. Among many large dwellings and a mosque, two mansions excavated by Thomassey suggest something of its scale and comfort. One of these was about sixty-six feet long and forty-two feet wide, and had seven rooms opening out of one another on two stories connected by an efficient staircase. The other was still larger, and had nine rooms. Built mainly in blocks of slatelike schist cemented with banco, their interior walls had been decorated with a yellow plaster of which a little is still preserved. No objects in silver or gold were found, but a large store of objects in iron, indicating, as Mauny has commented, "an already advanced civilization, both urban and agricultural." Among these iron objects were lances, knives, arrowheads, nails, a varied collection of farming tools, and one of the finest pairs of scissors of early medieval date ever to be found in any country. A large quantity of glass weights, evidently for weighing gold, were recovered; many fragments of pottery of Mediterranean provenance; and seventy-seven pieces of painted stone, of which fifty-three bore verses of the Koran in an Arabic script, while twenty-four others had decorated motifs.

Trade and tribute were the sources of its wealth. Ghana lay between the salt deposits of the north and the gold deposits of the south, and profited mightily from exchange between the two. Such was the southern need of salt that a gold-producing people called the Ferawi, according to El Bekri, would buy it for an equal weight of gold. But gold was also the commodity that the north wanted most. Thus the imperial ambition of successive states in the Sudan, drawing their wealth from this international trade, would be to monopolize the southern sources of gold — the "mysterious" land of Wangara and its gold-bearing soil that lay in fact somewhere near the sources of the Senegal River — and, secondly, to capture the principal salt deposits of the north, notably those at Taghaza in the northern desert, as well as to dominate the caravan roads. Ghana managed the first but not the second. Mali, after Ghana, would go far toward succeeding in both.

The rulers of Ghana not only knew the supreme trading value of gold, they also understood the need and the means of upholding it. El Bekri makes this clear. "The best gold in the country," he says, "is found at Ghiarou, a town that is eighteen days' journey from the capital, lying in a country filled with Negro peoples" and covered with their villages. "All nuggets of gold that are found in the mines of this empire belong to the king; but he leaves to his people the gold dust that everyone knows. Without this precaution gold would become so plentiful that it would practically lose its value."

They equally understood the value of trading tribute. The king of Ghana "exacts the right of one dinar of gold on each donkey-load of salt that enters the country, and two dinars of gold on each load of salt that goes out." Salt and gold would always be staple commodities; but others were important. "A load of copper" — entering Ghana from the copper mines of the southern Sahara — "pays him five mithcals, and each load of merchandise ten mithcals." * Here one glimpses the familiar picture of a centralized government which has discovered the art and exercise of taxation, another witness of stability and statehood.

In 1054 the Almoravid rulers came south to make converts to Islam and to chastise pagans, but they also came for loot. They had the salt deposits under their control; they sought now to capture the gold deposits as well. Their coming was brief but disastrous. Three hundred years after El Bekri, Ibn Khaldun would summarize the experience. The Almoravids "spread their dominion over the Negroes [of Ghana], devastated their territory and plundered their property. Having submitted them to poll tax they imposed on them a tribute, and compelled a great number of them to become Moslems. The authority of the kings of Ghana being destroyed, their neighbors, the Sosso, took their country and reduced its inhabitants to slavery." By the thirteenth century the state and cities of Ghana, or such as survived, were far gone in decay.

But the pattern of trade and tribute which had made Ghana strong over many centuries was not destroyed. If anything, it was strengthened. With Ghana and after Ghana, other states appeared. Conquest from the north, never more than spasmodic, repeatedly gave way to prolonged periods of peaceful trading; and it was the desert intermediaries in this trade, marauding

* The *mithcal* was about one-eighth of an ounce of gold.

Tuaregs and their kind, who regularly threatened this peace rather than the Arabs or Berbers of the north.

By 1213, according to a more or less respectable tradition, Allakoi Keita had founded the Mandingo state that would pass into history as the empire of Mali, or Melle; and twenty-five years later his successor, Sundiata, overthrew the Sosso rulers who had established themselves in Ghana not long before. Sundiata took the then capital of Ghana from the Sosso in 1240, destroyed it, and established his own capital (or the first of his capitals) in the south, perhaps at Niani or Jeriba on the upper Niger. He and his successors would dominate much of the Western Sudan for another hundred years.

They would dominate weaker rivals and enfeoffed subjects. For by this time the whole country of the Niger bend and its hinterland — more than half a million square miles of high and often well-watered grasslands — was drawn into the control of more or less centralized states. Some of these have achieved a place in history, through slender surviving records; others have left behind them no more than the curious echo of their names. Meanwhile far to the eastward, and at about the same time, another great savannah region was undergoing the same detribalizing and centralizing process; and would throw up, then and later, the states and empires of the Hausa and Fulani, of Kanem and Bornu and Darfur.

In this crystallizing process one strong power and ruling people, or federation of peoples, would rival or succeed or coexist with another, sometimes overlapping in time and place, sometimes continuing its life under different names and dynasties. In a limited sense the Mandingo empire of Mali may be said to have followed Ghana; and Songhay may be said to have followed Mali just as Bornu would follow Kanem. But any picture of one empire simply ousting another in mechanical succession would be false; the development across the whole region was rather a continuous growth of governing institutions interrupted by dynastic rivalries, foreign invasion, and the individual changes and chances of history.

And in all this there were parallels with contemporary Europe. The peoples of Europe and the Sudan might be as different from each other as the latitudes they lived in: the fundamental patterns of their social growth were often surprisingly alike. In both there was the steady organization of central power and tribute against an economic background of peasant agriculture, pastoralism, and an expanding use of metals. Trade, in both, was a great driving motor.

Timbuktu and Djenné, Walata, Gao, Agadès — these were the Milans and Nurembergs of the medieval Sudan: much less magnificent, indeed, yet rich and powerful and imposing in their time and place. Trading cities first and foremost, they welcomed the caravans which came in stumbling thirst out of the northern desert with loads of copper and salt, Venetian beads, the sword blades of Europe and Damascus. They assembled and dispatched the caravans which embarked again northward on that fearful journey, often with slaves, and the merchants with their ever more precious purseloads of gold. Their reputation spread across the world.

6 *Mali*

TIMBUKTU AND DJENNÉ, BOTH TO BECOME FAMOUS THROUGHOUT the Islamic world for their commerce and learning, seem to have grown into cities by the twelfth century. But their eminence dates from Mandingo supremacy and its empire of Mali. Then it was, in 1307, that the most renowned of all the monarchs of the old

Sudan, *Mansa* (sultan or emperor) Kankan Musa, inherited power over Mali and began to extend its dominion. After much success in conquest and diplomacy, this remarkable man followed others from the Western Sudan on pilgrimage to Mecca, and gave the world a proof of the widespread loyalties of Islam as well as a chance of measuring the wealth of Sudanese civilization.

His going through Cairo in 1324, his camel trains and servants and his wives and gifts and arrogant horsemen, all the trappings of a king whose realm would soon comprise a land as large as western Europe and as civilized as most of its kind in Europe, still lingered as familiar gossip in North Africa a hundred years later; for Kankan Musa went with a pleasantly memorable supply of gold as well as pomp and circumstance. An interesting contemporary estimate of Cairo's opinion was later recorded by a senior official of that city. Although El Omari's *Africa without Egypt* was written some time later, the writer was in a position to found his chapter on Mali from information gathered by men who had seen the Mandingo monarch on his way to Mecca.

He quotes a jurist of Cairo, who had talked with Kankan Musa, as having heard from the emperor that the length of his realm was "about one year." El Omari adds that he heard the same from another source, "but Ed Dukkali considers that it is four months long and as much wide; and this opinion of Ed Dukkali is preferable, since Kankan Musa may very well have swollen the real size of his realm." We know in fact that Mali at the time of Kankan Musa's journey, or soon after, had enclosed within its governing system the approaches to the salt deposits of Taghaza on the northern fringes of the Sahara, as well as the approaches to the gold country in the far south on the southern fringes of the savannah; while to the west it reached as far as the Atlantic, and eastward held the copper mines and caravan center of Takedda and probably the lands beyond.

This realm had grown during Kankan Musa's pilgrimage. In

1325 his army commander, Sagaman-dir, took the Songhay capital of Gao on the middle Niger; and with Gao there fell to the dominion of Mali the whole wide trading area which the Songhay had already captured to the north of them. Thus for size and wealth if not for the number of its people, who were comparatively few when compared with the empires of the East, Mali was one of the greatest states in the world of its time. Kankan Musa returned home by way of Gao, enjoying his general's conquest and receiving the submission of the Songhay king and notables, and went on upstream to Timbuktu.

There in Timbuktu he caused new mosques to be raised, mosques that would long be famous in the whole Sudan. They are said to have followed the design of a poet of Granada in southern Spain, Abu Ishaq es Saheli, whom the emperor had come to know in Mecca and persuaded to return with him. Ibn Battuta, visiting Timbuktu some twenty years later, says that he saw the grave of this "meritorious poet," while the Sankuré mosque of Timbuktu, attached to Abu Ishaq's name, would long be famous. And soon after Kankan Musa's visit, according to tradition, the earliest flat-roofed houses were built in Gao and Timbuktu. In any case the wealth of these cities must greatly have expanded from this time, for Mali had succeeded better than Ghana and now controlled the country to the north as well as the country to the south — many sources of copper, salt, and gold, as well as the caravan trails between.

Centers of commerce and religion, these cities became centers of learning. Scholars sheltered in their relative ease and security. The literate culture of the Western Sudan, already in existence for several hundred years, flowered in Timbuktu during years that saw, in Europe, the ravage of the Hundred Years' War. No one now can say how much it flowered, nor what fruits it bore, for the books that men read or wrote there are lost or not yet found; but Leo Africanus, two centuries later, gives some measure of the city's intellectual life. "In Timbuktu," he says, "there are numerous judges, doctors and clerics, all receiving good salaries from the king. He pays great respect to men of learning. There is a big demand for books in manuscript, imported from Barbary. More profit is made from the book trade than from any other line of business." The king in question was Mohammed Askia of Songhay; but conditions would not have greatly differed in the years of plenitude that came in the wake of Kankan Musa's conquest.

This was a civilization in its own right, standing to North Africa in much the same relationship of influence as Kush had stood to Egypt, and achieving, as Kush had achieved, its own original and independent growth. Peace reigned over the long caravan trails. Men were free to travel and trade and prosper as they could. There would be interruptions in this security, true enough — Mossi raiders would pillage Timbuktu only eight years after Kankan Musa's visit — but they would remain interruptions, disturbing rarely the everyday peace that Ibn Battuta found. And they must have disturbed even less the peasants and pastoralists who dwelt and throve on the banks of the Niger and out across the plains beyond. Many of these remained pagan even at the height of Islamic fame in the cities and gave, with their stolid clinging to the ancient ways, another native and authentic accent to this Sudanese civilization.

The excellent Ibn Battuta has left some pleasant travel notes of Mali. Always interested in women, he found those of Walata of "surpassing beauty" — no mean compliment, perhaps, from a man who had seen so many nations; moreover (and this he found upsetting as well as remarkable) they were "shown more respect than the men." The state of affairs at Walata, which he calls "the northernmost province of the Negroes," was "indeed extraordinary. Their men show no signs of jealousy whatever. No one claims descent from his father, but on the contrary from his mother's brother. A person's heirs are his sister's sons, not his own sons. This is a thing which I have seen nowhere in the world except among the Indians of Malabar. But *those* are heathens; *these* people are Muslims, punctilious in observing the hour of prayer, studying books of law, and memorizing the Koran. Yet their women show no bashfulness before men and do not veil themselves, though they are assiduous in attending prayer . . ." Even Islam had not succeeded in overthrowing matrilineal succession in the Sudan. Though strictly orthodox, Islam here would develop a distinctively Sudanese outlook in ethical and social matters.

These women, Ibn Battuta found to his surprise (and, one may think, to his delight), had "friends" or "companions" amongst men outside their own families, and the men in the same way had "companions" amongst the women of other families. "A man may go into his house and find his wife entertaining her 'companion,' but he takes no objection to it. One day at Walata I went into the qadi's house, after asking his permission to enter, and found him with a young woman of remarkable beauty. When I saw her I was shocked and turned to go out, but she laughed at me, instead of being overcome with shame, and the qadi said to me 'Why are you going out? She is my companion.'" And yet this qadi, says Ibn Battuta, "was a theologian and a pilgrim to boot."

With the conquests of Kankan Musa the rulers grew wealthier; and the cities, profiting from their control of the caravan terminals and their increasing monopoly of the more important products, followed suit. Perhaps Djenné was the greatest of them. "It is because of this hallowed town," the author of the *Tarikh es Sudan* would write some three hundred years later, but the comment will apply to the dominion of Mali as well as to the later dominion of Songhay, "that caravans come to Timbuktu from all points of the horizon." Crossing southward over the Sahara in the mid-nineteenth century, Heinrich Barth could still find potent evidence of the extent and wealth of this far-flung trading system. Though reduced by then to proportions that might be insignificant when compared with the carrying trade of nineteenth century Europe, it made a still convincing witness to the commercial machinery which had helped to build and maintain states and long-enduring dynasties in this savannah country of the Middle Ages.

Even through the eyes of this late observer, the scene grows wonderfully clear and vivid. Precise and intelligent, Barth was never content with general observations; he had the good reporter's attachment to fact. He always went to the heart of the matter and wanted to know the scale of trading profit, not only for his own day, but also for the past. "The importance of the trade of Agadès, and the wealth of the place in general," he comments in one of his typically factual observations, "appear very clearly from the large tribute, of 150,000 ducats, which the king of Agadès was able to pay to that of Songhay" — some 250 years, that is, before Barth himself would visit the place.

In the same thoughtful probing manner he looked into the value and the nature of the salt trade, a trans-Saharan staple whose handling would not have greatly changed over the centuries, and has left an admirably detailed account of the means whereby bold and enterprising men could profit from it. During the dominion of Songhay, he found, the second-in-authority at Agadès — one of the south Saharan caravan stations — had had to levy tax on all merchandise imported into the town. (It would not have been much different under the earlier dominion of Mali; and the king of Ghana, long before that, had done the same on his narrower frontiers.) This office had been of great importance in providing royal revenue, but also in the means of individual enrichment.

For the chief duty of this official, Barth found, was "to accom-

pany annually the salt caravan of the Kel-Gerès, which supplies
the western part of the Middle Sudan with the salt of Bilma,
from Agadès to Sokoto; and to protect it on the road as well as
to secure it against exorbitant exactions on the part of the Fulbe
[Fulani] of Sokoto. For this trouble he receives one *kantu,* that
is to say the eighth part of a middle-sized camel load . . . a contribution which forms a considerable income in this country,
probably of from eight to ten thousand Spanish dollars; the
caravan consisting generally of some thousand camels, not all
equally laden, and the *kantu* of salt fetching in Sudan from five
thousand to seven or eight thousand *kurdi,* or shells, which are
worth from two to three dollars. Under such circumstances those
officers, who at the same time trade on their own account, cannot
but amass considerable wealth."

Tales of fabulous kingly wealth had always been common. El
Bekri had long before reported the king of Ghana as having a
nugget of gold so large and heavy that he could safely tether his
horse to it. But with the growth of Mali and its trading network
the fables acquired a more statistical shape, and ceased perhaps
to be fables after all. Kankan Musa was said to have taken five
hundred slaves on the Mecca pilgrimage, each carrying a staff of
gold that weighed about six pounds. On his baggage camels there
were said to be eighty to one hundred loads of gold, each weighing about three hundred pounds. And anyone who has chanced
to see a modern durbar of chiefs and traditional rulers in West
Africa, a parade flashing with scores and hundreds of golden
staffs — wooden staffs, no doubt, yet covered with beaten gold —
will not find this so hard to credit.

Accumulation of wealth promoted trade, but it also promoted
industry. "The great advantage of Kano," Barth wrote of that
north Nigerian town, but medieval Timbuktu and Gao and
Djenné would have reproduced something of the same pattern,
"is that commerce and manufactures go hand in hand, and al-

most every family has its share in them. There is really something grand in this kind of industry, which spreads to the north as far as Murzuk, Ghat, and even Tripoli; to the west, not only to Timbuktu, but in some degree as far as the shores of the Atlantic, the very inhabitants of Arguin [on the Atlantic coast] dressing in the cloth woven and dyed in Kano; to the east, all over Bornu, although there it comes into contact with the native industry of the country; while to the south it maintains a rivalry with the native industry . . ."

Trading links multiplied. By 1400, according to Ibn Khaldun, annual caravans across the Sahara by way of the Hoggar Mountains counted no fewer than twelve thousand camels; and this was only one of half a dozen well-used routes. But the caravans went in many directions as well as to and from the northward and the Mediterranean; the whole Sudan was crisscrossed by their patient profit-seeking trails. Thus Bornu — in what is now northeastern Nigeria — bought copper from Wadai, its neighbor to the eastward; and Wadai had this copper in turn from Darfur, again to the eastward. Mali imported vastly from the Mediterranean as well as from Egypt, whether by way of the eastern or the northern routes — silks and damascened blades and horses in quantity. Schoolmen of the Muslim seats of learning traveled back and forth. Pilgrims walked to Mecca. Currencies evolved in gold or copper or shells or weight of stuffs, or in salt or metal pieces. Only to the southward could these savannah kingdoms seldom penetrate, but even there, beyond the forest barrier, they had their trading interest; and cola nuts from southern Nigeria were much in demand.

Against this restless enterprising background of conquest and centralizing government and continental trade, the kingdoms and empires rose and fell across a thousand years and more; yet only now perhaps, while the Western Sudan stands on the threshold of a regained independence, can their achievement win its full perspective and importance. This achievement was large and memorable, and is relevant to the re-emergence of an independent Sudan. When Kankan Musa died in 1352 he left behind him, in Bovill's words, "an empire which in the history of purely African states was as remarkable for its size as for its wealth; and which provided a striking example of the capacity of the Negro for political organisation."

7 *Songhay*

THE SONGHAY EMPIRE OF THE MIDDLE NIGER CAME TO POWER AFTER Mali had passed its apogee, and carried the civilization of the Western Sudan some further steps toward maturity.

Today the Songhay, a Negro people who may number some six hundred and fifty thousand, live along the Niger in their ancient home between the region of Timbuktu and the frontiers of modern Nigeria. They till the soil and raise cattle, and essentially are the same as they have always been: a people whose destinies and habits are inseparable from the river on whose wide banks they live. For much more than a thousand years they have occupied this middle reach of the Niger as it flows and broadens through rolling sun-scorched grasslands; and usually they have had dominion over it.

Their literate culture, at least in Arabic, goes back some nine hundred years; while it was a man of this nation, though writing in Timbuktu, who composed the *Tarikh el Fettach* in the last years of the sixteenth century. Thus the city of Gao was to the Songhay, for learning and for trade and government, what Timbuktu and Djenné were to others: and Gao, indeed, has yielded some of the most interesting inscriptions in the whole of Africa. Found in 1939 at Sané, some four miles from the center of modern

Gao, these appear in Arabic on a number of royal tombstones dating to the first part of the twelfth century. "Here lies the tomb of the king who defended God's religion, and who rests in God, Abu Abdallah Mohammed," declares one of them, adding that the king died in the year 494 after the Hegira, which is 1100: proof both of the early establishment of Islam in Gao, and of early regard for letters and for learning.

The origin of this Negro people is obscure, and that of their kings confused with many stories of eastern or northern provenance. At some remote time the whole of this river region is said to have been populated by a people divided traditionally into "masters of the soil" and "masters of the water"; and these are said to have belonged in turn to an ancient family of West African peoples. To these early inhabitants, migrants were added. Tradition says that these migrants included the Sorko, a fisherfolk coming from the east (perhaps from Lake Chad by way of the Benue River), and the Gow, who were hunters; and these two appear among the founders of the Songhay nation. Their most important settlement was at Koukya, or Gounguia; almost certainly this was near the falls of Labbezenga in the Dendi country, lying on the northwestern frontiers of what is now Nigeria.

Another tradition says that a group of Berber migrants arrived at Koukya, perhaps in the seventh century A.D., being connected with the Lemta of Libya; and established themselves as chiefs of the Songhay people. Disturbed by this, the Sorko people are said to have migrated upstream and founded the settlement and later city of Gao, and even to have pushed on westward as far as Mopti in the lake region above Timbuktu. The "Berber" kings of Koukya later followed them: in A.D. 1010 Dia (or Za) Kossoi took Gao from the Sorko and established the Songhay capital there, and it is from then that the state and later empire of Gao may be said to have begun. One need take neither the dates nor the traditions too seriously. All that comes out as relatively sure is that the

Songhay empire of Gao had its organized beginnings in the region of Dendi; that its civilization was the product of native initiative stimulated by migrant incursion; and that, with others, it took its rise in early centuries after the western Sudan had fully entered its Iron Age.

King Kossoi of Gao is said to have accepted Islam in 1009; and here, perhaps, tradition is well founded. This was the period that came before the Almoravid ravages and conquests, and no doubt those Almoravid armies would have had zealous men, whether merchants or scholars, to go before them. There is also another and persuasive light on this. According to the *Tarikh el Fettach* — written by a man well placed to know the traditions of his own people — this early Songhay monarch was converted by argument of the merchants of Gao, whose position at the southern end of one of the great caravan trails (the same, indeed, as the Garamantes may have used a thousand years earlier) had already made them rich and commercially persuasive. Their neighbors to the north — Lemtuna Berbers of the Adrar region — were energetic Muslims in their time; and commerce and religion had evidently moved together into Gao. And then conquest — as it generally would in Africa — easily followed commerce and religion: Dia Kossoi made himself master of Gao and accepted Islam.

This is what tradition says; and tradition, in this case, may be taken as largely in the right. The names and dates and details are no doubt subject to correction; thus the twelfth-century tombstones of Gao, made of marble brought piously from Spain, give royal names that are different from those of the *Tarikhs*. Here, in any case, the substantial point is that Islam, like Christianity elsewhere, would prove a great solvent of peoples and founder of states. It cut across tribal gods and ancestor beliefs as Christianity had done in Europe, and gave new scope for the building of many-peopled kingdoms and constellations of power. Long afterward, in the nineteenth century, European missionaries would see in "Christianity and commerce" a sovereign combination for civilizing and unifying tribal Africa; and it may not be unreasonable to imagine that Dia Kossoi and men like Kankan Musa, who governed on a much grander scale than he did, must have seen "Islam and commerce" in something of the same light.

These river people grew strong, at all events, from the stability of their mixed economy of farming and fishing and cattle-raising, from the importance of their trading cities, and from the success they had in uniting themselves against rivals. In growing strong they moved from merely tribal loyalties and forms of organization into the many-peopled empire of Gao. Their tribute-paying submission to Mali, imposed in 1325, lasted little more than fifty years. Thereafter their infant state survived invasion by another Sudanese people, the Mossi, as well as repeated attacks by desert Tuareg during the century that followed. And in course of time, through this tough compacting process, they aspired to greatness. The eighteenth ruler of the line of kings founded by Kossoi in A.D. 1010, Sonni Ali, came to power in 1464 and made Songhay the most powerful state in the Sudan of his time, except perhaps for Bornu to the eastward.

Like Kankan Musa of Mali, Sonni Ali established a single hegemony over much of the river and its hinterland, and accumulated, through a now familiar process of tribute and trade, wealth and power that were no less brilliant in the eyes of the men of his day. His predecessors had built on strong foundations; Sonni Ali, extending them, seized Timbuktu and Djenné from their Mandingo rulers and made these cities part of his dominion.

Of the motives that inspired him, or the shape they may have taken in his mind, the meager record says little. Sonni Ali has come down through tradition as a man of unusual courage and strength of purpose who, though probably not himself a pagan, had more than a little sympathy for the pagan traditions of the Songhay people. Muslim biographers invariably regard him as an enemy of their faith, or at least of orthodoxy;* and his descendants, by way of seeming to confirm this, are popularly invested with a reputation for skill and power in the magic arts. More probably, Sonni Ali cared little for the principles of other people's religion but much for the tactics of his own ambition. He recalls, faintly though the records murmur, the kings of the Europe of his day — bold in the field and cunning in council, playing off one enemy against another, superstitious in the manner of his fathers, given to fits of furious impatience with the logic-chopping of religious schoolmen; but loyal always to the cause of a strong central power which he, and he alone, should dominate.

One approaches nearer to the reality of those days of empire-building with his successor, Mohammed Askia, who comes luminously from the record. This man, whose name was Mohammed Touré but who took the title of Askia, and became Askia the Great, mounted the Songhay throne in 1493 and reigned for nineteen momentous years. He pushed the frontiers of the Songhay empire as far as Segu in the west and the sub-Saharan region of Aïr in the northeast, realizing once again something of the unified control of far north and far south that Kankan Musa had achieved. Yet his real triumph was to endow Songhay with an administrative system which marked a new and long advance towards a truly centralized state.

Sonni Ali and his predecessors had established and maintained a state power that was still, essentially, a tribal power obliged to take account of tribal boundaries and rivalries. Mohammed Askia seems to have gone much beyond that. Muslim biographers are loud in their praises of him; and there is little doubt that the Askia saw in "Islam and commerce" a powerful and dependable ally for this centralizing work. And just as Timbuktu and Djenné had owed much of their importance to the unifying power of Kankan Musa, so now did these and other cities of the Western

* The orthodoxy, here, of the Malekite rites of Islam.

Sudan expand again and flourish after a difficult interregnum. It is characteristic of this expansion that the men who wrote the *Tarikh es Sudan* and the *Tarikh el Fettach* (and other men, among them the renowned Ahmed Baba, whose writings are altogether lost or still to be found and republished*) should have lived in Timbuktu during and immediately after Mohammed Askia's reign.

This Songhay empire which Sonni Ali and Mohammed Askia forged and founded in the years, crucial to Europe, which saw the first maritime travels to West Africa and the rise of England as a naval power, lasted in the flower of its independence for little more than a century.

The Western Sudan in the time of its institutional growth was less fortunate, if one may contemplate the parallel for a moment, than Western Europe. For Europe suffered its last destructive invasions from without during the Magyar raids of the ninth and tenth centuries — the period of Almoravid penetration and conquest in the Western Sudan. But in 1591 the Moroccan armies of El Mansur emerged from the Sahara, captured Gao and Timbuktu, scattered the armies of the Songhay ruler, Askia Ishak, and ruined the state. Though as brief as the Almoravid invasion of five centuries earlier, this Moroccan experience was hardly less destructive. Decline set in. Timbuktu and Djenné retained their tradition and practice of scholarship, but within narrower limits: even Gao, a little more fortunate, could not afterward claim more than a small provincial fame. By 1600 the great days of the Western Sudan are over.

* A diligent inquirer has lately found, it seems, a manuscript of Ahmed Baba's in the library of the British Museum.

8 The Sao and Kanem

GHANA AND MALI AND SONGHAY DO NOT OF COURSE EXHAUST THE story of the Western Sudan in its centuries of major growth and change. O:her states and cities also underwent their gradual transformation from tribal groups to multi-tribal groups, and from these into centralized states and empires. Other strong peoples besides the Mandingo and the Songhay grew strong enough to nourish wider ambitions than their forefathers and to see the chance of larger and perhaps better ways of life and livelihood. By the time of Dia Kossoi's founding of the Songhay capital at Gao, early in the eleventh century, the Hausa states of what is now northern Nigeria were already in existence. These Hausa states were temporarily united, later on, into the larger state of Kebbi; and Kebbi would be strong enough to hold out against Mohammed Askia even after the Songhay armies had taken Kano. Two hundred years after that conquest another Sudanese people, the Fulani or Fulbe, would crown many wanderings and vicissitudes by establishing their hegemony over Hausaland.

To the east, moreover, there was Kanem, largest of many states that would emerge in the wide grasslands which run between the Niger and the Nile, and, with Bornu its successor, longest lived of all the states of the Sudan. Its origins, going back to the same remote period as the origins of Songhay, also interweave by tradition with the arrival of migrant peoples from the east and northeast. And tradition is easy to believe in this case, for these old trails from the valley of the Nile must have known many who fled from wars and invasions set going successively by the collapse of Kush and the conquests of Axum and the coming of the Arabs. Even the contemporary traditions of the peoples of Chad and Bornu suggest layer after layer of migratory incursion. But what gives acute interest to the origins of this empire of Kanem — established perhaps as early as the eighth century and enduring under one overlordship or another until the seventeenth — is neither its long life nor its usefully documented later period, but the archeological record of the Sao.

With the appearance of the Sao in the neighborhood of Lake Chad, there is both an end to the civilizing trail which had led from the valley of the Nile and the beginning of another civilization. For the Sao constructed towns, fashioned rams' heads in pottery, worked in bronze with the method of "lost wax" (as the smiths and artists of Benin would later work), elevated women to influence in government, and generally elaborated a mode of life that was plainly a new synthesis of the African east and African west. In some respects, indeed, they seem to have stood to Kush as Kush had stood to Egypt.

Who they were and whence they came is more or less completely unknown, though one tradition asserts they were "blacks" from the Bilma oases north of Chad. Some have tried to explain their achievement — in a once familiar manner of explaining away all notable achievements in continental Africa as the work of non-African peoples — with a suggestion that the Sao were descendants of the Hyksos conquerors of ancient Egypt. Lebeuf has disposed of this fable, though, and puts the date of their arrival in the Chad region at not long before the tenth century A.D. Urvoy, somewhat pushing back this date, regards them as being firmly settled on the east bank of Lake Chad by the eighth century as well as possibly in the savannah country to the north of Chad. Contemporary legend makes them appear as giants who easily subdued the "little men" whom they found;* and perhaps the Sao, or some of them, were really people of Nilotic origin, and unusually tall like many Nilotic peoples of today.

The Sao have disappeared, and excavation of their curious civilization is far from complete. But the results of three fruitful

*See page 17.

French expeditions by Lebeuf and Masson-Détourbet between 1936 and 1948, gathered together and summarized in 1950, suggest that it may eventually offer a satisfactory link in the story of cultural interplay between Nile and Niger. The Sao and their successors (the Kotoko, who wrote their own language with an Arabic script) were fully in the age of metals. "Such of their works as we know," wrote Lantier in 1943, "already witness to a mastery which presumes a long industrial past." Were they after all the lineal successors of migrants from declining Meroë? They worked in bronze and copper and, together with their jewelers and smelters, "appear blacksmiths who worked in iron." Their cities to the southeast of Lake Chad, their complicated burial procedures, their elaborate pottery and wide range of artistic production in clay — cult figures, toys, animals — and their success in using metals combine to give the Sao more than a hint of eastern origin, or at any rate influence, as well as a strange and unforgettable accent that is entirely their own.

Between the little-known but interesting settlements of the Sao to the east and west of Lake Chad and the emergence of the state of Kanem there remains a long and difficult gap. Could the Sao be said to constitute a nation in that remote time when they suffered migrant invasions from outside? Had they formed a state? Probably not. But out of their fusion with these migrants there came the peoples who would make the state of Kanem and the Kanembu nation; and these would prove as influential and important as civilizing and centralizing pressures on the varied peoples to the east of the Niger as Mali proved to be on those to the west. Here again there was the same drive towards political and military concentration: the rulers of the old empire of Kanem, taking its rise in the eighth century and continuing into the thirteenth, evolved new forms of government, centralized government, as well as more effective kinds of warfare and conquest. Here again one has the same underlying factors of iron-smelting and international trade;

and although they had no gold mines to tap and draw upon, as had Ghana and Mali to the westward, Kanem could and did seize the caravan trails that led northward through the Fezzan to the Mediterranean coast and eastward to the Nile.

The old Kanem empire is associated with the rule of the Sefuwa dynasty, which, so far as may be seen from later records, evolved an interesting and original pattern of tribal feudalism. This was exercised through a "great council" of twelve principal officers of the empire who discussed and applied (or failed to apply) the more important decisions of the ruling sultan. In the beginning this council appears as little more than a family affair, or even, as Urvoy has suggested, as little more than a family business, each "member of the firm" having real power as well as a title to power. But the titles and the power were given only for life, and were inheritable only by custom; later on, as the empire grew and the wealth of its rulers with it, disputes gave rise to dynastic wars, and nobles fought for "rights" they had once held only by the sultan's gift.

Yet in spite of these dynastic wars, and of wars with neighboring peoples, of usurpations and long periods of disaster, the identity of Kanem (or of Bornu which followed the old empire) remained stable down to the sixteenth or seventeenth centuries, and its fundamental structure is in some respects intact to this day. Thus it may be said, with Urvoy, that "Kanem was truly in the Middle Ages the civiliser of the central Sudan just as Mali, inheritor of Ghana, was the civiliser of the western Sudan. These were the centres which saw the elaboration of Sudanese civilisation as we know it today: so different from the civilisation of the Arabs and from that of the more purely Negro tribes of the south."

9 In Darfur

THE OLD EMPIRE OF KANEM, PRODUCT OF GROWTH AND INNOVATION through four or five hundred years, seems to have achieved its widest frontiers under *Mai* (sultan, emperor) Dunama Dibbalemi, who reigned from 1210 to 1224. The son* of Selma, another Kanem ruler famous in tradition, Mai Dunama is said to have pushed his eastern limits to the banks of the middle Nile; he likewise controlled the trading routes northward into the Fezzan, and through his countries there would have passed much of the commerce that linked Mali and the rest of the Western Sudan to the Near East.

But the "family business" of the reigning dynasty, so potent and successful in unifying these unbounded plains to the east and northeast of the Niger, now began to fall apart. "Until then there were no disorders," says the written tradition of the Bornu Chronicle, set down many years later; the Mai ruled supreme. But in the time of Dunama Dibbalemi "a civil war broke out that was due to the greed of his children." The princes "retired each to their different regions." Infallibly, these barons of Kanem made war for their feudal "rights." Sultan Dunama won this war and two or three more or less peaceful reigns followed; but then the feudal rivalries broke out again, and continued for two centuries. To these troubles were added a war of conquest against the Sao settlements round Lake Chad, and finally, bringing the old empire to a close, defeat at the hands of an invading people called the Bulala. These Bulala would dominate Kanem until the third quarter of the fifteenth century; and then at last, in their wake, the "new empire" of Kanem would emerge — the empire of Bornu of which the sultan-

---

* Or *Chiroma* — a title still in use, for example, among the emirs of northern Nigeria today.

ate of Bornu in northeastern Nigeria today is the direct if much reduced successor.

This potted history suffers greatly, of course, from the dynastic preoccupations of those whose business it was to remember tradition and hand it down. It may fairly be concluded that the everyday life of these lands between the Nile and the Niger was little more disturbed by such troubles and incursions than was that of the English people during the Wars of the Roses. Trade and interchange of ideas might be disrupted; they would seldom have come to a stop.

For at least three hundred years before the sixteenth century, and no doubt for much longer, caravans would have toiled back and forth between Nile and Niger — and, as seems likely from Mathew's work in Somaliland in 1950, between the Niger and the Somali coast of the Indian Ocean; and wars would scarcely have stopped them. Inland from that Indian Ocean coast there existed the kingdom of sultanate of Adal, destroyed by wars with its neighbors in the sixteenth century and now vanished altogether, but rich enough, before that, to have built cities whose walls still stand, here and there, to a height of eighteen feet; and the wealth of Adal was primarily the wealth of trade. "It would seem," says Mathew, "to have lain at the end of a long and tenuous trans-continental trade route that led west to the kingdom of Bornu and to the towns of the upper Niger" — linking the Indian Ocean, that is, with Mali and with Songhay and their lesser contemporaries.

Was Kanem regularly linked northeastward to the middle and lower valley of the Nile — and thence to the delta-heart of Egypt and the Near East by way of Sinai? The answer, probably, should be both yes and no. If this present outline could be more than fragmentary it would be necessary at this point to embark upon a description of those Christian kingdoms of the middle Nile whose achievement was to give fresh unity to the successor-peoples of

Kush and to introduce among them, as Shinnie says, "a time of flowering of artistic endeavour and of political power." Converted in the sixth century by missionaries from the eastern Mediterranean, these Nubians of the middle Nile remained Christian until overwhelmed by Islamic invasion not much less than a thousand years later. Their culture left a permanent mark on the eastern Sudan, mainly through the Nubian language; but its visible remains today are little more than a handful of ruined red-brick churches, some fine murals or fragments of murals, and a great deal of handsome painted pottery. Only future research can show how far these Christian kingdoms of Nubia served as a link between the lands to the west and the lands to the north and east, or how far they raised a barrier.

In the hills of Darfur, though, lying some six hundred miles across scorching semidesert plains to the west of the middle Nile, or nearly halfway between the Nile and the Niger, a group of ruins of widely different period and appearance can still yield some notion of the extent and variety, whether Islamic or Christian, of these east-west contacts through many centuries.

Nothing but the stark Sahara will appear, on the map, as empty as the plains and hills of Darfur; but the impression, at least in the matter of medieval history, is a false one. Many ruins of the past are scattered here, ranging from the ancient city of Jebel Uri with its nine-stepped "audience hall" to graves of the vanished Daju people; fine buildings in red-brick of a much later period; and, as unexpected evidence in 1958 would suggest, at least one Christian church and monastery.

Of all these ruins that are hidden away in remote Darfur, Jebel Uri is perhaps the most interesting and impressive. Hard to reach today except by tough motor transport, it lies among the sudden peaks of the Jebel Furnung, glittering outliers of the Jebel Si, some six hours' driving to the northwest of El Fasher, the present capital of Darfur. Beyond a wadi called Ain Soro, while skylines flatten again for the immensities of Wadai to the westward and the desert to the north, a path swings off leftward into lank grass and thorn. Another half-hour's wandering back and forth delivers this path to the brink of a downward-falling valley; and beyond this valley, making its farther wall, rises the hill called Jebel Uri. Even from here, if one knows what to look for, there may be seen a zig-zag boulder causeway that goes steeply upward to the peaked summit a thousand feet above. Around the foot of this causeway, though hidden from a distance, lie the "palaces" and streets and multitudinous ruined dwellings of one of the largest of the lost cities of Africa.

This city of Jebel Uri was built of stone within a strong encircling wall that winds, for the most part, along the lowest escarpment whence the long climb to the summit begins. Here in this well-seized defensive place there must have lived a numerous population; and they must have lived here, by archeological evidence that is still incomplete, for a long time — perhaps for three or four centuries. Its builders took local stone for their dwellings, using no mortar, nor bothering to bond their walls whenever these struck each other at an angle; and yet working with such skill and care that several of their structures are still intact to a height of ten or twelve feet.

The causeway which they built to the top of their peak is also an impressively solid affair, being often of huge blocks of stone; and three walls enclose or fortify the narrow summit. At the lower end of the causeway, within many encircling walls and circular stone-built huts long since unroofed to the sky, there is the ruin of a much larger building which tradition calls a palace or kingly seat. The high guardian walls and well-made gateways of this place surround what is recognizably some kind of hall or meeting place. Although its age may be as much as seven hundred years, a nine-stepped stairway remains in fairly good repair, and mounts to a broad platform. A little below is another "palace"; though local opinion is strongly of the view, in which it may be right, that this was not a palace but a mosque.

Jebel Uri, like other sites in Darfur, is not yet finally explained. In Arkell's view, buttressed by a good deal of evidence, the likeliest explanation is "either that Uri was the headquarters of the Kanem adminstration of Darfur during the tremendous expansion of the empire of Kanem under Dunama Dibbalemi"— that is, in the thirteenth century — "or that it was at some time during their supremacy a capital of the Bulala" in the fourteenth and fifteenth centuries. It would have belonged, on either view, to the trading system of Kanem and have shared in the prosperity which that implied. Here, perhaps, was one of the relay-intermediaries for exchange of goods along the transcontinental trail between the Niger and the Indian Ocean.

Beyond this medieval outline, though, other and earlier outlines faintly suggest themselves. There is archeological evidence in Darfur that men and goods passed this way, coming from east or west or both, since times of remote antiquity. Did that earliest of Egyptian pioneers into the far south and west, Harkhuf of the sixth dynasty (c. 2400-2200 B.C.), reach these hills of Darfur? Arkell thinks so; and no one has yet denied it. The Derib el Arbain, that appallingly dry "Forty Day Road" which still takes Darfur camels into Upper Egypt every year, is in any case of great age.

There are cattle brands, Arkell says, "connected with [Darfur's] earliest traditional sultans, the Daju, that still survive in Dar Sila, and can only be explained as having been originally Egyptian hieroglyphs." The nine-stepped audience chamber of the palace of Uri, he suggests, "may well be a rough copy of the platform on which the Meroitic king"— whose family had fled, and probably fled westward, from Axumite conquest —"gave audience near his palace." Indeed, "there are so many parallels between the institutions of the divine kingdom of Darfur and those of the divine kingdom of Kush that it seems probable that they are due to the foundation of a kingdom in Darfur by the exiled royal family of Meroë after the fall of that city."

This would have occurred at some time after A.D. 350. Within about five hundred years of that date, and perhaps a good deal less, the Sao "giants" would be working in bronze and iron not more than six hundred miles to the westward of Uri. Had the immigrant ancestors of the Sao reached Lake Chad by way of Darfur?

These are interesting ideas; true or not, they have behind them the solid fact of old and varied contact between Nile and Niger. Whether or not these ruins of Jebel Uri commemorate the centuries of Meroitic disappearance, they remain in any event of monumental significance to the medieval history of Africa. Like the great system of artificial soil terracing on Jebel Marra, not many miles to the south of Uri, they reassert the astonishing unity in diversity that underlay so many of the societies of what, for convenience' sake, may be called the African Iron Age. Like Kumbi Saleh two thousand miles away across the western plains; like Djenné and Walata, Gao or Timbuktu or the grand walls of Kano; like Darfur's palaces and mosques of red brick; or the flash and glitter of that well-horsed cavalry which James Bruce saw beneath the walls of Sennar on the Blue Nile, this city of Uri and its honeycomb of dwellings, in their veil of yellow grass, speak unmistakably of prolonged growth and innovation.

Some twenty miles to the south of Uri, again among the gray rocks and thorn of the Jebel Furnung, there is another ruin that is famous in Darfur: the dilapidated fragments at Ain Fara of another though much smaller city of circular dry-stone dwellings, but crowned, unlike Uri, with the remnants of a fine red-brick palace and an equally fine mosque in the same well-found material. Or so it was believed until yesterday.

But Ain Fara, in 1958, would provide an archeological surprise. For it suddenly appeared probable, and perhaps certain, that this tumbled structure on the crown of a bare hill, its haggard ruin sharp against the sky of middle Africa, was not the ruin of a palace but the ruin of a monastery of Christian Nubia. Nobody had ever thought that Christianity had come as far as this, nearly halfway to the Niger, or even that the Nubian kingdoms had reached beyond the western fringes of the middle Nile.

It likewise appeared that the large square "mosque" nearby, built with L-shaped pillars within its wall, had been really a Christian church; that a smaller mosque along the hillside had been founded as another Christian church (though converted later to a mosque); and that the small red-brick "rooms" along the razor's edge of hilltop above this smaller "mosque," had not always been — as local tradition holds — the rooms of the ruler's harem, but were built initially as cells for Christian monks.

The reason for this abrupt revision is a good example of the changes and chances of archeology. In 1929 a British visitor to Ain Fara — a charming place for picnics (as for medieval settlement) with its deep cold pools paving a sheltered gorge beneath the ruined hillside — had collected in the large "mosque" a number of agreeably decorated fragments of pottery. But in 1958, rearranging her possessions, this visitor presented two of them (the others were lost) to Dr. Arkell at London University; and Dr. Arkell immediately recognized them as Nubian Christian ware. One of them — and the Christian evidence could hardly be clearer — is the fragment of a saucer finely painted with a fish and a cross, and the other is a piece of terra cotta stamped with a dove's head and a cross. Both of them may date to about the tenth century.

With this the blurred picture of Ain Fara — previously ascribed to builders from Kanem or Bornu — came sharply into new focus. Two fragments of Christian pottery might be slender evidence for changing a palace into a monastery and a mosque into a church; and this, moreover, in a place where Christianity was never known to have reached. But then it was remembered that the L-shaped pillars peculiar to the "mosque" at Ain Fara were very much like those on which the little churches of Christian Nubia, up and down the middle Nile, had raised their domes. It was seen that the plan of the "palace" made much more sense as the plan of a monastery, and it was recalled that the monasteries of the Nile had often stood on hilltops above their parent churches. The uniquely large bricks of Ain Fara — some of them three or four times larger than bricks usually are — could be found, moreover, in the ruins of Christian Nubia; but not elsewhere.*

Nubian Christianity was submerged by Islam in the fourteenth and fifteenth centuries. Its outpost in Darfur — if the evidence for Christianity there be accepted — suffered the same fate. The churches became mosques; the monasteries became palaces or seats of government. Perhaps the conqueror was Mai Idris Alooma of Bornu, who ruled the "new empire" of Kanem-Bornu between 1571 and 1603; perhaps it was another and forgotten ruler. However that may be, Darfur became an independent kingdom after the death of Mai Idris; and from now onward the local sultans of the Keira dynasty of the Fur people of Darfur would build their own palaces and mosques among the hills. Their dynasty would continue until 1916, when its last sultan, Ali Dinar, would lose his throne to British rule; and the ruins of their buildings, many of them tall and strong, may be found at many places on the slopes of Jebel Marra.

The fuller history of Darfur, when it can at last be written, will therefore reproduce the same varying process of steady unification, institutional stability, and dynastic warfare that appears elsewhere across the Sudan from the Nile to the Atlantic. Yet why, having endured so long and grown to its own maturity, should this civili-

---

* I am indebted to Dr. Arkell for these notes on Ain Fara: his written opinion was not yet published when this book went to press.

zation of middle Africa have fallen into ruin — have sunk so far into eclipse, apparently, as to enable a later world to ignore it altogether?

One should not overstate the ruin. Three hundred and fifty years separate us from the Moorish destruction of the Songhay state, from the death of Idris Alooma and the disintegration of the empire of Bornu, from the writing of the *Tarikh es Sudan* and the intellectual eminence of Djenné. While Europe went through an industrial revolution and emerged in its present shape and state of mind, these civilizations of the Sudanese plains continued their slow life, their stable interchange of goods, their calm disordered journey through the years. They declined, but they did not disappear. The bare and yet resilient fabric of their farming and cattle-raising life could take hard shocks, and if merchants fell on thin times, many would none the less survive.

The difference through these latter centuries — and much of Africa would show it — was less in the shrinking of Sudanese civilization than in the expansion of Europe. What Heinrich Barth could find in the Western Sudan a hundred years ago would not have greatly differed in its social life and limits from the Mali of Ibn Battuta, five hundred years before. But the Europe that Barth knew was altogether different from the Europe that Ibn Battuta could have known. Yet even when allowing for this difference in the scale of judgment — a difference that has encouraged many Europeans to suppose that Sudanese civilization never existed, or not as anything worth the name — the question may recur in another form. If the civilizations of middle Africa did not greatly decline in their social and economic structure, but continued onward at about the same level, why did they so continue instead of moving to newer and more "modern" levels?

10 *Eclipse and Survival*

Part of the answer to this question is clear enough.

Happily for what is known of Songhay — and of some other Sudanese states — there is the work of Leo Africanus. Born at Granada in southern Spain, in the same year that Askia the Great deposed the successor of Sonni Ali, this useful witness was expensively educated at the schools and libraries of Fez, whither his parents had removed from Christian persecution. On coming to manhood, he made several journeys in the Maghreb and the Western Sudan. He was well placed to observe and well qualified to profit by his observation.

Christian pirates captured him in 1518, or thereabouts, while he was sailing from Istanbul to Tunis. These had the sense to realize they had laid their hands on someone out of the ordinary; and instead of selling him along with other Moorish captives in the slave marts of maritime Italy, they took him to Rome and gave him to the Pope. This Pope was Leo X, son of Lorenzo de' Medici and member of a brilliant family grown rich and powerful on international trade as well as on the government of Florence.

What rich and powerful men in the commercial life of Europe at that time wished eagerly to know was the state of the world beyond the Muslim barriers in North Africa; and it was precisely this, the gratified Pope soon found, that his intelligent young Moor could tell them. Leo X gave him freedom and a pension, and, with conversion to Christianity, the name of Giovanni Lioni, hence Leo Africanus, as the European world would soon know him. His description of Africa, completed in 1526, was first published by Ramusio in 1563. An English edition came out in 1600, translated by a friend of Hakluyt's, and was acclaimed with eager curiosity although its information, by then, was long since out of date.

Leo Africanus gave no brilliant or romantic picture of the Western Sudan, but confirmed its curious variety, civilized achievement, and trading wealth. "It is a wonder," he said of Gao, which he seems to have visited, "to see what plenty of merchandise is daily brought hither, and how costly and sumptuous all things be"; while more gold was on offer there than the market could absorb. Europe took careful note of this. But the Moors of North Africa, who had known all this earlier and known it much better, were still more attentive. Morocco had long grown rich as the northernmost intermediary in the trans-Saharan trade; armed with the musket, its armies now embarked on conquest in the south.

Mohammed Askia — Askia the Great — was deposed in 1529. Eight successors bore the royal title; and Songhay grew in stability and substance. Moorish temptations likewise grew. In 1585 the Moroccan sultan, Mulay Ahmed el-Mansur, seized from Songhay the great salt deposits of Taghaza, and took thereby the first step toward the sources of Sudanese gold which Moroccans believed they could capture just as the Almoravids long before them had believed. A few years later they invaded Songhay itself. In 1591 the armies of Songhay were overwhelmed by a Moroccan force which had crossed the desert under the command of a Spanish renegade named Judar. Although Judar had only four thousand men he had some two and a half thousand firearms — arquebus or matchlock — while the much larger armies of Songhay had none. These armies were beaten, and Judar seized Timbuktu and Gao.

Something of the loot they took may be measured from an English merchant's account of Judar's return to Marrakech eight years later. "Six days past," wrote Jasper Tomson on July 4, 1599, "here arrived a nobleman from Gao, called Judar Pasha, who was sent by this king ten years past to conquer the said country, wherein many people of this country have lost their lives.

"He brought with him thirty camels loaded with *tibar*, which is unrefined gold . . ." — valued by Thomson at 604,800 pounds — "also great store of pepper, unicorns' horns and a certain kind of wood for dyers, to some one hundred twenty camel-loads; all of which he presented unto the king, with fifty horse, and great quantity of eunuchs, dwarfs, and women and men slaves, besides fifteen virgins, the king's daughters of Gao, which he sendeth to be the king's concubines. You must note all these," added the careful Thomson, "to be of the coal black hair, for that country yieldeth no other."

This invasion of Songhay is said to have cost the Moroccans some twenty-three thousand deaths in warfare and disease, for resistance was stubborn and well conducted. Although they got much loot, the Moroccans were defeated in their hopes of capturing the sources of gold; and they soon found — as others would find elsewhere in Africa — that the gold dried up and vanished with invasion. After twenty-five years of trouble, Sultan Mulay Zidan abandoned Songhay in 1618.

But if their invasion cost the Moroccans much more than it was worth, it cost Songhay its place in later history. For it demolished the unity and administrative organization of the state, and while it left Timbuktu and Gao and Djenné as considerable cities, it robbed this civilization of its vitality, for it temporarily ruined the trans-Saharan trade as well as much of the internal trade of the Sudan. With this ruin there came a long and miserable depression. "From that moment," says the chronicle, "everything changed. Danger took the place of security, poverty of wealth. Peace gave way to distress, disasters, and violence."

The Songhay state fell apart. By 1660, when the last additions to the *Tarikh es Sudan* stop short, the Songhay Negroes of the river region had absorbed the descendants of their Moroccan conquerors, the Arma, but their authority was feeble. Further south, in Dendi, princely ambitions had partitioned the country. Thereafter Songhay was an easy prey. In 1670 the Bambara of Segu, further up the Niger, made Timbuktu their vassal; and the Tuareg, returning from the desert for yet another onslaught on the sown, did the same with Gao. A century later the princes of the Fulani, assembling in *jihad* at the call of Usman dan Fodio, launched their quilt-mailed cavalry on neighboring peoples, and on the Songhay of Dendi among them.

The wars continued. Of all the greatness and extent of Songhay only the little "state" of Anzuru, on the left bank of the Niger, managed to remain independent. Then, at last, Europeans imposed a colonial peace. In 1884 the French attacked along the Niger from the west. They took Timbuktu in 1894, Gao in 1898, and finally drove off the Tuareg in 1900. In 1959, to round off the story, the Western Sudan along with the rest of French West Africa was in course of acquiring a new political identity. After three hundred and fifty years of stagnation or subjection, this wide region would once again embark upon a life of its own.

What might not have happened, though, *without* the Moorish invasion and its destructive interference in all that trading circuit upon which the power of Songhay (as of Ghana and Mali and Kanem before it) ultimately depended? It is reasonable to think that Songhay would have continued with the long process of unification and civilization which had begun in the Western Sudan about a thousand years earlier. And here one may return to an earlier point — that the Western Sudan, in this respect, was less fortunate than Western Europe. In his monumental study of European feudalism, Marc Bloch has underlined the key importance of the fact that *outside* invasions ceased to trouble Western Europe as early as the tenth century, and were never renewed except at the periphery.

"However rich in lessons the study of these invasions may be," he says of medieval Europe, "we ought not to allow it to conceal a much greater fact: the end of the invasions. Until then these ravages from without, this great jostling of peoples, had framed the history of the west . . . From now on, the west would be exempt: in contrast, or almost so, with the rest of the world. Neither the Mongols nor the Turks would do more than clamour at the gates. There would certainly be quarrels: but within a closed space. And from this there came the chance of a cultural and social evolution that was much more regular, and was immune from the damage of outside attack or the submerging flood of foreign migration . . . We may think that this extraordinary immunity . . . was one of the fundamental components of European civilisation."

And yet, though Moorish ravages may explain a good deal in the course of Sudanese eclipse, there were other reasons too. One of these was the decline of Moorish civilization itself: by the seventeenth century the coastal civilizations of North Africa had lost their medieval eminence, and, with that, much of their power of transmitting ideas and techniques, along with expanding trade, back and forth across the deserts of the south. Never isolated from the medieval world — the world of Arab greatness — the Sudan became isolated from the post-medieval world, the world of technical advance and industrial revolution.

Behind this again lay the fact of oversea discovery by Portuguese and Spaniards and Italians. The wealth of the Western Sudan, as of the west coast of Africa, had seemed great to men who listened to Leo Africanus; comparatively, it was so. Yet in those very years when the Moorish armies of Sultan el-Mansur were laying waste to Songhay, the distant ships of Columbus and of Diaz were discovering the seas of America and the seas of India. Compared with the loot of those continents, African wealth would soon appear small and doubtfully worth the cost of getting; and European investment would go increasingly into expeditions elsewhere. It was hardly surprising. After sailing round the world Sir Francis Drake could show a return in 1580, it is said, of 1,500,000 pounds on an investment of 5,000 pounds. Understandably, his *Pelican* was renamed *The Golden Hind*. No one in England had ever before seen wealth collected on a scale like that. The reputation of Sudanese gold would lose its glitter.

And then geography remained obtuse. Always difficult to cross, the Sahara became no easier. Shipping improved; in the fifteenth century, powerfully helping long-range travel on the seas, shipwrights in Europe learned how to make better rudders, how to step three masts instead of two, how to strengthen their hulls with transverse bulkheads. Navigation improved. Ships bore increasingly into the wind. But nothing supplanted the camel in the wastes of the Sahara. What Ibn Battuta had written of its miseries and perils in 1350 would remain as true in 1650 or 1850.

Those miseries and perils were many and real. "We passed ten days of discomfort at Taghaza," records Ibn Battuta, "for the crossing of the desert which lies beyond it, which is a ten nights' journey with no water on the way except rarely . . . At that time we used to go ahead of the caravan, and when we found a place suitable for pasturage we would graze our beasts. We went on doing this until one of our party was lost in the desert: after that I neither went ahead nor lagged behind . . .

"We came next to Tasarahla, a place of subterranean water beds, where the caravans halt. They stay there three days to rest, mend their waterskins, fill them with water, and sew on them covers of sackcloth as a precaution against the wind. From this point the *takshif* is despatched. The *takshif* is a name given to any man of the Massufa tribe who is hired by the persons of the caravan to go ahead to Walata, carrying letters from them to their friends there, so that they may take lodgings with them. These persons then come out a distance of four nights' journey to meet the caravan, and bring water with them . . . It often happens that the *takshif* perishes in this desert, with the result that the people of Walata know nothing about the caravan, and all or most of those who are with it perish.

"That desert is haunted by demons: if the *takshif* be alone, they make a sport of him and disorder his mind, so that he loses his way and perishes. For there is no visible road or track in these parts — nothing but sand blown hither and thither by the wind. You see hills of sand in one place, and afterwards you will see them moved to quite another place . . . We hired the *takshif* on this journey for a hundred gold mithcals* . . . On the night of the seventh day we saw with joy the fires of the party [from Walata] who had come out to meet us." Men would not undertake such journeys unless the rewards seemed great. And by the seventeenth century these rewards had begun to seem small.

Such changes underlay the eclipse of the Western Sudan. But other factors, human factors, confidence and temperament, the texture of social life, were there as well. To thoughtful men in Timbuktu, regarding the disaster of Moroccan invasion, the fault appeared to lie in Songhay itself. Thus the writer of the *Tarikh es Sudan*, completing his book under Moroccan occupation of Timbuktu, thought that God had wished to punish his fellow-countrymen for their lack of faith and their loose morals. "As to adultery," he says, "it had become so frequent as to seem the normal thing. Without it — no elegance, no glory: to such a point did the sons of the sultans commit adultery with their sisters." The taint of decay seemed already in the air.

It is worth insisting, though, that much of the fabric of Sudanese life survived. Even in Barth's day — in the middle of the nineteenth century — the internal trade of the Western Sudan was no mean thing.

From Kano, Barth thought, no fewer than three hundred camel-loads of cloth came annually to Timbuktu — a commerce worth not less, he reckoned, than five thousand pounds. "In taking a general view of the subject," he went on, "I think myself justified in estimating the whole produce of this manufacture"— of

* About twelve and a half ounces of gold.

Kano dyed cottons — "as far as it is sold abroad, at the very least at about three hundred million *kurdi*; and how great this national wealth is, will be understood by my readers when they know, with from fifty to sixty thousand *kurdi*, or from four to five pounds sterling a year, a whole family may live in that country with ease, including every expense, even that of clothing; and we must remember that the province is one of the most fertile spots on the earth, and is able to produce not only the supply of corn necessary for its population, but can also export; and that it possesses, besides, the finest pasture grounds."

It was not an ideal society. "A very important branch of the native commerce of Kano," Barth adds, "is certainly the slave trade . . . Altogether I do not think that the number of slaves annually exported from Kano exceeds five thousand;* but of course a considerable number are sold into domestic slavery."

Yet against the background of Victorian sweatshops and human degradation that Barth knew, this Sudan seemed a gentle and a pleasant country. "If we consider," he says of the Kano textile manufacture, "that this industry is not carried on here as in Europe, in immense establishments degrading man to the meanest condition of life, but that it gives employment and support to families without compelling them to sacrifice their domestic habits, we must presume that Kano ought to be one of the happiest countries in the world; and so it is so long as its governor, too often lazy and indolent, is able to defend its inhabitants from the cupidity of their neighbours, which of course is certainly stimulated by the very wealth of this country."

---

* Fifty years earlier, during the last decade of the British slave trade, Liverpool ships had exported West African slaves at an annual rate of about thirty thousand.

four

Between the Niger
and the Congo

The Negroes of Guinea are very haphazard in their habits of eating. They have no set time for meals, and eat and drink four or five times a day, drinking water, or a wine which they distill from palms. They live for the best part of one hundred years.

Anonymous European opinion,
c. 1540

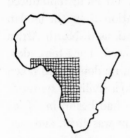

1 Beyond the Savannah

W<small>HAT WAS HAPPENING, MEANWHILE, IN</small> the lands that lay beyond the forest verge? This green frontier was as much a barrier to the peoples of the savannah as were the deserts of the north. They traded with the forest peoples when they could, or whenever commerce served, as it did with gold and cola nuts and slaves; their rule could seldom or never penetrate there. Not even Kankan Musa or Askia the Great or Idris Alooma made entry there in any significant or enduring depth, although trade and the missionaries of Islam would gradually open a breach.

Yet earlier migrations had evidently penetrated southward beyond the barrier of forest. Many Negro peoples of tropical West Africa believe that their remote ancestors came from the north and northeast. The Akan people of modern Ghana, for example, have a tradition that their forefathers came from the north in the eleventh century. Their king lists go back to a period which may be the end of the thirteenth century — to the foundation of their ancient capital of Bono Mansu, the ruins of which (or of subsequent building) are about a hundred miles north of Kumasi in modern Ashanti. There is a story that these founding fathers of Bono Mansu had come from "the great white desert" in the north; and good reason exists for supposing that this migration legend has within it a core of truth.

It is obvious in any case that these strong and vigorous peoples of the forest belt were not the mere product of migration from the northward. They borrowed much from the north. They received many newcomers from the north. But they no more reproduced the shape and pattern of Sudanese civilization than the Sudan reproduced the shape and pattern of civilizations in North Africa and Kush, from which it, in turn, had borrowed. They took ideas and techniques from the north (as the north, no doubt, had taken some from them), but they worked them into a civilizing synthesis of their own: an interweaving process which had begun in Africa at the other end of recorded time, when Egypt was great, and continues to this day. Nothing is to be learned about the course of African history from supposing a mechanical imitation of more advanced peoples by less advanced peoples. The truth is not so simple. Technologically "backward" peoples borrowed ideas from less "backward" peoples and tried to apply them to their own conditions; in applying them, they invariably modified them. The product was a compound, never a mere amalgam.

Thus it is true — or so it appears on present evidence — that the peoples of the forest belt acquired the knowledge of mining and smelting and working iron from neighbors to the northward, that they acquired this knowledge in the last centuries of the pre-Christian era, and that in acquiring it they began the slow revolution of their Stone Age tribalism into new forms of social organization. But it is not true that they followed the same lines of social and economic development as those from whom they had received this knowledge. On the contrary, they attained to important achievements of their own.

For the history of this forest belt and its varied peoples there is little or no help to be got from the Arab writers of the Middle Ages. Like the learned men of Timbuktu and Djenné, they knew next to nothing of the subject. But with the second half of the fifteenth century documents accrue from another source. By 1475 Portuguese captains had pioneered along the coast as far as the bights of Benin and Biafra, the great sea angle of west and southwest Africa; and Ruy de Siqueira, it seems, had actually landed on the coast of Benin as early as 1472.

Early European records of the west coast are of erratic value. Often enough they throw more light on European than African history. Sometimes they fall to a standard of literacy so low as to make them practically worthless; and seldom do they reach the descriptive skill and curiosity of the best of the medieval and post-medieval Arab travelers. These early Europeans on the coast were pirates and adventurers of whom no more than a handful could write their names; none of them would have had the literary sophistication and much-traveled background of men like Ibn Battuta or Leo Africanus. Yet they were bold and enterprising men, these captains; and so long as their crews would risk it they would generally sail into the unknown, concealing though it might a host of devils and monsters beyond number. Their records are much better than nothing.

They made little contact with the interior. Their object was to secure gold and pepper and slaves and anything else that would fill their hulls and yield a profit on returning. In the service of their masters — usually the sovereigns of western Europe — they established trading stations on the coast (rarely more than a dozen miles from salt water) and here and there, with growing confidence and fat returns, transformed these into coastal forts which they garrisoned in spite of every kind of killing fever. Many of these old castles survive today as picturesque ornaments along the coast: the Prime Minister of modern Ghana, with an agreeable irony, lives in one of them.

So that what these venturers could tell of West Africa was little more than its coastal aspect — its coastal aspect, moreover, as seen from the decks or trading counters or gun emplacements of men who had no interest in the country and its people except for the chance of trade. Valuable elsewhere in the non-European world, the records of early Christian missionary endeavor have disappointingly little to add. Unless the archives, still no more than partially explored and published, have unexpected treasures to contribute from that source.*

All of this might have been otherwise but for one great intervening factor. This was the frantic growth and murderous enlargement of the oversea slave trade.

2 The Great Distortion

THE SCALE OF THE OVERSEA SLAVE TRADE SO MUCH SURPASSED ANYthing of its kind before or since as to be quite distinct, in its impact on Africa, both from overland slaving — long practiced by the Arabs and many Negro states — and from the domestic slavery of African Iron Age feudalism. It was much more than the merely peripheral bleeding of vitality that was represented by overland slaving. It was quite different, in its catastrophic effects, from the subjection of weak peoples to stronger peoples that occurred through African warfare and conquest. Often as deadly as the medieval Black Death, which is said to have carried off a third of Europe's population, the oversea slave trade was much worse in its social consequences. For the Black Death was over in a handful of years; but the oversea slave trade endured for more than four centuries. It degraded thought and action, African as well as European, through generations of engrained contempt for human life.

European demand for African slaves had been first satisfied as early as 1444, when a consignment taken north of the Senegal estuary was put ashore at Lisbon; and it was continuously satisfied,

* As this is written, some fifteen thousand unpublished documents in the libraries of Goa, Lisbon, and the Vatican await publication by the Arquivo Histórico de Mozambique and the Central African Archives.

for hundreds of years after that, as the Portuguese and their rivals pushed further down the coast and established themselves there. By the early sixteenth century there were parts of Portugal where the number of Negro slaves was said to be larger than the number of native Portuguese. But the demand for slaves in the Caribbean and Brazil was infinitely greater still; looking at the records, it appears as practically insatiable. It enormously and radically swelled the trade. Millions were taken away or perished in the wars that oversea slaving provoked and lived from.

Round figures are deceptively easy to digest. A few examples may stick more instructively in the throat. Thus a Portuguese historian has lately estimated that about one million three hundred eighty-nine thousand slaves were taken from the coast of Angola *alone* in the years between 1486 and 1641, or about nine thousand a year from this never densely populated land. A report to Philip I calculated the number of slaves taken from Angola to Brazil in the years 1575 to 1591 as fifty-two thousand fifty-three, or nearly two thousand a year. Cadornega put the total number of slaves imported into Brazil — mainly from Angola and Mozambique — between 1580 and 1680 as about one million, or about ten thousand a year for a century; the figures, later on, would become larger still. And Angola and Mozambique were only two of many zones of collection.

Liverpool records of a century later show that in the eleven years of 1783 to 1793, about nine hundred Liverpool voyages were made for slaving and carried over three hundred thousand slaves worth about fifteen million pounds; the net return being reckoned as something more than twelve million pounds, or more than a million pounds a year. Barth, in the middle of the nineteenth century, could still complain not only of the Sudanese overland slave trade from Kano and elsewhere, but also of the oversea slaving of American ships in the Bight of Benin. Easily accepted over the centuries, the slave trade proved exceedingly hard to stop.

What the full effects of it really were is difficult and perhaps impossible to say. They were ruinously destructive of society and civilizing growth. At many points they were probably fatal to both. The wars provoked by slaving — and it was oversea slaving that made the pace in most of tropical and southern Africa — had no "progressive" side in that they stimulated rivalry between peoples, and hence invention and initiative, and thus material progress — as some have liked to argue. They were, on the contrary, completely negative in their effects on Africa — they stained and ruined much of the fabric of African society while permitting nothing better to replace it.

As the slaving wars continued, men grew more callous. African demoralization matched European cupidity. Slave revolts, sudden and ferocious in despair, added to the misery and bloodshed. "As very few of the negroes can so far brook the loss of their liberty," says an account of 1788, "and the hardships they endure, as to bear them with any degree of patience, they are ever upon the watch to take advantage of the least negligence in their oppressors. Insurrections are frequently the consequence, which are seldom suppressed without much bloodshed. Sometimes these are successful, and the whole ship's company is cut off. They are likewise always ready to seize every opportunity for committing some act of desperation to free themselves from their miserable state; and notwithstanding the restraint under which they are laid, they often succeed."

The writer was abolitionist, and sympathetic to the slaves. Yet, as Herskovits has shown, "from the beginning vast numbers of negroes refused to accept the slave status without a struggle." When they failed in revolt before they reached the Americas, they revolted there; and Toussaint l'Ouverture of San Domingo was only one of many slaves who reasserted human freedom in the Caribbean or the mainland of America.

One needs to remember this long story of insurrection when

considering the native attitudes of West Africa. That the chiefs and some of the tribes of the coasts were easily corrupted into wholesale slave trading is obvious enough: the step from domestic slavery, which they had always practiced, to the sale of slaves was all too easily made. Their attitude might not be the same as that of the Elizabethan slaver, John Hawkins, whose much respected coat-of-arms embodied "a demi-Moor, proper, in chains." It might be different from the state of mind of those European bishops of the Congo who sat, decade after decade, in an ivory chair on the quayside of Luanda, and extended their merciful hand in wholesale baptism of the slaves who were rowed beneath, going in chains to the ships that would carry them upon the "middle passage" to Brazil. But it was substantially at one with both: society permitted slavery, and therefore permitted slaving.

The coastal chiefs and peoples, or some of them, might willingly accept all that, for they were soon linked by trading interest to this insatiable European demand (just as, at other times and places, others would be linked to an Arab demand). But the notion that the whole of African society entered and endured the slaving centuries with greed, docility, or dumb acceptance — a notion somewhat favored by those who have argued, or still argue, the "inherent inferiority" of Negroes and the "slavish nastiness" of African society — has no foundation in the record. The weak might go to the wall; they did not therefore like it. African society had been relatively peaceful and generous and even gentle; the world these peoples were thrown into was one of death and horror. The best and strongest took the first or second chance to resist or revolt; the rest endured. But endurance did not mean acceptance.

It is easy to imagine the process of demoralization — the hunt for a few slaves changing into the hunt for many; and, with that, the gradual ruin of every sentiment of decency and restraint. It is more difficult to measure the ruin which this wholesale slaving visited upon many of the states and societies it cursed. "Gradually," Ihle has written of the Congo, and the same would be true elsewhere, "the last social links were broken, and the whole structure utterly destroyed. Certainly there had been slaves in the Congo before the coming of the white man. They had formed an organic part of the social framework, however, and had in it their clearly determined place. But after the growth of the slave trade the possession of slaves was transformed into a savage manhunt. Not only did the stronger man sell the weaker, but even the bonds of family life were broken, and parents sold their children or children their parents as generally worthless objects to the Portuguese, who branded them with a hot iron as if they had been sheep."*

Something of the measure of this decadence and ruin may be seen from comparing the condition of African peoples who suffered the slaving centuries with the condition of other African peoples — or what can be learned of them, for most of these lay far into the hinterland — who did not. Or one may look, for better understanding of the matter, at the contrasts between European narratives of the fifteenth and sixteenth centuries, when the trade was in its infancy, and European narratives of three or four hundred years later. These contrasts are especially instructive in the case of the notable kingdom of Benin, not far from the coast of modern Nigeria.

The British fought their way into Benin in 1897; and what they found there was afterwards described by Commander Bacon, who led that expeditionary column. "Truly," says Bacon, "has Benin been called the city of blood. Its history is one long record of savagery of the most debased kind. In the earlier part of this century, when it was the center of the slave trade, human suffering must here have reached its most acute form; but it is doubtful if even then the wanton sacrifice of life could have exceeded that of more recent times."

* Branding was practiced, of course, by all the European slaving nations.

The true history of the city-state and empire of Benin, of course, was anything but "one long record of savagery of the most debased kind"; yet at the time Bacon got there it may reasonably have seemed so. "Blood was everywhere . . . On the right [of the main compound of the king] was a crucifixion tree with a double crucifixion on it, the two poor wretches stretched out facing west, with their arms bound together in the middle . . . At the base were skulls and bones, literally strewn about, the debris of former sacrifices, and down every main road were two or more human sacrifices. . . ."

What cupidity and fear and despotism may do to rulers everywhere has been lately seen in Europe and in Asia, while the Aztecs of Mexico, whose society had nothing to do with oversea slaving, were also cursed with ritual murder. Yet the link between the scene that Bacon described and the fact of four centuries of oversea slaving must surely be a crucial one. Colonialist Europe may have succeeded, here and there, in fastening on African minds a sense of special guilt for the slaving centuries; but the truth is that the guilt was shared all round, and that Africans were not the prime movers in the matter. The peoples of the interior of central and southern Africa, beyond the long arm of the slavers, seldom or never reproduced those holocausts. When they did, these were occasional and despotic variants from a generally pacific rule. Nor did medieval Benin suffer in this way.

Four centuries before Bacon's expedition, at a time when slaving had yet to be on any great scale, the Portuguese had found a different scene. Pushing up the delta rivers —"small shippes of fifty tunnes" could go as far as Guato, "nine leagues with a good road" to Benin itself — they found a city-state that was prosperous and greatly skillful in the working of metals and of wood, "about a league long from gate to gate," without a wall but "surrounded by a large moat, very wide and deep, which sufficeth for its defence."

"I was there four times," says Pacheco, writing at the end of the fifteenth century. "Its houses are made of mud walls covered with palm leaves." This city-state had extended its rule over the neighboring countryside and was altogether "about eighty leagues long and forty wide." It was "usually at war with its neighbours." These wars provided slaves for domestic use, much as in medieval Europe; but the dignitaries of Benin, with the coming of Europeans, soon found their profit in selling them. "We buy [slaves]," adds Pacheco, "at twelve or fifteen brass bracelets each, or for copper bracelets which they prize more."

In spite of warfare with rivals, peace and order were the rule in that old Benin. The accounts are bare; but so much, at least, they make plain. In 1486 Affonso d'Aveiro took a small trading and exploring mission into Benin on behalf of the king of Portugal. He died there, but before dying had managed to send out a cargo of pepper, the first of that commodity to reach Europe from the Guinea coast; "and presently," says another Portuguese account, "samples of it were sent to Flanders and to other parts, and soon it fetched a great price and was held in high esteem."

At the same time the king of Benin — the *oba* as he was called — sent an ambassador to Portugal "because he desired to learn more about these lands, the arrival of people from them in his country being regarded as an unusual novelty." And when this ambassador — "a man of good speech and natural wisdom" — returned to Benin, he brought with him presents from the king of Portugal, a number of Catholic missionaries, and "new agents of the [Portuguese] king, who were to remain in that country and to traffic for the said pepper and for other things, which pertained to the trades of the king." Slaving, that is, was still of minor importance.

How these agents and missionaries fared in Benin is the substance of another Portuguese report, characteristically short on descriptive detail if long on implication, of 1516. "The favour which the king of Benin accords us," wrote Duarte Pires, then Portuguese royal agent in the city, "is due to his love of your highness; and thus he pays us high honour and sets us at table to dine with his son, and no part of his court is hidden from us but all the doors are open."

The missionaries were being well received, says Pires, but Christian labors much hindered, apparently, by the king's being engaged in warfare with his neighbors. On returning from one of his wars, however, the king "gave his son and some of his noblemen — the greatest in the kingdom — so that they might become Christians; and also he ordered a church to be built in Benin; and they made them Christians straightway; and also they are teaching them to read, and your highness will be very pleased to know that they are very good learners." A tactful report, perhaps; but not a troubled one. By 1554, when the Englishman Richard Windham got there, he found the king "could speake the Portugall tongue." Windham bought from him — against goods and the promise of goods on his next returning — "fourscore tunne of pepper." But he bought no slaves.

Similar reports, brief and scattered and seldom more than incidental to the business of mariners and traders, have survived from European visits to several other kingdoms and city-states along the coast, from the estuary of the Senegal River in the west to the estuary of the Congo in the south. They reveal the existence of many centers of tribal power, often at rivalry, often bound together by feudal ties, invariably working in metals, with a wide range of religious systems from simple animism to intricate forms of divine kingship; and offering so many apparent tokens of similarity with feudal Europe that the Portuguese had no difficulty in transferring a simple European explanation to many of their customs. In the kingdoms of the Congo estuary, indeed, they very soon persuaded the paramount chiefs and counselors to accept titles of nobility along with baptism, so that counts and dukes and marquises soon flourished there; though neither titles nor baptism can ever have conveyed the same arrogance of meaning for those who received them as they undoubtedly conveyed for those who offered them. The painful hierarchies of Europe were unknown to most of Africa.

These peoples had always believed in a single divine power ruling the ultimate destinies of their world: the Christian god, in that respect, was no different from their own — with the difference that baptism, for them, could be nothing but an amiable ceremony. They had usually accepted a hierarchy of power — with the difference that their hierarchy was subject to laws of the collective, while the hierarchy of feudal Europe had long become a law unto itself. These differences explain why the titles disappeared and the missionaries failed: neither could survive the strong pressures of a society which, though feudal in many of its appearances, was tribal in its essence.

Tribal — but not therefore primitive. Here, of course, it is dangerous to generalize. Primitive societies existed in Africa then, just as they still exist here and there in Africa today; although the word "primitive," even with them, can be properly applied only in a narrow sense of material or technological simplicity. But the tribalism of these Negro and Bantu-speaking peoples who had spread and multiplied across the central and southern continent, and some of whom the Portuguese reached in the fifteenth and sixteenth centuries, had long evolved their own Iron Age patterns of society and forms of organization. They had shaped their own original course and evolution, and the word "primitive" could have no more application to them than it could to their contemporaries in Europe. So much is clear, to look no further, from the early art of Ife and Benin.

3 *Benin*

THE BENIN EXPEDITION OF 1897 BROUGHT BACK SURPRISING TRO-
phies. As well as of blood and sacrifice, Bacon also told of "several
hundred bronze plaques, suggestive of almost Egyptian design, but
of really superb casting," and of "magnificently carved tusks."
When these objects were examined in Europe the reality was seen
to be still more remarkable than Bacon had suggested. Serenity
and peace breathed inexplicably from this place of "savage chaos."

More were found, a decade later, by the German Africanist, Leo
Frobenius, who attributed them to the heritage of Atlantis, the
"lost continent." Other Europeans, meanwhile, thought these
works of art must be of classical Greek lineage; or perhaps the
creations of some solitary European of long ago who had arrived
in Benin and conceived, by amazing genius, all these "un-African"
masterpieces. Others again thought they were obvious products of
the European Renaissance — and for thinking that the wonderful
sensitivity and idealized naturalism of these heads gave them some
excuse; or simply put them down to "Portuguese influence." *

Good chance brought to light, in 1938 and 1939, another great
assemblage of bronzes — or, more precisely, of brasses — at the
palace of the Oni of Ife, traditional ruler of another city-state that
lay about a hundred miles from Benin. More are still being
found; and today these works of early Ife and Benin, whether in
terra cotta or cast in metal, are famous everywhere. All are now
accepted as entirely African and most of them are thought to have
been made between the thirteenth and the eighteenth centuries,
with the best work belonging to the early part of this period.†

---

* "The bronze art of Benin," wrote Sir Harry Johnston in 1910, "is almost
entirely due to the inspiration of the Portuguese."

† Later degeneration seems to have gone hand-in-hand with kingly autocracy and an increase in human sacrifice.

They are the product, that is, of Iron Age maturity in one of the pre-European states of the West African forest belt.

A satisfactory description of the African societies which produced these works of art and others like them must await the findings of much more research, some of which is now in progress. Dike and others are at present engaged in preparing a detailed history of Benin. After new excavations at the palace of Benin in 1957, Goodwin has shown the possibility of establishing a long series of pottery types. The palace itself, he found, had at least four consecutive floors. Willett, in the same year, reported about thirty thousand pieces of pottery from Yoruba sites near Ife, and these are now being studied in conjunction with pottery from a hundred well-shafts dug there in 1953 and 1957 by the Nigerian Antiquities Service. "Yoruba archaeology," Willett comments, "has hitherto justifiably concentrated on the rescue of art objects from the shrines of Ife; and, as no study has been made of the pottery of the Yoruba, there is no chronological context for these pieces. [But] there is now a very large quantity of material from the two most important Yoruba sites, and it is hoped that their study will eventually produce a chronological framework."

Yet an outline does emerge. It would seem that these societies of what is now southern Nigeria, remarkable for their art and religion, stand in midstream of inheritance both from ancient West African origins and from other influences that took their rise in the north and east. It was long thought that their art, so different from the abstract styles of Africa, was somehow extraneous to themselves — was an accidental borrowing, as it were, from outside. This is now seen to be wrong: their art was part of their own growth. That was proved once and for all when Bernard Fagg uncovered at Abiri, some ten miles from Ife, five terra-cotta heads in the same grave: two were highly stylized, but the other three were of a finely conceived naturalism. Just as at Nok, many centuries before, abstract art and "portrait art" here went hand in hand — a

rare and challenging phenomenon for which religious explanations must probably be found.

Much too little is known, as yet, to say what links — if any —
may have led from the art of Nok to the art of Ife. And the case
is not much better when one comes to consider the question of
"outside influences." The Yoruba people of Ife and its neighborhood, a Negro people, say that their ancestors "came from the
east"; and Biobaku has even felt able to suggest that "the Yoruba
must have migrated to their present homes from a region where
they came under ancient Egyptian, Etruscan and Jewish influences." He places these "Yoruba migrations from the Near East" as
somewhere between A.D. 600 and 1000.

However that may be, the evidence for eastern influence on
Yoruba culture is not small. There is first of all the religious evidence. "The kings," an anonymous Portuguese pilot wrote in
about 1540 of the Guinea coast, but more especially of Benin and
Congo, "are worshipped by their subjects, who believe that they
come from heaven, and speak of them always with great reverence,
at a distance and on bended knees.

"Great ceremony surrounds them, and many of these kings never
allow themselves to be seen eating, so as not to destroy the belief of
their subjects that they can live without food. They worship the
sun, and believe that spirits are immortal, and that after death
they go to the sun." And although the gods of Kush like those of
Egypt may first have taken shape in ancient Africa to south and
west of the Nile, the echoes of Kushite divine kingship here seem
plain enough. To these, as we have seen,* can be added the evidence of the Yoruba national god, Shango, being worshiped with
a ram's mask that is strongly reminiscent of Kushite or Old Egyptian origin. From the same grave that yielded the five heads mentioned above, Bernard Fagg also recovered a ram's head and a
coiled serpent, both familiar in the religions of the ancient Nile.

* Page 61.

Did the ancestors of the Yoruba know that great city of Meroë? The Meroitic temple at Naga (c. 100 B.C.–A.D. 100) has a fine coiled serpent climbing on its façade.

And then it is true that the art of Ife and Benin — as of other centers of early civilization in West Africa — made extensive use of casting in bronze and brass by the "lost wax" method which the peoples of the Nile had used. Castings by this method appear first at Ife and then afterwards at Benin, not far away; and they appear, as though by sudden importation, in the full splendor of their sensitivity and fine technique. Yet the use of this technique, even if it came originally from the Nile, could not have come suddenly or quickly. The art of Ife appears to have reached its zenith in the thirteenth century, a thousand years after the collapse of Meroë; and the explanation of its sudden maturity is probably no more obscure than that its lineal forerunners have not yet been found.

There comes to mind, in this connection, a parallel with the fine bronze casting of the Shang dynasty of China in the second millennium B.C. When those magnificent pots and beakers were first considered in the nineteenth century they too seemed to have sprung fully formed from the lap of the gods. Only much later, and with much research, was it understood that they came not from sudden importation or invention, but from long years of trial and error. They were the culmination, the beautiful and spacious summit; beneath them was the piled-up soil of long experiment.

What Creel remarked of archeological and artistic discovery in China can be usefully applied to Africa as well. "Until about 1920," he observed some twenty years ago, "it was doubted that Stone Age men had lived in China at all. When large numbers of Neolithic sites were found it was said 'Yes: but we have no Palaeolithic.' Palaeolithic remains were found in the Ordos in 1923, and it was said 'Yes: but not in China proper.' In 1928 traces of Palaeolithic man were found in the valley of the Yellow River between

Shensi and Shansi, and now we have skeletons from the very region of Peking. What may yet be found in China, only a bold man would predict." This skepticism that Creel was hitting at may have its value, but it is damaging when made into a principle. If considered in isolation, the astonishing art of Ife and Benin might seem the sudden product of an outside inspiration; but it ought not to be considered in isolation.

This art, like the societies which created it, belongs rather to a complex and capacious tradition of its own: a tradition which grew and evolved with the coming of Iron Age civilization to this wide forest land beyond the southern verge of the plains of grass. It may have an unusually distinguished position there; yet cut away from its cradling world it can no more be explained than the bronzes of the Shang dynasty can be explained apart from the early civilization of China.

4 Unity in Diversity

WE ARE ONLY AT THE BEGINNING OF UNDERSTANDING WHAT THE "Nok culture" really meant. It is only a handful of years since the achievements of the Sao, in the region of Lake Chad, became known and were added to the story. "Lost wax" gold castings from the Ivory Coast, to the West of Yorubaland, yield little or nothing in skill and forcefulness to the work of Benin; while "lost wax" brass industries "which, at least in their nonfigurative work, are remarkably similar and occasionally even indistinguishable in appearance" belong to the Dan-Ngere peoples of Liberia, French Guinea and the Ivory Coast as well as to grassland peoples of the Cameroons.*

* William Fagg in *The Sculpture of Africa*, p. 60. His essays and Eliot Elisofon's photographs in that volume offer a masterly guide to the whole subject.

The famous golden death-mask of an Ashanti king that is stored now in the Wallace Collection, in London, is another example of highly skilled metal-working that obviously belongs, in its bold combination of realism with symbolic abstraction, to a strong but strongly varied cultural heritage. And one could almost endlessly extend the list — to the masks of the Baoulé, to the wood-carving of equatorial Africa, to the work in wood and metal of the Bambara of the upper Niger and a host of others: the products of an African consciousness and cosmogony and care for the decorative arts of life that made, and make, a world of their own.

To this creative synthesis many sources brought their contribution. These peoples borrowed much; but they also invented much. Somewhere behind the ideas and techniques that we seem to recognize as North African or Nilotic lies the broad onflowing river of native adaptation and invention: the figurines of Nok, the strange head of Jemaa, the ancestor figures of the Sao and Kotoko, flowing out of a remote antiquity which may well return, as discoveries in the Sahara now suggest, to that most memorable of all the artistic works of purely African antiquity — the seated man and woman who were painted on a rock at Séfar, in the mountains of Tassili, when the earliest kings of Egypt were not yet born.

This distinctive Negro evolution had no near frontier in the south. Once we are into the forest belt, beyond the savannah, the trails wind away southward and southeastward across the continent; and it becomes impossible to know with any certainty where they begin or where they end. Many ancient usages — the erection of megaliths among them — seem to link much of continental Africa together. But the manner and direction by which they traveled, and when they traveled — or even *if* they traveled, and were not adopted independently by different peoples — are problems to which there is no present solution. If, for example, it is relatively easy to suggest where ram worship and divine kingship came from, it is anything but easy to suggest why a people of southern Ethiopia should regard a crest on the forehead (in their case, a markedly phallic crest) as a sign of triumph and nobility, while the people of Ife and Benin evidently did the same. Did these two widely diverse peoples arrive at the idea independently of one another? Or was there not perhaps a common ancestry in forehead-crests — an ancestry returning once again to Meroë and its crested kings?

Further southward, a clearer pattern begins to define itself. This is largely because the rise of Iron Age society coincided — and no doubt made possible — the progressive spread and multiplication of Negroid peoples across the southern continent. Thus the same patterns of divine kingship, cultivation, tribal collectivism, metalworking, building in stone, are found again and again. Such objects as iron gongs, such techniques as hillside terracing for soil conservation and for irrigation, such skills as carving in wood: all these make links between regions wide apart.

Except in East Africa, where pastoral barbarians from the north would intervene in medieval and post-medieval times and destroy the sedentary Iron Age societies which had existed there, together with their settlements and their cities and most of their arts and crafts, we come here into the presence of closely related cultures which influence a greater part of the central and southern continent. These cultures are Bantu; but the fact that they are Bantu today does not necessarily mean that their origins should be attached to the arrival or emergence of the peoples who now possess them. There may have been pre-Bantu or proto-Bantu Iron Age cultures in central and southern Africa just as there evidently were in East Africa — a point that is worth holding in mind, even at this early stage in knowledge, if only to avert the danger of supposing that culture-successions in this central and southern continent have been identical with successive waves of migration. Migrating peoples came southward, bringing new ideas and new technologies, but they met others in their path, and with these others they intermingled; and the result of their intermingling was cultural change — a complex process, anything but automatic or predictable.

And then, opening another wide horizon to this evolving Iron Age in the central and southern continent, there is the steady growth of trade across the Indian Ocean. It accompanies the whole period of the age of metals in regions to the south of the Sahara, and its contribution to the origins of contemporary Africa is perhaps no less important than the contributions of ancient Egypt and of Kush, of the Lybico-Berber peoples of North Africa, of the maritime states of southern Arabia.

Persia, India, Indonesia, China: all these impinged for centuries on the long eastern seaboard of Africa; and all have left much behind them. "I have never in my life seen so much broken china," Sir Mortimer Wheeler said in 1955, after a brief stay in Tanganyika, "as I have seen in the past fortnight along the coast here and the Kilwa Islands: literally, fragments of Chinese porcelain by the shovelful . . . In fact, I think it is fair to say that so far as the Middle Ages are concerned, from the tenth century onwards, the buried history of Tanganyika is written in Chinese porcelain."

This Indian Ocean trade would not touch West Africa. A solitary sherd of Chinese ware, true enough, was lately found in the ruins of a missionary chapel at Mbanza within two hundred miles of the Atlantic coast — in the "duchy" of Mbata, a dependent of the old kingdom of Congo — but is evidently of seventeenth or eighteenth century manufacture and thus of accidental provenance.*

But what trans-Saharan trade and influence did for the Sudan and perhaps for the whole of western and central Africa, this

---

* I am grateful to M. Maurice Bequaert, of the Musée Royal du Congo Belge, for this information; the sherd in question was examined in Holland by M. Delorme in 1946.

Indian Ocean trade would do for eastern and southeast Africa. It would bring the ancient people of those distant plains and hills within the civilizing circuit of the outside world. It would help to develop other Iron Age societies and promote other civilizations; and it is a large part of the story of pre-European Africa.

five

To the Southward

Two days' sail beyond, there lies the very last market town of the continent of Azania, which is called Rhapta, and has its name from the sewed boats already mentioned; in which there is ivory in great quantity, and tortoise shell.

Periplus of the Erythraean Sea about A.D. 60

The mariners of Oman go on this sea as far as the Island of Kanbalu in the sea of the Zanj.

El Mas'udi A.D. 947

 # 1 *The Southern Zanj*

THOSE MARINERS OF OMAN, WHO SAILED
the "blind waves" of the seas of East
Africa through medieval times, took with them in the year 912 or
a few years later a passenger of unusual value. This "sea of the
Zanj," he would afterwards remember, was the most perilous of
all the seas of the world he knew — and his travels had been many.
Its long ocean rollers were called "blind" just because "they grow
into great mountains and open deep gulfs between them." Yet he
went with the mariners of Oman far down the coast — perhaps as
far as Madagascar, perhaps in one trading ship after another as
occasion served — and returned to Arabia, by the same route, three
years later. After many other journeys that consumed his youth
and middle years he settled at last in Fostat, old Cairo; and there
he wrote books. In 955 he composed the last of these, and died a
year later.

This man, Abdul Hassan ibn Hussein ibn Ali El Mas'udi, was
among the best informed of travelers in the medieval world. He
became, as Ibn Khaldun would write more than four centuries
after his death, "the model of all historians and the authority
upon which they rely for the critical estimate of many facts which
form the subject of their labors." Born in Baghdad of a family of
the Hedjaz towards the end of the ninth century, El Mas'udi traveled and studied and wrote for nearly forty years. Though only
two of his works are known, their value is unrivaled for an early
knowledge of the Arab trading world, and especially of the East
African coast. The more famous of these books he called *The
Meadows of Gold and Mines of Gems*, because, he said, he
wished "to excite a desire and curiosity after its contents, and to
make the mind eager to become acquainted with history." Evi-

dently finished in about 947, the whole of this splendid work was translated into French and published in Paris in 1864. An English translation of its first section had already appeared in 1841, but a complete English version has still to be made.

The Meadows of Gold lives up to its startling title: aside from its great quantity of information, it is surely the best of all the medieval travel books. Not until Marco Polo's story of his journey to China and back, three hundred years later, would anything so good appear. What El Bekri would do at second-hand for the kingdoms of the old Sudan in the middle of the eleventh century, El Mas'udi had done at first-hand, and a hundred years earlier, for the peoples of the eastern seaboard. This means that the medieval history of East Africa can start, with pretty solid evidence, in those years that saw the state of Ghana reach the zenith of its power.

At that time — which saw in West Africa, as well, the beginnings of the empire of Mali and the city-state of Ife — the peoples of the eastern coast of Africa were, to the Arabs, known universally as the Zanj. These were the Negroes or "black people" who lived beyond the land of Ethiopia. Ibn Hordadbeh, who mentions them first in A.D. 886, laconically observes that "whoever goes to the land of the Zanj, surely catches the itch." Suleiman the Merchant, having sailed from the Persian Gulf to Canton and back in the ninth century, says that this "land of Zanj is vast. The plants that grow there, such as *dura* [sorghum] which is the foundation of their diet, sugar cane and others, are all black in color." Then comes El Mas'udi, and the records emerge from hearsay and sailors' fable.

To El Mas'udi, traveling to the southward with the mariners of Oman and the merchants of Siraf, and sojourning on the coast for several years, these Zanj were evidently a people of many tribes. In some references they appear to be "all the blacks"; in others, only "some of the blacks." Their tribes include the Berbera, which is enough to show that El Mas'udi made no distinction between the Zanj of what might now be called "Hamitic" type and the Zanj of Negro type. Other Arab writers, doubtless drawing on El Mas'udi, say the same. Writing on hearsay in 1030, El Biruni says that the coast of the southern continent and islands are populated by "the various tribes of the Zanj."

The origins of the word remain mysterious. Perhaps they were Persian. It first occurs, at all events, in a Persian inscription of 293 B.C., which records that Narseh the King had relations with "Zhand Afrik Shah," though whether this king of the Zanj was an African ruler or merely a prince of southern Arabians who were then established on the East African coast is unknown, and probably unknowable. Modern Zanzibar — "coast of the Zanj" — perpetuates the word. Even today, Zanj is common usage in the Arabic-speaking world for Africans whose skins are dark.

This numerous group of peoples, says El Mas'udi, lived in a country seven hundred parasangs in length (about twenty-five hundred miles down the coast, or roughly the distance from the Horn of Africa to Mozambique), "a country divided by valleys, mountains, and deserts of sand, abounding in wild elephant," and reaching to the southward as far as Sofala (near modern Beira, in Mozambique), "which is the most distant frontier of the territory that is reached by the ships of Oman and Siraf."

Beyond that, then or later, the Arabs did not go; or if they did, the records of their voyaging have disappeared. It is easy to sail on southward from here, but hard to return, for once you enter the channel between Mozambique and Madagascar, the monsoon wind fails at last, and a southward current sets in; moreover, trading interest would have carried the Arabs no further than Sofala, where ivory or gold was plentiful. Their writers generally speak of the country beyond Sofala as "the land of Waq Waq," which may have meant Natal, just as the Waq Waq (who were evidently not considered to be Zanj) may have been Bushmen. Yet it seems more likely that they merely ignored the coast beyond Mozambique, and that "the land of Waq Waq" was the island of Madagascar. Medieval Arabs generally believed that land somehow swept eastward from the foot of Africa and joined, or at any rate, led toward the great eastern islands they knew, and Ferrand has argued that "eastern Waq Waq" was Java or Sumatra.*

Some of the Zanj whom Mas'udi knew were undoubtedly — as we shall see later — the forerunners of present Swahili populations and of present "Hamitic" populations. But others seem to have been the forerunners of those more distinctively Bantu-speaking peoples who now occupy much of the coast and the hinterland. In this connection the most useful part of El Mas'udi's surviving work is where he speaks of the kingdom of the Waqlimi; for it is here that one gains a first authentic glimpse of the growth and development of Iron Age society in southern Africa. Here too is the first historical notice of the mines of Rhodesia.

These Zanj of the Waqlimi are those who built their capital in the far south, in the land of Sofala, "which produces gold in abundance and other marvels." He does not say exactly where, though it was evidently not in the same place as the Arab trading station of Sofala itself; but Ibn Said, writing on hearsay two hundred years later, puts this capital at Sinna. This was certainly the Sena of later Portuguese discovery, lying about one hundred fifty miles up the Zambesi River from the sea. Edrisi, at about the same time, has Sinna as a town "on the borders of the land of Sofala"; and we may reasonably take it that the capital of these southern Zanj, in Mas'udi's time, was on the lower reaches of the Zambesi.

When was this capital built? Mas'udi makes no comment on this either, but he evidently means that they had built it long before his time. For he begins his account of East Africa with the old migration legend which recounted how those sons of Kush, sons of Canaan, who "turned to the rightward, between the east and the west," and peopled the eastern and southeastern African

* In Grottanelli, p. 54.

lands, were "the Nubians and the Beja and the Zanj"; but he adds that "only the Zanj" persevered in making their way into the far south "beyond the upper waters of the Nile."

Having built their capital, says El Mas'udi, "they elected a king whom they called Waqlimi. This name . . . was that of their kings from time immemorial. The Waqlimi commands all the other kings of the Zanj and has three hundred thousand riders." This last, of course, was a traveler's fable; in his very next sentence Mas'udi goes on to explain that "the Zanj use the ox as a beast of burden, for their country has neither horses, nor mules, nor camels, and they do not even know these animals." Nor was their country ever visited by snow or frost: only with Abulfeda, three hundred years later, would the snows of Kilimanjaro appear in Arab writing — and Abulfeda is careful to add that he does not believe in them. That Mas'udi should not even mention them is pretty clear proof of the Arabs having known next to nothing of the hinterland in the tenth century.

These Zanj were skilled workers in metal, and energetic traders. They hunted the elephant for its ivory, but made "no use of its ivory for their daily needs." They were jet black, with "hanging lips," and prized iron above gold. They ate the banana, but the staple of their diet was sorghum and a plant called *kalari*, dug from the ground like a truffle. They also ate honey and meat and possessed many "coconut islands" whose fruit was important for them.

They were great orators. "The Zanj are elegant speakers, and have orators in their own language. Often a devout man among them, entering a crowd, will make a speech inviting his listeners to conform to the ways of god and obey god's orders. He tells them what punishments must follow disobedience, and recalls the example of their ancestors and former kings."

All this suggests a long-settled people or group of peoples who lived by mixed agriculture, cultivating grain and grazing cattle, and by trade; and who understood the smelting and manufacture of metals. It is indeed a clear and convincing account of the early Iron Age cultures of east and southeast Africa which archeology would begin to uncover a thousand years later.

But it suggests more than that. Through Mas'udi's detailed and often vivid accounts one may see that the spread and multiplication of Negro peoples across the southern continent was far advanced by the tenth century. One may catch the echo, faint but sure, of the spiritual and material ideas with which they traveled, and which they carried to every part of their remote land. Here in southeast Africa of the tenth century these ideas and techniques were present as emphatically as they were present elsewhere. They were important in the forest belt of West Africa. The Portuguese would find them in the Congo of the fifteenth century. They still have their molding influence in parts of Africa today.

This continuity of culture and its wide spreading through migration are worth some emphasis, for they are keys to an understanding of African history. Consider, for example, the astonishingly close parallel between El Mas'udi's description of the ideology of the southern Zanj with a modern anthropologist's description of one of the peoples of the southern Sudan today.

The Zanj of southeast Africa, says Mas'udi, have no codified religion. "Everyone worships what he pleases, a plant, an animal, a metal." Their religion, that is, was animist. But it comprised a "divine kingship." Waqlimi, the title of their kings, "means son of the great god: they call him thus because they have chosen their king to govern them with equity. As soon as he exercises a tyrannical power and departs from the rules of justice, they kill him and exclude his posterity from royal succession, because they say that in acting thus he has ceased to be the son of the great god — that is, the king of heaven and earth."

Now turn to Professor Evans-Pritchard and the Shilluk of the southern Sudan a thousand years later. These Shilluk are one of those "black peoples" whom contemporary Arabic-speaking Sudanese also call Zanj. They number about one hundred ten thousand, and live in hamlets on the west bank of the White Nile near the town of Malakal. They are mainly a cattle-keeping people, but they also cultivate a little grain, and have blacksmiths of their own. They elect their kings and think them divine; and in none of this do they behave differently from the tenth century Zanj of the remote land of Sofala.

All these Shilluk kings, says Evans-Pritchard, "are believed to be descended from Nyikang, the leader of the Shilluk in their heroic age, who led them to their present homeland, conquering it from its inhabitants and dividing it among the lineages of his followers; and Nyikang, or, as we would say, the spirit of Nyikang, is believed to be in every king or to have passed from king to king down the line of his successors. Nyikang is thus a mythological personification of the divine kingship which itself symbolises the national structure, a changeless moral order . . . We can only understand the place of the kingship in Shilluk society when we realise that it is not the individual at any time reigning who is king, but Nyikang who is the medium between man and God, and is believed in some way to participate in God as he does in the king."

The parallels continue. Mas'udi explains that the southern Zanj kill or depose their kings whenever they go astray. "Our authorities," says Evans-Pritchard, "say that the Shilluk believe that should the king become physically weak the whole people might suffer, and, further, that if a king becomes sick or senile he should be killed to avoid some grave national misfortune, such as defeat in war, epidemic, or famine. The king must be killed to save the kingship and with it the whole Shilluk people." The root ideas, clearly, were the same.

The Zanj of Sofala, says Mas'udi at another point, "choose their king to govern them with equity." The Shilluk of the upper Nile, explains Evans-Pritchard, "elect their king" because "the kingship belongs to all the people and not to the royal clan."

Now the point, of course, is not that these Zanj of the upper Nile are in any close relation of inheritance to the southern Zanj of medieval times. The Shilluk, as it happens, are rather a new nation. Dak Fadiet, the divine king whom they elected in 1945, was only the thirty-first of his line, which might put Nyikang, their hero-founder, somewhere in the seventeenth or eighteenth centuries. The point is that the spread and multiplication of African peoples across the southern continent was an organic process, having its own rules and ideologies, its own dynamism, its own strong civilizing growth; and that all this remains persistent and powerful enough to make it possible to study the remote African past, at least in some degree, through the African present.

Yet today, looking back and trying to discern the lines of growth, the most reliable indicator in this organic process remains undoubtedly the use of iron. These peoples might have spread and multiplied without iron tools and iron weapons; but only much more slowly, much less successfully. Hunting, farming, craftsmanship in wood and leather and bone, the conquest of forests and the defeat of rivals — all these, with iron, became infinitely less difficult. Stone and bone and wood might continue to be used; iron would progressively supplant them. As elsewhere in the world — however different the circumstances — iron in southern Africa would give society a new and firmer technical foundation, and open the path to cities and to civilization.

Now the use of iron was extensive among the Zanj of Mas'udi's time. By the twelfth century, as will be seen, southeast Africa was actually exporting large quantities of iron. But where in these southern lands — so far from Kush and Libya — lay the beginnings of the use of iron?

Archeology has lately had new and clear things to say about

this. With Desmond Clark's recent discoveries at the Kalambo Falls, the chronology of early southern African society — forerunner of the medieval states and city-states of Rhodesia and the coast — begins to emerge from the mist, and takes on round and solid shape.

2 *Discoveries at Kalambo*

THE BROAD SEQUENCE OF TRANSITION FROM OLD STONE AGE TO NEW Stone Age to Iron Age is far from clear, as yet, in southern Africa. Rich in evidence of people who hunted and fished and gathered their food, southern Africa is poor in evidence of people who practiced agriculture before they knew the use of metals.

In East Africa a mature neolithic — agriculture without metal — may go back beyond 1000 B.C. Earlier than this we seem to meet transitional cultures that were on the road to growing food but had not yet quite got there. The earliest of these transitional cultures so far found, the site at Hyrax Hill in Kenya that was excavated in 1937 by Dr. and Mrs. Leakey, is dated to about 3000 B.C. Here the Leakeys discovered a neolithic settlement complete with cemetery and stone-walled enclosures, as well as some pit-dwellings of a different culture. People had apparently lived here for some three thousand years.

Similarly transitional cultures also seem to have existed in what is now Rhodesia. In Northern Rhodesia the "woodland Nachikufu" people — whose earliest phase is dated by radio-carbon tests to about 4000 B.C. and who painted interestingly on rocks — used weighted digging sticks, grindstones, pestles, heavy scrapers and spokeshaves of stone, awls of bone and polished adzes. Like the people of Hyrax Hill, they were beginning to extend their range of food; but they cannot have extended it very far, if only because the yam is the only food plant, among those now grown in Africa, which is known for certain to have existed there. They may have cultivated the yam. They certainly ate vegetables of one kind or another, for some of the carbonized remains of these have been found. But they were still a long way from that command of environment which would accompany — and make possible — the great migrations of Iron Age Africa.

Up to a few years ago it was no more than suspected that the beginnings of iron metallurgy in southern Africa might go back to the early centuries of the Christian era. Then, as scientists began to look for evidence in archeologically empty territories like Rhodesia, a little firm evidence came to light. Thus Desmond Clark found that he could report from Barotseland, in north-western Rhodesia, potsherds of a type that was generally agreed to be early iron age in date: the so-called channeled ware of Rhodesia. A radio-carbon result for fragments of oxidized ferri-crete from the same site has since given an approximate date of A.D. 90.*

But in 1953 the doubts were swept away. Clark began work on a site at the southern end of Lake Tanganyika, hard by the spectacular falls of the Kalambo River as it plunges over the brink of the Rift Valley; and proved beyond all question that an Iron Age culture really did begin here more than fifteen hundred years ago.

"Here in old lake beds dating either to the interpluvial or to the very beginning of the succeeding Gamblian Pluvial of Upper Pleistocene age," Clark has written of his work at Kalambo, "were found final Acheulian and later camping floors in association with partially carbonised tree trunks preserved in waterlogged clays, fine silts, and sands." Radio-carbon test of this "final Acheulian" — the end, that is, of the early stone age in south-central Africa — has yielded a date of "more than 36,000 years before the present."

* Dr. Clark in a letter to the writer.

But people went on living at the Kalambo Falls. Level after level of their occupation has emerged from the careful prodding of spade and trowel. And at our end of prehistoric time, as it were, another radio-carbon test (probably reliable although, in common with all other radio-carbon tests, not conclusive by itself) has offered an important Iron Age date. It was applied to material from the closing stages of early Iron Age layers at Kalambo; and returned an answer of about A.D. 1000. "There is no reason," Clark comments on this, "to assume any contamination; and one may therefore conclude that the beginning of the early Iron Age 'channelled ware' occupation was somewhere in the first half of the first millennium A.D., or somewhat earlier."

One can thus begin to see a little more clearly. The use of iron appeared in south-central Africa at about the same time as it appeared in the forest belt of West Africa, or not much later: in the last centuries of the pre-Christian era, that is, or the first centuries of the Christian era. It was either developed there independently or was brought down by migrating peoples from the north, and perhaps in the first place from pre-Christian Meroë, that "Birmingham of ancient Africa." If the latter, though, this migration of iron-using technique must have moved with surprising rapidity, since little more than two or three hundred years would in that case have separated the development of ferrous metallurgy on the middle Nile from the making of smelting tuyères in Northern Rhodesia.

By the tenth century A.D. the peoples of the Lower Zambezi, as we know from El Mas'udi, were in strong growth and development of their Iron Age culture. We also know from the archeological evidence that this was true of other peoples in the hinterland. Thus the Zanj and their fellow peoples had experienced, by the tenth century, the social and economic revolution which took them out of the Stone Age. Again one sees, here as in West Africa, that it is the second half of the first millennium A.D. — the period, let us say, between A.D. 500 and 1000 — which is crucial to the study of contemporary African origins.

This technical revolution was the more remarkable, in most of south-central Africa, in that it seems not to have involved any metal before iron, such as gold or copper. Elsewhere in the world a Copper Age and Bronze Age preceded Iron Age society; yet the earliest techniques for smelting metals throughout south-central Africa seem to have been techniques for smelting iron. This is why it appears reasonable to speak of these pre-European states and polities in southern Africa as "Iron Age." Some authorities — among them Professors Goodwin and Malan — prefer the term Metal Age, because, they point out, gold and copper may have been worked on a small scale before iron, especially by the Hottentots of South Africa, who used, however, an ironworking technique; and both, as well as tin, were certainly worked at the same time as iron. The smiths of the old Transvaal certainly understood the making of bronze; and those of the Katanga — in the far southeastern corner of the Belgian Congo — just as certainly understood the "lost wax" method of casting that many others had used in the north and west. These points have their weight; yet it nonetheless seems true that no metal, before the coming of iron, was sufficiently important as to cause any significant change in economic and social organization.

Although they worked copper and gold extensively, the technical and military superiority of the dominant and most developed societies of medieval southern Africa was in any case founded on their skill in working iron. Ironstone being common in most regions of Africa, the production of wrought iron would depend — once its reduction by charcoal in hand-blown clay furnaces was understood — only on the demand for it and on the availability of timber. There was no lack of timber, and the demand was evidently an ample one. Iron could become an everyday convenience; and so, of course, could gold and copper, for these are smelted at a lower temperature than iron. There is plenty of written evidence to show that all these metals became an everyday convenience.

This evidence rests not only on Mas'udi, and his reports of commerce in the tenth century. Even more eloquent of the commercial and therefore social stimulus of the ocean trade — to the peoples of the coast but also to the peoples of the hinterland — is the evidence for use of iron and export of iron that is contained in the writings of another Arab historian.

3 The Foundations of Southern Civilization

E<small>DRISI'S</small> DESCRIPTION OF THE COAST OF EAST AFRICA WAS WRITTEN in Sicily, for a Norman king, in about 1154; and there exist at least three manuscript copies of it. The first was evidently made at Almeria in southern Spain in 1344; the second was found in Egypt but is undated; and the third, an abridgment, was published in Rome in 1592. Composed a full two hundred years after El Mas'udi had died, it appears to rely a good deal more on hearsay and second-hand report; and Edrisi, unlike his great predecessor, seems not to have traveled down the coast himself. Yet his painstaking exactness and wealth of detail are outstanding for an age which generally cared for neither; and it was perhaps for these, as much as for his breadth of knowledge, that this Andalusian nobleman enjoyed his reputation among Norman scholars of his day.

He is writing against a background gained by countless venturers in Arab trading through every quarter of the eastern seas as far as northern China; and it is clear that in these two hundred years since Mas'udi's time the Indian Ocean trade with East Africa has enlarged and grown more various. To those who read of it in Sicily, or heard Edrisi talk of it, this eastern trade must have seemed rich beyond dreams, a strange and glittering Eldorado where Europeans, if only they could reach it, might enter on an altogether larger kind of life.

Yet Edrisi is nothing if not practical in his reports. He knows about the gold and ivory trade, of course, for it is famous by now throughout the Arab trading world. But his emphasis is not on ivory or gold — or slaves — but on iron. It is wealth in iron — wrought iron — that makes the trade important. And the aspect of the coast has altered much since Mas'udi's inquiring voyages: more towns and ports are there, and much more trade. Iron is the basis of this trade.

This point is worth some thought, for nothing more clearly shows the full importance of the Indian Ocean trade to the early development of the coast. Thus Malindi, "city of the Zanj" — the Gedi that Kirkman would excavate in 1953? — has become a "big town"; yet Malindi is not even mentioned in El Mas'udi, though he may have known of it as an obscure trading settlement. The Zanj of Malindi own and work iron mines, trade in wrought iron, and make large profits from so doing; two days to the southward, continues Edrisi, the small town of Manisa (Mombasa in two of the manuscripts) does the same: a clear enough indication that the coastal peoples were already in regular trading contact with peoples of the hinterland behind the coast.

Throughout the land of Zanj, he explains, the main products are iron and tiger skins.* Even in the southern land of Sofala, prized for its gold, it is iron that the merchants want. Of two small towns of the land of Sofala, Dendema and Djentema (Quilimane and Chindi?), Edrisi reports that the inhabitants depend entirely on the iron trade for their livelihood, while "a great number of iron mines are found in the mountains of Sofala."

"Hither come the people of the islands of Zanedj [variously

* Presumably leopard skins. A modern translation and commentary on Edrisi are greatly needed.

rendered, and possibly the Maldives and Laccadives off the southern coast of India] to buy iron and transport it to the mainland
and the islands of India, where they sell it for a good price; for it
is the object of a big trade there, and is in big demand." This iron
of Sofala, he says, is known to be much better than the iron of
India, as well for its abundance as for its good quality and its
malleability. "The Indians are masters in the arts of working it."
They make the best swords in the world from Sofala iron. Nothing
cuts better than this iron of India. "Everyone knows that, and
nobody can deny it."

Now this "Indian iron" is none other than that famous *wootz*
steel which India sold throughout the medieval world: the steel
from which the swordsmiths of Damascus made their much-sought
blades. When the Crusaders invaded Palestine they found a well-
armed enemy; and there is every chance that the best of the Sara-
cens' weapons and chain mail were of steel which successive
craftsmen had mined in southeastern Africa, forged in southwestern India, and fashioned in Persia and Arabia. East and
southeast Africa had become an integral part of the widest trading
circuit the medieval world would know.

If it is true, then, that the crucially formative period of the
eastern and southern African Iron Age can be narrowed down to
the middle centuries of the first millennium A.D., it is also true that
the crucially developmental period was already far advanced by
the middle of the twelfth century, when Edrisi wrote.

Within these centuries an Iron Age in eastern and southeastern
Africa gave rise to new societies and civilizations: along the coast
but also in the hinterland. To this, as we shall see, archeology
brings vivid confirmation.

These societies and civilizations were native to eastern and
southern Africa. Yet they no more developed in a vacuum than
the kingdoms and empires of the old Sudan or the states and city-
states of the forests to the south. Progress relied, in both regions,

on the installation of iron-extracting industries within their own culture; just as it relied, in both regions, on continuous and expanding trade with another and technically more advanced part of the world. Kush and Carthage seem to have played towards West Africa, in the diffusion of iron technology and the evolution of social and religious ideologies that received this new knowledge and grew out of it, the same stimulating role as the Mediterranean, a few centuries earlier, had played towards western and northern Europe. In southern Africa this same stimulus may also have come from Kush — and perhaps from West Africa; beyond any doubt, it came as well from the Indian Ocean trade.

For what the Sahara was to West Africa, one may emphasize, the Indian Ocean was to east and southeast Africa. There was no essential difference but that camels crossed the one and sailing ships the other. In times of Moorish invasion of the Western Sudan, indeed, the parallel comes so near as to show trans-Saharan expeditions actually crossing the desert with the aid of nautical instruments. One Moorish invader, Ammar Pasha, even took with him a captured French sailor who could travel upon the sand by quadrant and compass.

Along the southern borders of the Sahara, wherever the caravan trails ended or began, commerce by the thirteenth and fourteenth centuries had long-established trading marts where merchants and cameleers, travelers and every kind of hanger-on would mix and mingle, linger or settle: Arabs and Berbers, Negroes and desert Tuareg and Fulani. Riding northward on his return from the Western Sudan in 1353, Ibn Battuta saw these desert-bordering marts in the flower of their prosperity. He stayed in the red-stone houses of Tagedda and marveled at the "luxury and ease" of their possessors. These, he wrote, "have no occupation but trade. They travel to Egypt every year, and import quantities of all the fine fabrics to be had there and of other Egyptian wares." Like the mariners of Oman and the merchants of Siraf, far to the east, these people of Saharan Tagedda were powerful intermediaries in trade between North Africa and continental Africa.

And in much the same way the commerce of the Indian Ocean, growing century by century from remote beginnings, had long-established trading cities where the ships of India and Arabia could discharge their goods and load again with the goods of Africa. And here too the coastal peoples — those sharp-eyed populations of east coast maritime cities — would show a mingling of many racial stocks. The people of Malindi, observed Barbosa in about 1501, have "fair stone houses" with "flat roofs after our fashion." They are "both black and white" — "Hamite" and Arab, no doubt, Indian and Bantu — and "great barterers, who deal in cloth, gold, ivory, and divers other wares . . . and to their haven, every year, come many ships with cargoes and merchandise."

It is a striking parallel. The peoples of the Western Sudan grew with Iron Age technology and ideology, and with trans-Saharan trade, into strong centralized states: Ghana, Mali, Songhay, were among the fruits of this growth. But the same underlying pattern would repeat itself in these eastern and southern African lands which entered their Iron Age and developed their oversea trade and their civilization at much the same time; and threw up the kingdoms of the Waqlimi and the Monomotapa, and settled in Sena and Zimbabwe and Mapungubwe and their like.

Thus the records of the Indian Ocean trade, or such as have survived, are inseparable from the history of eastern and southern Africa. Arabia, India, China, would leave their influence here; just as the maritime cities of Malindi and Mombasa, Kilwa, Sofala and half a hundred others, the terraced inland settlements of Azania, the mines of the interior and the empire of the Monomotapa, would make their own contribution, certain if obscure, to the history of Arabia and India and China.

six

Traders of the
Indian Ocean

The ships that sail the southern seas and southward are like houses. When their sails are spread
they are like great clouds in the sky . . .

Chin Chhü-fei in A.D. 1178

The Zanj have no ships of their own; but they use
the ships of Oman and of other countries . . .

Edrisi in about A.D. 1154

1 Sheba's Cities

Voyaging eastward in one of the earliest of the Portuguese fleets to India, Duarte Barbosa saw that the people of the East African seaboard were great sellers of gold and ivory and wax. The merchants of the Indian kingdom of Cambay to whom they sold these goods, he found, "make great profits" from this trade, "and thus, on the one side as on the other, they earn much money." To seize these profits and control the trade that yielded them would become the great "forward element" in Portuguese maritime endeavor.

Though new to the Portuguese in 1500, this trade was of long antiquity. Egyptians of the early and middle dynasties had sent to Punt for much the same goods; and Punt, even if not the coast that Barbosa knew, belonged commercially to the same region. Two and a half thousand years before Barbosa's voyage the navies of Hiram, king of Mediterranean Tyre, had brought gold from Ophir; and Ophir, if almost certainly the southern tip of Arabia, was likewise part of this same trading region.

Solomon's records are witness to this southern commerce's reputation. "For the king had at sea a navy of Tarshish with the navy of Hiram. Once in three years came the navy of Tarshish, bringing gold and silver, ivory and apes and peacocks. So King Solomon exceeded all the kings of the earth for riches and wisdom."

They make their first real appearance, these southern origins of wealth and wisdom, in the Sabaea of Queen Belkis, she "who gave the king an hundred and twenty talents of gold, and of spices very great store, and precious stones: there came no more such abundance of spices as these which the Queen of Sheba gave to King Solomon."

Now these early civilizations of southern Arabia have vanished as completely from the map and memory of man as the much less elaborate but not much less important civilizations of East Africa. Yet they were famous in the old world. Great maritime investors, they grew strong and wealthy in their control of the carrying trade between Asia and Africa on the one hand, and Egypt and the Mediterranean on the other. Safe in terraced cities which they built on the hillsides of the Yemen and the Hadhramaut, they held the Red Sea straits in their fast grip, and for centuries exacted dues from all who would pass through them. No nations of the world were so wealthy as these Gerrhaeans and Sabaeans, declared Agathacides of Alexandria in about 150 B.C., for they were placed "in the center of all the commerce which passes between Asia and Africa." They had every profusion of luxury in plate and sculpture, the furniture of beds and household embellishments; and their expense of living rivaled the magnificence of princes.

This Arabian prosperity spanned two thousand years. Even as late as the tenth century A.D. one may catch its smooth assuring echo when a writer of San'aa, ancient capital of the Sabaeans, recalls the sweet land of his birth. This city "is regarded by all the peoples," says Hamdani, "as one of the gardens of the earth." In a land implanted with great castles and marbled life-endowing dams and irrigation aqueducts, "it enjoys the autumn rains at the time when the sun reaches Leo and faces it in Taurus, and the spring rains at the end of March and the beginning of April. It is rich in spices, vegetable products, and fruits; and boasts of a variety of aromatic plants, flowers, roses, and several kinds of birds. The smallest house has at least one or two cisterns; the cesspools are deep, built at a distance from one another, and, because of the hard gypsum tiles, the spotless plaster and the clean floors, are free of any stench or obnoxious odor. A lavatory remains in use from one century to another without needing either to be drained or cleansed."

This was the San'aa that El Mas'udi, whose family had come
from Hedjaz, would have known. Some four centuries later
Ibn Battuta wrote of Zabid — "after San'aa the largest and
wealthiest town in Yemen" — that "it lies amidst luxuriant
gardens with many streams and fruits, such as bananas and the
like." Its inhabitants were charming in their manners, upright
and handsome, while the women — and this was an aspect of
civilization that never failed to interest him — "are exceedingly
beautiful." Thereafter the irrigation would fail; the wars and dis-
sensions and invasions would breach the dams and aqueducts
and spoil the spotless lavatories: the Yemen would retire into
isolation and decay. Yet for medieval people this Yemen and its
neighboring Arab lands would count among the most civilized
countries of the world.

Thus it was no barbarian commerce which first developed the
African coastal trade. From the time of the Queen of Sheba in
the tenth or ninth century B.C. — and perhaps from an earlier
time — the trade passed successively from the control of one
Arabian state to another. In the first century A.D., whence comes
the earliest documentary evidence, the coast of what is now
Somaliland, Kenya and Tanganyika could still be known to
Red Sea mariners as "the Ausanitic coast," although the southern
Arabian state of Ausan had gone into eclipse before 600 B.C. After
Ausan there had come Qataban; and then Sabaea once again; and
then the Himyarites. After the Himyarites there falls an interval
— with Ptolemaic Egypt and Roman power grown strong —
and then control of the trade goes over to the southern side of
the Red Sea straits and is held by Axum, until, in the eighth
century A.D., the Arabs of Islam acquire supremacy. They will
hold this supremacy until the coming of the Portuguese in 1498.

Beyond the Red Sea straits, within which the struggle for monopoly of the incoming ocean trade was always restrictive, two
factors governed and greatly extended the number and national-

ity of shipping in the trade. The first was the growing strength and unity of states in western India, Ceylon, Indonesia, and China; and the second was the steady improvement in naval technology. Both would influence the subsequent history of eastern and southeastern Africa.

2 Sailing Down Africa

A GREEK PILOT CALLED SCYLAX OF CARYANDA IS THE FIRST KNOWN mariner to have passed the Indian Ocean. He is said to have sailed to the Red Sea from the mouth of the Indus in 510 B.C.; and the earliest surviving pilot-book, or periplus, though written some two hundred years later, was given his name. Others followed, among them Alexander's famous pilot, Nearchus, who sailed to the Indus and back in 327-26 B.C. Many must have gone this way, and of many nations.

In those early centuries they followed the coast, working and weaving slowly round from harbor to harbor; then, gradually, they learned to use the monsoon winds which always scour the Indian Ocean. Blowing from the northeast at more or less fixed and regular times of the year, these winds reverse themselves thereafter and blow back again from the southwest. They will take sailing ships reliably in either direction, according to the season of the year, and up and down the East African coast as far south as Cape Delgado, at the entrance to the Madagascan channel.

Little by little, with better ships, mariners learned to cut the northern corner of the ocean, venturing ever more boldly across the empty waters that lie between western India and southern Arabia; at the same time they pushed southward down the African seaboard. There is no means of knowing the early progress of this venturing. By the middle of the first century A.D., at all events, Greek pilots had learned that it was possible to sail directly from the exit of the Red Sea to the port of Barygaza, on the northwest Indian coast, and not long after that they were sailing directly to Malabar on the southwest Indian coast. Down Africa, in the wake of Sabaeans and Himyarites, they were sailing as far as the borders of what is now Mozambique.

By the first century A.D., that is, Alexandria and Rome were gathering a fairly detailed knowledge of the African coast for a long way towards the Madagascan channel. Of this the most famous of the old pilot-books, the *Periplus of the Erythraean Sea*, gives eloquent proof. Written probably by a Greek of Alexandria who had manifestly sailed the southern coast himself, it appeared in about A.D. 60 and offers an intelligent and factual manual, about 7,500 words in length, of the maritime usages and trading stations of the African coast as far south as Rhapta. This Rhapta was certainly on the coast of Tanganyika, and probably between modern Dar-es-Salaam and Tanga. Only in the last few years has archeology even begun to tackle the implications of what it has to say.

The author of the *Periplus* describes trading routes which many before him must have followed. By this time the coastal voyage is divided into a number of well-recognized "daily runs" with regular ports of call and markets; and the goods that each of these ports and markets will supply and ask for are clearly known. An outline of political conditions, such as trading captains ought to have, is mentioned in passing.

He says that it was customary to sail from Egypt for the market towns of the "far side" — the ocean side, that is, of the Red Sea straits — about the month of July. In these "far side ports," facing the Indian Ocean, ships from the Red Sea could trade with ships from India, or they could pursue their voyage down the African coast; in either case the trade would be varied and extensive.

"And ships are also customarily fitted out from the places across the sea, from Ariaca and Barygaza,* bringing to these far side market towns the products of their own places: wheat, rice, ghee, sesame oil, cotton cloth, girdles, honey from the reed called sacchari. Some make the voyage especially to these market towns; and others exchange their cargoes while sailing along the [African] coast. This country is not subject to a king, but each market town is ruled by a separate chief."

Some of these coastal chiefs are independent; others are subject to the Himyarite princes of southern Arabia. They import tools and weapons of iron that are made at Muza on the Red Sea coast. Could they make iron tools and weapons for themselves? On this the *Periplus,* which is interested in maritime instructions and trading hints, has nothing to say: presumably the answer is that they could not. No doubt the coastal trade helped to bring iron technology southward; yet by A.D. 60, we may note, the Iron Age culture of the Kalambo Falls, in northeastern Rhodesia, was already in its infancy.

"There are imported into these markets" — of this coast of Azania, the coast of Kenya and Tanganyika — "the lances that are made at Muza especially for this trade, and hatchets and daggers and awls, and various kinds of glass; and at some places a little wine and wheat, not for trade, but to serve for getting the goodwill of the savages." Exported from these ports of Azania were much ivory, rhinoceros horn, tortoise shell, and a little palm oil. "And these markets of Azania are the very last of the continent that stretches down on the right hand" from the Red Sea.

They would remain so for several centuries. Yet the establish-

---

* The northwest Indian coast, that is, of Cutch, Cathiawar, Gujerat.

ment of pre-Islamic Arab trading connections went steadily on —
by settlement, intermarriage, and continuous exchange of goods;
and, with this, a further extension of the trading area to the southward. How far to the southward? A coin of Constantine I (early
fourth century A.D.) has turned up in northern Madagascar, so the
Himyarites may even have sailed as far as that. And in 1950
Gervase Mathew, British pioneer of east coast archeology, made
important discoveries on a group of small islands off southern
Tanganyika. (See map on page 204.)

On the islet of Sanje ya Kati, near the somewhat larger islet of
Kilwa, he found amid tall undergrowth the ruins of a settlement
of "small oblong houses of carefully dressed masonry, grouped
round a citadel whose walls still rise to sixteen feet." It is the
earliest of the coastal trading settlements so far traced; and its
iron-using culture may well have been pre-Islamic by several
centuries — southern Arabian, that is, or perhaps southern Indian.

Nearby, on another coral islet called Songo Mnara, Mathew
opened a sudden and splendid vision of the grand scale of this
developing trade. During preliminary excavation of a deserted
medieval town in this forgotten place, screened by mangrove
swamps on the fringe of a glittering ocean, he was "able to examine and identify glazed stoneware almost certainly from Siam,
and a mass of Chinese porcelain . . . dated from late Sung to
early Ming [c. A.D. 1127-1450]. Among the coins discovered in
the same group of islands there are specimens from mints in
Mesopotamia and from Mongol mints in Persia, while among
the beads there are pierced cornelians from India, and others of
amber and crystal and topaz."

Even yesterday these old cities — Kilwa Kisiwani, Songo Mnara,
Sanje ya Kati, Kua, and their like — were forgotten or lost to all
but a handful of men. But in medieval times the civilized
commerce of the whole eastern world had filled their streets and
warehouses.

3 The Nature of the Trade

IF THE EARLY CHRONOLOGY OF THIS SOUTHWARD PROBING IS STILL impossible to state in any detail, its method is clear enough from one of the most illuminating passages in the *Periplus of the Erythraean Sea*.

The people of the ports of "the continent of Azania" — of Kenya and Tanganyika — were "men of piratical habits, very great in stature, and under separate chiefs for each place"; but the coast itself was claimed by a southern Arabian potentate "under some ancient right which subjects it to the dominant state in Arabia" — successively, as we have seen, to the princes of Ausan, Qataban, Sabaea, and Himyar. Muza in Himyar had the upper hand when the author of the *Periplus* went down the coast. The merchants of Muza, accordingly, sent there "many large ships, using Arab captains and agents who are familiar with the natives and intermarry with them, and who know the whole coast and understand the language."

Behind this simple description there must lie whole centuries of experience — centuries when trading Arabs and coastal Africans evolved an individual culture that would gather much from both. When Europeans first saw this coast, some fifteen centuries later, this culture was long since mature, and possessed an accomplished language, Swahili, of its own. Derived from an Arabic word meaning "of the coast," this Swahili language, like Swahili culture, is not an Africanized Arab product but an Arabized African product: its basis and most of its elements are African — Bantu-speaking African — but with a strong Arab infusion, the influence of all those centuries of trade and settlement. This Arab infusion would be deepened, in early medieval times, with more intensive settlement and colonization from Arabia and the Persian Gulf.

Religious and dynastic wars in Arabia promoted that. By the

seventh and eighth centuries, trading cities on the coast of Somaliland and Kenya and even Tanganyika were being transformed by Arab refugee immigration into cities that were strongly Arabic in culture. This Arab predominance seems seldom to have extended to more than a ruling group or "extended family," except perhaps on the islands off the coast, where the refugees often settled. But while the ports and cities of the mainland stayed essentially African, their culture became increasingly Islamic.

By the tenth century, as El Mas'udi makes clear, Arabs were installed as far south as Sofala in the kingdom of the Waqlimi. At the other end of the eastern world, by then, they were long installed in southern China, in Malaya, in the ports of India and Ceylon. Thereafter, and in growing numbers, laden ships would pass from China to Africa and back again, going from port to port, their cargoes handled by one trading people after another; until the whole of the vast ocean seaboard would be linked by an intricate system of transport and exchange. Songo Mnara and its fellow cities would know the porcelain of Chekiang and the stoneware of Siam.

Yet it was India that remained, for East Africa, the most important market and supplier. If Chinese coins and porcelain, at least from the late twelfth or thirteenth century, can now offer useful guides to the dating of coastal history (and, here and there, to the dating of the history of the hinterland as well), Indian beads become valuable in this respect as early as the eighth century. When more is known of them, beads from Indonesia and Indo-China and Malaya may become the same.

Indian textiles, if only they could have survived, would tell a great deal more, for they were brought into these East African ports through many centuries. As supplier of goods to Africa and consumer of goods from Africa, or as entrepôt for goods sent eastward from Africa or Africa-ward from the further east, the rising civilizations of western and southern India would act and react on east and southeast Africa for many hundreds of years; and only future research can tell the full extent of this.

Edrisi has shown what part was played by the Indian demand for African iron. Ivory had always been important in the same way. Tusks sold by the Zanj, says Mas'udi, "ordinarily go to Oman where they are sent on to China and India. That is the way they go, and if it were not so, ivory would be plentiful in Muslim countries. In China the kings and civil and military notables use chairs of ivory: no official or other prominent individual would think of visiting the king in a chair of iron, for ivory alone is used for such a case." In India too, he says, ivory is much in demand: they use it there for sword hilts and dagger hilts, and for making chessmen.

Gold was another staple. Large quantities of gold must have gone to India from the ports of southeast Africa through a period of five or six centuries, adding greatly to those glittering piles that Europeans would excitedly discover after 1500. Tortoise shell was another valued African export. Slaves were another: there were enough African slaves in Mesopotamia, by the end of the seventh century, to enable great slave revolts that would continue on and off for two hundred years. But slaving nonetheless remained a subsiduary: it never overwhelmed the early Arab connection with the coast as it would later overwhelm the European connection (and, later again, the nineteenth-century Arab connection). Iron, gold, ivory — these were the African goods that the eastern world principally wanted.

Though funneled into Europe through the Red Sea straits, this trade was shared by Asia among many maritime peoples. From the second century A.D., with the rise of their island states in Java and Sumatra, the Indonesians certainly took a hand. They colonized Madagascar in the centuries that followed, although the sea routes they traveled are unknown. They coasted up the African seaboard as far as the Horn of Africa, and have left traces of their passage in the long string of islets, the Bagiuni islands, which lie off the coast of Somaliland. The Bantu-speaking people of these islands still use outrigger canoes which resemble Indonesian models.

Yet it is perhaps through the Chinese connection that one may glimpse most clearly the wealth and long endurance and extent of this African trade with the countries of the east.

The story of this Chinese connection is the story, largely, of a naval technology in which the Chinese long excelled and led the world. The trials and voyages which enabled their arrival on the African coast in 1417 or 1418 and again in 1431 or 1432, traveling with fleets whose crews and complements are variously estimated for the later of these voyages to have numbered between twenty-seven thousand and thirty-seven thousand men,* make part of a long and vivid record. And this record, as it happens, gives illumination to the ways and manners of the men who plied these Indian and African waters, and the ships they traveled in, and the perils they encountered, and the countries they could know.

4 China and Africa

THOSE SHIPS THAT SAILED THE CHINA SEAS AND SOUTHWARD IN THE twelfth century, and whose sails when spread were like "great clouds in the sky," were the product of many centuries of experiment. For at least a thousand years, by then, Chinese mariners had crossed the skylines of the ocean.

One vivid account survives. Through it there echoes at least a little of the fear and peril that were suffered by all those nameless heroes, pilots, pressed men, mariners, captains, merchants and as-

---

* Pelliot has twenty-seven thousand five hundred fifty for the voyage of 1431; Duyvendak thirty-seven thousand.

sorted travelers who voyaged on those early seas. A Chinese pilgrim to the Buddhist shrines of India went home in A.D. 413. Fa Hsien had come overland to India through Turkestan and through the great Snow Mountains of the north but desired to go home by sea. Having sailed in fourteen days from the mouth of the Ganges to Ceylon, and lingered there to see the Buddha's Tooth and other famous wonders of the land, he took passage on "a large merchant vessel" that was bound for Java.

Carrying two hundred people, this merchant ship towed a smaller vessel for safety's sake; but the precaution was a slender one. When they ran into a gale, two days out of port, and "the merchants wished to get aboard the smaller vessel," the men on this smaller vessel, "fearing that they would be swamped, quickly cut the tow rope." Fa Hsien's narrative shows that panic followed. Bulky goods were thrown overboard to lighten the ship; and Fa Hsien, the pilgrim, "also took his pitcher and ewer" — pathetic contribution of a puzzled scholar — "and threw them into the sea"; but saved the pious books and images he had brought from India.

For thirteen days and nights they ran helplessly before the gale until "they arrived alongside an island, and there, at ebb tide, they saw the place where the vessel leaked and forthwith stopped it up, after which they proceeded on their way." Their troubles were not over. "This sea," explains Fa Hsien, "is infested with pirates, to meet whom is death. The expanse of ocean is boundless, east and west are not distinguishable; only by the observation of the sun, moon, and constellations is progress to be made."

They sailed onward. And "in the darkness of the night," Fa Hsien remembered afterwards, "nothing was to be seen but the great waves beating upon one another and flashing forth light like fire, huge turtles, sea lizards, and such-like monsters of the deep. Then the merchants lost heart, not knowing whither they were going."

How many must have foundered! But Fa Hsien made Java in safety, and after a stay of five months again shipped in a large vessel, this time for Canton—a journey normally reckoned, he says, at fifty days. Another gale was nearly his undoing for a second time. On this occasion the merchants with whom he traveled, not agreeing with his Buddhist persuasion, thought they might as well appease the fates by casting him into the sea. He was happily saved by a "religious protector" who threatened to report the merchants, when he got to China, if they should drown Fa Hsien.

"Meanwhile the sky was constantly darkened and the captain lost his reckoning. So they went on for seventy days until provisions and water were nearly gone . . ." But at last they made a landfall, "and seeing the old familiar vegetables, they knew it was their fatherland . . ." The long voyage was over at last. It was made, one may note, exactly one thousand years before European mariners embarked on their great period of discovery down the west coast of Africa.

Fa Hsien's first ship, from Ceylon to Java, was no doubt Ceylonese or Javanese; but the second was probably Chinese. Maritime links between China and the Red Sea are attested for late Han times (A.D. 25-220), and writings published during the Three Kingdoms period (A.D. 221-265) speak of four-masted and even of seven-masted ships with some kind of fore-and-aft rig being used by the Chinese of Canton and Annam. And although the great sea-going junk of medieval times was developed mainly in the two Sung dynasties (A.D. 960-1279), a naval architect called Yang Su was already building long-haul vessels with as many as five decks, and measuring more than a hundred feet from truck to keel, by about 600. Thereafter, under the T'ang emperors (A.D. 618-906), maritime trade grew apace; and the T'ang Kuo-shi-pu, written in the ninth century but drawing on earlier records, says that the ships of the southern seas were so high out of the water that ladders several tens of feet long were needed to get aboard them.

The wealth of the trade, and the great distances involved, pressed continually for better ships and surer means of navigation. Eastern captains had long known how to navigate by the stars, as Fa Hsien's story shows; but those of Sung times also steered by the magnetic compass. "The exact date at which the magnetic compass first became the mariner's compass, after a long career ashore with the geomancers," says Needham, "is not known; but some time in the tenth century would be a very probable guess." It was certainly in use by 1086, about a century before it is known to have come into use in the Mediterranean.*

Another invention was that of transverse watertight bulkheads, noted with admiration by Marco Polo at the end of the thirteenth century, but possibly introduced a good deal earlier. The axial or stern-post rudder seems to have appeared in T'ang times, perhaps as early as the eighth century; and T'ang and Sung sailors also knew how to sail into the wind. Their taut mat-sails are described as going round the masts like a door on its hinges, thus enabling ships to beat up to windward in a manner beyond the reach of Mediterranean sailors for a long time thereafter. These ocean-going vessels with their pivoting sails were known as "boring into the wind" ships.

By the twelfth century, in any case, Chinese ships were technically capable of sailing wherever sailing ships could go, then or later; although only in the fifteenth century would the famous admiral Cheng Ho make landfalls on East Africa. At Angkor Vat, amid the royal ruins of old Cambodia, there survives a stone engraving of what is generally agreed to be a Chinese junk of

---

* In writing this chapter I have had the great advantage of being able to read, in advance of its publication, the sixth volume of Dr. Joseph Needham's history of science and civilization in China, in which he deals with Chinese naval technology; and I am greatly indebted to his generosity and help.

Kwangtung or Tongking. Carvel-built, it has two masts with sheets and square matting sails, its anchor is hoisted by a windlass, and it seems to have a true axial rudder. Its date is 1125 — the earliest surviving picture of an ocean liner.

For all their technical mastery, the Chinese do not seem to have penetrated beyond the eastern waters of the Indian Ocean, even though their ships and equipment were capable of taking them much further. On this, though, there is no general agreement among the experts; and Pelliot, an eminent French sinologist, has said that Han dynasty ships (before, that is, A.D. 220) used to go as far as the western end of the Indian Ocean. Perhaps they did. Chinese goods were certainly reaching the Red Sea and the Mediterranean, by the sea routes, as early as the beginning of the Christian era. The bronze pots that Meroitic smiths copied at about this time probably came by sea. There were also Chinese-Roman exchanges; but these, like most of the trade, would have passed through many transshipments.

Thus a Chinese document of the first century B.C. explains how officials of the Imperial Department of Interpreters, together with "volunteers," went out to sea "to buy brilliant pearls, glass, rare stones, and curious products, for which they give gold and various silks." But having reached foreign countries, "the merchant ships of the barbarians transport them so as to make them reach their destination, and they also draw much profit from this trade."

With Sung expansion in the twelfth century, the Chinese became strongly established at trading stations in southern India, the port of Quilon being their principal entrepôt. They had certainly reached Arabia much earlier. El Mas'udi, writing in 947, says that the ships of China used to go "to Oman, to Siraf, to Obillah and Basra, while the ships of those countries sailed directly for China." Edrisi, writing in 1154, has a passage relating how at some time in the past, when India was in confusion, the Chinese withdrew their trading posts to the islands of

Zanedj — possibly the Maldives or Laccadives, or perhaps the big islands of southeast Asia. Sung annals of 1083 speak of a second visit to the imperial court of a foreign envoy with a name whose last three characters may reasonably be read as "the Zanj." This ambassador had come from so far away that the Emperor Shön-tsung, "besides giving him the same presents which he formerly bestowed on him, added thereto two thousand ounces of silver." Unless future research throws up Chinese writings so far un-known, this early African envoy, if he really was such, is the only one recorded in China until 1414, when the city of Malindi sent ambassadors to the emperor and, with them, the gift of a giraffe.

But the trading records, as usual, are more eloquent. Although imperial China always had a court party which condemned med-dling with barbarians and foreign trade — an "inland party" as opposed to an "ocean party" — oversea trade by T'ang times was far too valuable to be ignored or suppressed. Maritime imports into T'ang China, says Suleiman the Merchant sometime before 850, included "ivory, frankincense, copper, tortoise shell, camphor, and rhinoceros horn." All this was highly taxed.

On arrival at Canton each ship was obliged to hand over its cargo to imperial agents, who stored it until the last ship of the season's fleet had arrived, when three-tenths of the merchandise was retained as import duty and the balance handed back to the owners — a truly imperial share in the profits of private enterprise. Even so, it failed to satisfy; and in 971, under the first Sung em-peror, the Canton inspectorate of maritime trade was reorganized so as to secure a still firmer grip on the profits of import and ex-port. And some time before 983 the whole maritime trade with foreigners was declared a state monopoly, and private trading with foreigners made punishable by branding on the face and exile to an island in the sea.

Yet the trade continued to grow. In 999 inspectorates of mari-time commerce were established at Hang-chou and Ming-chou

(Ning-Po today); and although through several centuries there-after traders continued to be mulcted of a third of their goods and sometimes of even more, there is no sign of their failing to deliver. Between 1049 and 1053, for example, Sung annals show that the annual import of ivory, rhinoceros horn, pearls, incense and other goods amounted to more than fifty-three thousand units of count: yet by 1115 this annual quantity had risen to five hundred thousand units of count. Within a hundred years of this, or not much more, Chinese porcelain began to reach the western ports of the Indian Ocean in considerable quantities; and princes and merchants in African cities like Songo Mnara could begin to embellish their houses and enjoy their tea — or had they still to learn about tea? — with the aid of celadon cups.

This large export of Sung porcelain is traceable to several causes. Chinese pottery technique made big advances at about this time. The African trade was getting into its stride; partly through Islamic Arab pioneering and settlement down the coast, partly through social growth in Africa itself, and partly through Chinese maritime expansion. But Chinese trading practices provide another explanation. The evidence shows that, by Sung times, Chinese payment for imports had taken the form of huge exports of coin. These were so large, it appears, that serious complaints of a drainage of metal were heard. Foreigners were to be paid, it was thereupon decided, not in cash but in goods.

"In 1147," says Duyvendak, "Chinese ships going abroad to trade, or foreign ships going home out of the ports of Kwang-tung and Fukien, were to be inspected in order to see whether they had cash on board. For taking out two strings of cash the punishment was one year's imprisonment, for more than three strings, execution; informers were to be rewarded." Another regulation, made in 1210, ordered that payment for foreign goods was to be in silk, porcelain, brocade, and lacquered wares instead of coin.

The drain seems to have continued. "Alas, that the gold and silver of the land should be flowing out in trade with savages from afar!" ministers of state reported to the throne in 1219. "Trading stations should be established on the borders at which our silks, brocades, gauzes, porcelain, lacquer and the like could be offered in exchange for their goods." In spite of all these regulations and intentions, it is sure that coin continued to go abroad; and many coins of the Sung period have turned up in East Africa and elsewhere. Yet the export of porcelain (and presumably of other and perishable goods) undoubtedly increased.

In the thirteenth century, after eclipsing the Sung, Mongol emperors reopened inland trading routes through Turkestan; and maritime trade became less important. Under the Ming emperors who followed, though, it achieved its greatest expansion until modern times. In 1405 Cheng Ho began his seven great voyages to the far west. Known to Chinese history as the Three-Jewel Eunuch, Cheng Ho was a Muslim of Yunnan who had reached high office at the imperial court. As intimate servants of the court — and especially of imperial ladies who wished for "the latest and the best" from oversea — eunuchs had often gone on foreign expeditions ever since the reign of Wu-ti in the second century B.C.; but Cheng Ho was undoubtedly the greatest of all these emissaries.

He sailed in command of many ships and of thousands, even of tens of thousands, of men, and made seven great voyages between 1405 and 1433. In 1407 he returned from India; in 1409 from India, Indonesia, Cochin, and Siam; in 1414 he was at Ormuz on the Persian Gulf; in 1417-1419 he went as far as Malindi in modern Kenya.* Three years later Cheng Ho was again at Ormuz, while some of his ships went still further westward; and in 1431-1433, completing this great record of ocean travel, he took another huge

---

* Kirkman's excavations at Gedi (a city unknown to East African history) suggest that it is in fact the site of old Malindi: eight miles, that is, southwest of modern Malindi.

fleet to the Persian Gulf and sent at least a part of it onward to·
Aden and East Africa. This time Brava is mentioned in the
records and so is Mogadiscio, which is said to have houses "four
or five stories high." His original reason for going as far as East
Africa in 1417, one may note, was to see safely home the ambassadors of Malindi who had come to Peking in 1415.

Yet although this story of Chinese maritime trade with East
Africa is part and parcel of the history of the coast, and to some
extent of the hinterland as well, it is disappointingly bare in the
documentary record. The earliest Chinese reference to Africa,
that of the *Yu-yang-tsa-tsu* sometime before 863, offers a gloomy
account of "the country of Bo-ba-li" that was obviously the Berbera region and its seaboard of the Horn of Africa. Nothing
useful is to be learned from this but what we should have known
in any case: the people were herdsmen and were much raided by
Arabs. They were, that is, Galla or Somali or perhaps Masai. A
somewhat longer but not much more useful account of this same
country of Bo-ba-li is in Chao Ju-kua's *Chu Fan Chi, Record of
Foreign Peoples,* completed in 1226 but drawing largely on earlier
sources. As commissioner for foreign trade at Ch'uan-chou in
Fukien, Chao Ju-kua had plenty of scope for collecting information from sailors and foreign traders; and his account of the
country of Tsöng-ba (Tsang-bat in Cantonese — a transliteration
from Arabic meaning "coast of the Zanj") is worthy of mention.

To westward, says this Chinese Hakluyt of the thirteenth century, "this country reaches to a great mountain" (this, presumably, means Kilimanjaro). Its inhabitants are of Ta-shi (Arab)
stock and follow the Arab religion; they wrap themselves in blue
cotton stuffs, and wear shoes of red leather. "Their daily food
consists of meal, baked cakes, and mutton." The land has "many
villages, and a succession of wooded hills and terraced rocks." In
this last it may be tempting to see a reference to the artificial hillside terracing of East Africa that was undoubtedly in extensive use

and maintenance at the time; but Dr. Needham, who has been good enough to look at the original on my behalf, thinks the passage can be made to mean no more than that the hills of the countryside were formed in natural terraces. The products of this region of the Zanj consist in "elephants' tusks, native gold, ambergris, and yellow sandal wood." Every year, it is explained, the ships of Hu-cha-la (the Indian kingdom of Gujerat) and of Arab localities along the coast come here for trade with white cotton cloth and red cloth, porcelain, and copper.

Cheng Ho's passengers ought to have been able to add a great deal to these bare fragments of mariners' talk; but the harvest is dismally small. This was probably not their fault. By 1450 the "inland party" at the Chinese court had decisively defeated its sea-enchanted rivals; and there is a likelihood that the records of Cheng Ho's expeditions were deliberately annihilated rather than left to tempt new mariners later on. A few contemporary charts have survived, and one, at least, which derives from Cheng Ho's voyaging to African shores. There are, as well, two inscriptions. The more important of these, put up by Cheng Ho himself in 1431 on the eve of his seventh and last expedition, has given us the dates of his voyages, recording too how "we have traversed more than one hundred thousand *li* of immense water spaces and have beheld in the ocean huge waves like mountains rising sky-high, and have set our eyes on barbarian regions far away and hidden in the blue transparency of vapors; while our sails, loftily unfurled like clouds, day and night continued their course."

These voyages were the crest and climax of Chinese oversea venturing, and were remarkable on any terms. Thereafter the falling off was steep indeed. In 1420 multiple-masted naval architecture had attained such status as to have an administrative board of its own, the Ta T'ung Kuan T'i Chu Ssu. Yet by 1500 the great shipyards were all closed down; the building of a sea-going junk with more than two masts had become a capital offense, while an edict of 1525 would authorize coastal officials to destroy all such ships, and arrest all mariners who continued to sail in them.

Why this sudden and determined turning away from the sea? Chinese shipwrights were the most advanced of any in the world. Time after time through previous centuries they had made revolutionary discoveries, and the tradition of their ocean sailing was unbroken through fifteen hundred years. Not until 1450 did Europeans develop three-masted ships for general use, and thus make possible those long voyages which discovered America, Africa, and the Far East. Yet Chinese yards had launched such ships for many hundreds of years before that. Their thirteenth century vessels were often larger than seven hundred tons burthen, and of well-proved sailing ability; yet "the average size of the ships of the Spanish Armada of 1588," Needham comments, "was still only five hundred twenty-eight tons . . . as against an average size of about one hundred seventy-seven in the English fleet." Notwithstanding all this — and at the very moment when they might well have gone on westward into the Atlantic and the Red Sea — the Chinese turned back and closed their yards, dismissed their captains and destroyed their ships.

The reasons belong to Chinese, not African, history. They appear to have lain in court rivalries between the eunuch class which had grown powerful on maritime discovery, and the official class which both feared the power of the eunuchs and looked down on maritime trade as extravagant, luxurious, and disagreeably entangled in contact with barbarians. In any case the officials won; but their triumph was more fateful than they knew. For in those very years when they were passing their edicts and burning their ships, European crews turned the Cape of Good Hope and entered the Indian Ocean.

Fair Cities of Stone

Kilwa is a Moorish town with many fair houses of stone and mortar, with many windows after our fashion, very well arranged in streets.

Duarte Barbosa in 1501

Madaka ya nyamba ya zisahani
Sasa walaliye wana wa nyuni.

Where once the porcelain stood in the wall niches
Now wild birds nestle their fledglings.

A *Swahili poet,* in 1815,
of the vanished glories of Pate.

1 A Forgotten Civilization

Four small ships came first, with Vasco da Gama in command. They went eastward round the Cape of Good Hope where Diaz had already led, and pushed bravely to the north. Behind them lay fierce months of solitary Atlantic voyaging; and their crews, as near to mutiny as da Gama's strong hand would ever allow, had lost all stomach for going further. But they went further.

Their greatest achievement, had they but known it, was over. For what was navigationally grand about da Gama's first voyage to the east was much less its course across the Indian Ocean, where countless ships had gone before him, than its bold crossing of the south Atlantic and its landfall on southwestern Africa. Diogo Cão and Diaz had followed the long inward-bending arc of the western coast; da Gama sailed straight across it.

But not until they reached the Madagascan channel could the Portuguese understand that their worst trials lay behind them. Then, onwards from Sofala, they passed from one agreeable surprise to another. After those months of gray Atlantic loneliness they were astonished to come upon busy ports and populous coastal cities. To their relief and joy they found themselves among sailors who knew the sea ways to India and beyond; who sailed with charts and compasses and quadrants as good as their own, or better; whose knowledge of the world was wider even than theirs. And yet they, in those years of 1488-1489, stood at the farthest point of European discovery.

They anchored in havens that were thick with ocean shipping. They went ashore to cities as fine as all but a few they could have known in Europe. They watched a flourishing maritime trade in gold and iron and ivory and tortoise shell, beads and copper and cotton cloth, slaves and porcelain; and saw that they had stumbled on a world of commerce even wider, and perhaps wealthier, than anything that Europe knew.

To these European sailors of the last years of the fifteenth century the coast of eastern Africa could have seemed no less civilized than their own coast of Portugal. In the matter of wealth and knowledge of a wider world it must have seemed a great deal more civilized. They were repeatedly surprised by the ease and substance of the ports and towns they saw and sheltered in and plundered. They found themselves repeatedly disregarded as strange and uncouth. "When we had been two or three days at this place," says the laconic logbook of da Gama's flagship, the *São Gabriel*, of an encounter at a port that was probably Quilimane, "two *senhores* of the country came to see us. They were very haughty; and valued nothing which we gave them. One of them wore a cap with a fringe embroidered in silk, and the other a cap of green silk. A young man in their company — so we understood from their signs — had come from a distant country, and had already seen big ships like ours." In truth, of course, he had seen much bigger ships. Compared with ocean-going vessels of the Indian Ocean of that time, these ships of da Gama's were small indeed.

Wherever they touched they found that what was thought remarkable about their coming was not that they should have come by sea, a common event, but that they should have come from the south. Marvel succeeded marvel. Even the land of Prester John, legendary in their Europe, was said to be near this wonderful coast. At Mozambique "we were told that Prester John resided not far from this place; that he held many cities along the coast, and the inhabitants of these cities were great merchants and owned big ships." This information, says the logbook, "and many

other things that we heard, made us so happy that we cried for
joy." It is, in fact, a pretty clear reference to that inland empire
of the Monomotapa which supplied the coastal trade with much
of its gold and ivory; and is interesting for its reference to the
owning of ships. As this is the only reference of its kind it should
be taken, perhaps, as meaning that the Monomotapa controlled
coastal cities busy with the maritime trade; and this conclusion,
as it happens, is suggested by other evidence.

They pursued their way northward in leisurely days that seemed
a mere promenade after their passage of the south Atlantic. They
knew now that they would find sailing routes to India, and that
the voyage would be relatively easy. They passed Kilwa and
Mombasa. At Malindi they were given a rousing welcome as
potential allies against Mombasa, and secured, though not without
some disagreement, a pilot who could take them to India. It was
not quite seventy years since the fleets of the Three-Jewel Eunuch
had last sojourned in these waters.

A southwestern monsoon carried them without mishap to India.
There they anchored in the Gulf of Cambay, off the city of
Calicut, and were met with understandable misgivings. Following
their custom at unknown ports, they sent ashore one of the con-
victs they carried for such occasions; he met with a "Moor of
Tunis," says the logbook, who could speak Castilian and Genoese. This Moor of Tunis must have been a man of parts: he at
any rate was in no doubt of the meaning of European ships in
eastern waters. "Devil take thee," he is said to have greeted the
Portuguese. "What brought you hither?" It was, after all, one of
the big moments in history.

For nearly a century after that the fortune-seekers of Portugal
would seek and find their fortunes. In the first twenty-five years
alone they commissioned a total of two hundred forty-seven ships
in small fleets that sailed to India nearly every year, a truly
challenging effort for a people as poor and few as were the Portu-

guese. Boldly and ruthlessly they grasped the Indian Ocean trade and bent it to their sole advantage. They cut savagely across those many complex strands of commerce which centuries had woven between these myriad ports and peoples of the east; and they wrecked the whole fabric of that trade, leaving behind them, when their force was spent, little but ruin and disruption.

Schooled in the bitter rivalries of Europe, they fell upon these tolerant and easy-going civilizations of the Indian Ocean with a ferocity and violence that were like nothing seen there through many centuries. "Cruelties," says Whiteway, "were not confined to the baser sort, but were deliberately adopted as a line of terrorizing policy by Vasco da Gama, Almeida, and Albuquerque, to take no mean examples. Da Gama tortured helpless fishermen; Almeida tore out the eyes of a Nair who had come in with a promise of his life, because he suspected a design on his life; Albuquerque cut off the noses of women and the hands of men who fell into his power on the Arabian coast."

The Portuguese, of course, were inherently no worse than other Europeans of their time, nor Europeans inherently worse than Indians, Africans, Arabs or Chinese. They were men of their day, but their day in Europe was one of violence and brutality. They reached India, as it happened, during a time of dynastic rivalry and religious war, so that their conquest of the coastal cities was made easy for them. No doubt they would have triumphed in any case. For the rules they fought by were different from the rules they found. Their own records show that they gave no quarter nor expected any. "There is here a power which I may call irresistible," St. Francis Xavier would write in 1545 of the Portuguese who came to India, "to thrust men headlong into the abyss, where besides the seductions of gain, and the easy opportunities of plunder, their appetites for gain will be sharpened by having tasted it, and there will be a whole torrent of low examples and evil customs to sweep them away. Robbery is so public and common that it hurts no one's character and is hardly counted a fault. . . ."

Warfare in India, by contrast with this murderous determination, had long become an agreeably conventional affair. "All fighting," records Whiteway, "was in the daytime when the sun had well risen. The opposing camps were pitched near each other and both sides slept securely. At sunrise the soldiers of both armies mingled at the tank, put on their armor, ate their rice and chewed their betel, gossiped and chatted together. At beat of drum either side drew apart and formed their ranks. It was creditable to be the first to beat the drum, but no attack was allowed until the other side had beaten theirs."

Europe triumphed over India and grew in the length of days into its own leisurely tolerance. In time, as they grew wealthier, Europeans came even to believe that they had always enjoyed a higher civilization than Indians or Africans. They forgot the past, which told another story. Yet the civilizations of India could not be effaced. Their monuments were too many, their prestige too great, their praises too loud and widely sung. The Indian Ocean trade might be ruined; there incontestably survived a good deal of the Indian greatness it had served.

But the coastal civilization of East Africa, less imposing, less wealthy, less deeply rooted in its hinterland, met with a different fate. These seaboard cities might seem as fine and comfortable as most of the maritime cities of Europe or India — set as they were beside a glittering ocean in white terraces of tall houses, ringed with strong walls, paved with firm quays, crowned by forts and palaces — and brave enough to stand for all eternity. Yet their fame barely survived; often it vanished altogether. Some of them, today, are entirely lost. Weird creepered ruins in the coastal jungle or bare mounds for the guessing of antiquaries, they are known only to the stray investigator; and he, often enough, can reach them only by paying men to cut a path for him through barriers of vegetation.

It was at Mozambique, during his first voyage, that da Gama exchanged the first shots. Back again on the coast in 1502, this time with a score of ships from home (the largest but one of all the fleets that Portugal would send to the golden East), da Gama threatens to burn Kilwa unless its ruler will acknowledge the supremacy of the king of Portugal and pay him yearly tribute in gold. Ravasio does the same at Zanzibar and Brava. Meeting resistance, Almeida storms Kilwa and Mombasa, burning and destroying. Saldanha ravages Berbera. Soares destroys Zeila. D'Acunha attacks Brava. And this last place, comments Barbosa, who went out in one of the earliest fleets and knew the sacking of Brava from the men who were there, "was destroyed by the Portuguese, who slew many of its peoples and carried them into captivity, and took great spoil of gold and silver and goods." There survives a letter from the ruler of Mombasa, after Almeida's disastrous invasion, to the ruler of Malindi. Returning to their blackened city after the Portuguese had gone, it says, the Swahili and Arab people of Mombasa found "no living thing in it, neither man nor woman, young nor old, nor child however little. All who had failed to escape had been killed and burned."

All this was as easy for the Portuguese, and for much the same reasons, as it was in India whenever they met with resistance to their greed and theft. They were better armed. They were trained to ruthlessness. They wanted more than a simple monopoly of trade, ruinous though that would be for the coastal cities; they wanted loot as well. African warfare, like Indian warfare, was designed to minimize casualties, not maximize them. These invaders had no such care.

Here again Europeans would afterwards believe that the Africans they found had lived in savage cruelty and chaos before the gently civilizing hand of Europe had come to stay their murdering conflict; the truth, in fact, was otherwise, just as it was otherwise in India. Consider, for example, how warfare really was among the Azande, a numerous people of central Africa whom Europeans have often credited with a lusty interest in killing and in conquest. "I was told," says Evans-Pritchard, one of those Europeans who have lately done so much to right the balance of fact and judgment, "that since the aim was to get the enemy to withdraw so that victory might be claimed with as little loss on your side as possible, you usually avoided complete encirclement (*kenge aboro*) for if the enemy was unable to withdraw they would, seeing that there was no hope, sell their lives as dearly as they could."

The Azande therefore "left a gap in the rear. Moreover, there was a further convention, that fighting should begin about four P.M., so that those who were getting the worse of it could withdraw under cover of darkness." This agreeable convention, he adds, was often not observed. The point, of course, is not that pre-European Africa was a garden of sweetness and light — the point is that its warlike manners were relatively merciful and gentle when compared with the warlike manners of conquering Europe. Not always so, of course — the Wazimba who sacked Kilwa in Portuguese times had a ferocious reputation — but often so.

What was then destroyed or ruined in Africa, and afterwards forgotten, proved hard to remember in later years. If the early Portuguese thought of Africa as the land of Prester John, of the gold of Ophir and the Queen of Sheba, marvelous and splendid, rich beyond dreams, those who came afterward would return to another extreme. Africa would become by reputation altogether a land of savage torment, moral and mental darkness, childlike or perverse.

In 1518 the Portuguese could celebrate the consecration in Rome of Africa's first Negro bishop — Henrique of Congo, son of the undoubtedly African king of Congo and his undoubtedly African queen — and help the tribal feudalism of the Congo states to all the gamut of nobility and its titles of aristocratic mark.

This seemed to them, as the Portuguese royal archives show, the right and natural thing to do: these African peoples might be different — they were not therefore to be despised. But opinion changed. Some four hundred years later — years, for the most part, of oversea slaving — the common judgment of the outside world would all too often think of Africans as history-less and helpless in their brutish misery.

Ruin of the Indian trade and eclipse of its African terminals, oversea slaving, colonial conquest and many things beside, would obscure and hide the African past. We can begin to see the picture more clearly now. But is it fair and just, when tracing African history, to use the evidence of these coastal city-states and kingdoms? Were they not, after all, Arab rather than African?

2 Arab or African?

BEFORE THE ARCHEOLOGICAL DISCOVERIES OF THE PAST FEW YEARS it was generally taken for granted that the vanished cities of the East African coast were not African, but Arab. The late Sir Reginald Coupland, author of a standard British work on East Africa, called them "Arab colonies" and recommended his readers "to speak of the chain of coastal colonies and their civilisation as Arab." He admitted some Persian influence, but seems to have thought that the African contribution was small or nonexistent. It is a view which still claims many supporters, though their ranks are thinning. For the archeological discoveries of the past few years have thrown doubt on this Persian influence, added many sites to the record, and given their African background and texture a new and fuller meaning.

Yet the orthodox view — that these city-states were plainly Arab — has had much to support it. All this bustling commercial life that was found by the earliest Portuguese on the coast — and reported by the admirable Barbosa — was cosmopolitan, with plenty of Indians, Persians, Arabs ("white moors," Barbosa called them) and mainland Africans of various tribes; but the Arab accent was undoubtedly a strong one.

Even at this primitive stage of investigation, historical or archeological, one may catch a little of the gleam and glitter of their life. "The manner of their trade was this," says Barbosa, who saw it just before the Portuguese made final havoc there, and properly, in his later narrative, uses the past tense: "They came [to Sofala] in small vessels named *zambucos* from the kingdoms of Kilwa and Mombasa and Malindi, bringing many cotton cloths, some spotted and others white and blue, also some of silk and many small beads, grey, red, and yellow, which things come to those kingdoms from the great [Indian] kingdom of Cambay in other and greater ships."

They dealt — and he is talking now of Aden in southern Arabia, greatest of all the Arab-African entrepôts and urgently in need of archeological investigation — in cotton, drugs and gems, seed pearl in abundance, carnelians, opium; in copper and quicksilver; in madder and vermilion and great store of rose water; in woolen cloth, colored Mecca carpets, gold in ingots, coined and to be coined (and some in strings); in rice and sugar and coconuts; in lacquer and sandal wood and aloe wood and musk . . . "so much so that this place has a greater and richer trade than any other in the world."

Vanished though they are, the trading cities of the African coast were not much less impressive. The ruins of Kua, into which Sir Mortimer Wheeler cut his way through dense bush in 1955, are now known to have covered not less than thirty-five acres, and to include a palace, more than thirty stone houses, seven mosques and three cemeteries. Here on the little island of Juani, off the larger island of Mafia, they have slumbered in complete

MEDIEVAL EAST AFRICA

abandonment since their sacking by Madagascan invaders about a hundred and fifty years ago. At Songo Mnara, another city that was probably founded in the thirteenth century, Mathew has found "fluted demidomes [that] rest on fluted pilasters and . . . elaborate vaulted chambers with a barrel roofing inset with a hundred circular cavities."

Hither came, as we have seen, the fine goods and luxuries of the eastern world. Of Reynal in India, a little way above Surat, Barbosa offers a gemlike description which might surely have been made of these African coastal cities as well, and reveals something of the leisurely civilization of all this ocean seaboard. The Moors who dwell in Reynal, says Barbosa (who finished his book in about 1518), "are wealthy and distinguished, fair in colour and of gentle birth. They use, in the front room of their houses, to have many shelves all round — the whole room being surrounded by them as in a shop, all filled with fair and rich porcelain of new styles."

But at Kilwa and at Kua, Songo Mnara, Mombasa, Malindi and elsewhere, in the palaces of rulers and the houses of the well-to-do, one could have seen the same thing: the pottery of Sultanabad and Nishapur, bold in shape and colour; the painted figures of Persian djins and princes in gay *Minai* pastels; the celadon of Sung China and lavish Ming bowls and ornaments; the beads and precious stones of India, figures and figurines in gold and ivory, jewelry of jade and copper, carpets of the Middle East and Mecca — all exposed for sale but also for enjoyment and embellishment.

The constant to-ing and fro-ing of all this clamant maritime life helps to explain why early voyagers from Europe and the Mediterranean were so vague and contradictory about the peoples who actually inhabited these ports and cities. Today a better estimate is possible.

The earliest known non-African colonizers of this coast — this old Azanian coast of the Greco-Roman world — had been the merchant princes of southern Arabia, they who descended from the royal line of Sheba and filled the merchant fleets of Tyre and Tarshish. They had come, as the record shows, for trade, and not for loot or conquest. They were few but they were constant; they made themselves agreeable, learned the languages of the coast, married local women, established trading stations. By the middle of the first millennium B.C. and probably earlier they began to give an Arab inflection to the culture of the coast.

Constantly absorbed by the peoples among whom they lived, these trading Arabs were as constantly reinforced from Arabia and the Persian Gulf; and they never quite lost their identity. Out of their presence came Swahili culture: authentic African synthesis of non-African ideas that nonetheless remained basically and predominantly African — Bantu-speaking African. Some of the exotic elements in coastal culture — such as the outrigger canoes of the Bagiuni islands — can be clearly traced; the origin of others, like the markedly phallic or pillar tombstones of both island and mainland, still elude an explanation. This early culture of the coast was syncretic; it took from many sources but it made a distinctive whole — but this whole was clearly African.

The picture needs extending a little. All round the seaboard of the ocean, ports and cities had sprung to life whose vivid various life illuminated the mingling of many peoples: Indians, Persians, Arabs, Indonesians, Malayans, Chinese, Africans. In the course of years these ports and cities grew into the grain of the cultures of the lands in which they lay, retaining only the echo and the distant accent of their hybrid origins. But this was as true of East Africa as of India and southeast Asia.

After the beginning of Arab expansion under Islam, in the seventh century, the picture somewhat changes. Refugees from Arabia come down the African coast; not for trade only, but for settlement as well. They found the earliest Islamic cities on the coast; and these, at least to begin with, are dominated or much influenced by Arab ruling groups. Eight sites of this period are so far identified, small trading stations for the most part, situated on islands off the coast which could easily be seized and, once seized,

MEROË
Statue in Plaster (Height about 4 feet), Undated

hartoum Museum, the Sudan Government

The Pyramids at Meroë

NAGA: The "Lion Temple"

NAGA: Ram of Amun-Re

NAGA
The "Lion God"

DARFUR
The Ruined City of Jebel Uri

Musawarat es Safra

easily held against invasion from the mainland. Typical for this period are sites at Unguja Kuu and Kizimi Kazi on Zanzibar island and at Sanje Majoma, another ruin on the coral islet of Songo Mnara.

These new colonists find African people who speak Swahili and feel themselves to be Swahili, and other African peoples on the neighboring mainland; and they also find, no doubt, many small Arab groups in earlier trading settlements. They establish themselves without much difficulty but in time they too merge and intermarry, giving Islam increasingly to the culture of the whole coast but absorbing into their Arab manners much that was purely or partially African. And in time, again, the descendants of these little dynasties — increasingly African — will fabricate long family trees which trace back "nobility of line" to powerful families in Arabia and Persia: they will play the same game that so many royal and aristocratic *parvenus* had played before them and would continue to play after them — they will seek for "noble ancestors," and, in so doing, muddle historians of a later day.

This Arab settlement down the coast became more frequent and self-assertive after the seventh and eighth centuries. On the island of Pate, for example, Islamic settlement is traditionally asserted for the end of the seventh century. Perhaps it is a little too early, but there is no doubt that by the end of the eleventh century many trading settlements up and down the coast were growing into cities ruled by Islamized Arab or Arab-Swahili or Swahili groups, or containing numerous colonies of such people. This was true for as far south as Sofala, the principal southern port for trade with the Rhodesian plateau of the hinterland.

These Arab and Arab-Swahili and Swahili ruling groups in emergent city-states up and down the coast went through many vicissitudes whose record escapes all detailed narrative; and archeological investigation along this coast has only just begun. Some of them remained distinctively Arab as well as Islamic; others, and especially those of the mainland like Malindi and Brava, seem never to have had more than a veneer of Arab culture. It may soon be possible to say much more about them. Freeman-Grenville has now completed a list of pre-European sites on the Tanganyika coast and islands — they number sixty-three — and considers that with further research "a satisfactory dating of pottery and porcelain should be possible from the second century B.C. to the end of the fifteenth century." He has examined some thousands of coins, Roman, Greek-Egyptian, Byzantine, Chinese, Turkish-Egyptian, and from the mint founded at Kilwa shortly before 1300, and is in course of publishing his results.

One fact that seems to emerge, meanwhile, is that there occurred in the thirteenth and fourteenth centuries a cultural change which caused many settlements to grow into cities. There appears to have been, at about this time, a tremendous expansion in the demand for African goods, and a culmination of the process which had gradually brought coastal Africans into trading settlements over previous centuries. Several cities appear to date from about this time: Gedi (excavated by Kirkman in 1953), Kilwa, Songo Mnara — although all of these were probably built on previous and more humble foundations.

But what, by now, was the people of these cities? El Mas'udi, Edrisi and other Arab writers of the tenth to the twelfth centuries had been consistent in saying that the dominant people of the coast was Zanj, Negro, and that some were Muslim. Dimasqui, in about 1300, speaks of "Mogadiscio of the Zanj" and says that the people of the coast are Negroes and infidels: they practice rites handed down from their ancestors and — echo of El Mas'udi — are famous for their eloquence at feasts. Although founded as a settlement in about 1100, the city of Gedi (old Malindi as it probably was) acquired its first stone mosque only in about 1450 — clear evidence that its inhabitants were not Arabs.

Around 1331 there turns up once again the indefatigable Ibn

Battuta. After visiting Kilwa he describes it as "one of the most beautiful and best-constructed towns, all elegantly built," and says that "the majority of its inhabitants are Zanj, jet-black in color, and with tattoo-marks on their faces." If that was true of the island city of Kilwa, it must certainly have been true of the main-land cities as well; and this is what the evidence, sparse though it is, also shows. Barbosa gives the ruler of Malindi, for example, as a "Moor"; but later evidence shows conclusively that he was in fact Swahili. At Brava in 1501 he finds another "great town of the Moors"; yet at Brava, even today, the common language of the city is not Arabic, nor even Swahili, but of more purely Bantu formation. This cosmopolitan culture of the coastal cities was predominantly an African culture.

The richness of early Swahili culture, little noticed or com-pletely ignored outside East Africa, confirms this. Poets here were writing down *mashairi*, or lyric songs, by at least 1150; and they were writing them down in the Swahili language, an African lan-guage, even though the script they used was a modified Arabic script and their style and language had many Arab echoes. They continued to write *mashairi* and *tendi*, epic poems, for all the cen-turies that followed; and they are writing them down today. They drew on foreign themes; but so, one may remark, did Shake-speare. They lived in cities which looked to southern Arabia and India for wealth and fashion, travel and adventure; much as Shakespeare's London looked to southern Europe and the Medi-terranean. Shakespeare's poetry was nonetheless English for that; nor was Swahili poetry any the less African. "Just as Spenser drew for incident upon foreign sources and yet wrote a truly national poem," in Harries' words, "so also the Swahili poets north of Mombasa have created a national literature from sources which are foreign."

To this the traditional chronicles, or such as have survived, bring their various reinforcement. Like the *Tarikh es Sudan*, some were written down in Arabic; others, like the chronicles of Mombasa and of Pate, were in Swahili with an Arabic script; some, like those of Kilwa, were in both. As late as 1824 Emery could find that "Swahili is generally used at Mombasa" — and this, indeed, after long Arab settlement there and recent conquest from Arabia; so that when the notables of that city presented him with a copy of the Mombasa chronicle, it was "in the Swahili language and Arabic character."

Even the later architecture of the coast, in Mathew's opinion, "forms a distinct variant among the medieval Islamic culture." When beginning archeological work on the east coast eleven years ago, he recalls, "I assumed that the ruins of the sites I was investigating were the remains of Arab or Persian colonies along the coast . . . but gradually I have come to doubt: now I am beginning to think that the history of the coast in the medieval period is more easily intelligible if it was the history of an African culture gradually Islamised than if it is merely the history of Islamic colonies from the Persian Gulf."

"Sometime in the thirteenth and fourteenth centuries," he goes on, "the culture of the coast became integrally Islamic. But even if the culture had become Islamic, still it would seem to be Negro." These merchant cities and trading kingdoms of the coast of the Zanj, we may conclude, were neither Arabian nor Persian nor Indian; they were African, and predominantly Negro African — just as were Timbuktu and Gao and Djenné, the kingdoms of the Hausa, the city-states of Ife and Benin.

3 *Steps* to the *Interior*

THE POINT NEEDS EMPHASIZING NOT ONLY TO RESTORE THE PAR-
entage of these east coast civilizations to their rightful owners, as
it were, but also because it bears directly on the next great problem.
If the long centuries of ocean trading helped to draw and stimulate
these coastal peoples into medieval civilization, what did they do
for peoples in the hinterland? Did they do anything? Can one trace
the history of the hinterland through these medieval centuries?

These questions are difficult to answer, partly for lack of archeological research, partly for other reasons. For as soon as one turns
one's back on the coast and confronts the mountains of the interior and the plains beyond, the uplands and the forests and the
gray-thorn mass of inner Africa, the evidence loses form and date,
the routes of influence confuse and blur and peter out, the lines
of growth wander and disappear.

The rest of this book is concerned with trying to answer these
questions. Some repetition may be unavoidable, for the obstacles
are many and problems still to be solved are legion. Yet this stumbling will be worth the trouble if only because here in the central
and southern hinterland the achievements of a purely African historical experience can be measured better than elsewhere. Here
one may scale the barricades of ignorance and long-enduring solitude and see, though distantly as yet, what pioneering humanity
could do in Africa when delivered over to its own resources.

Archeology has lately demolished several of the barricades or, at
any rate, has lowered them. Clark's work at the Kalambo Falls has
put the origins of the southern African Iron Age into a new and
meaningful framework; and others have labored in the same good
field. Here and there the outline regains something of its coastal
clarity and brilliance — to the far north in Ethiopia, and to the

south in Rhodesia. Here, and sometimes elsewhere, the sweep and vigor of Iron Age societies have left their potent mark.

These lands behind the long east coast do not make, and never made, a cultural whole. Earthworks in Uganda, some of the largest in any part of the world, point back to Iron Age societies whose inspiration was largely of inner Africa; other ruins, in Kenya and Tanganyika, seem related to the history of the coast but even more to that of southern Ethiopia. Far to the southward, meanwhile, merchant cities on the coast traded with new civilizations in the interior; and these last, climax of Iron Age culture in southern Africa, have left their ruins at Zimbabwe and Mapungubwe, Niekerk, Penhalonga, Khami and elsewhere.

Yet if Zimbabwe and its kind are the culmination of Iron Age growth in central and southern Africa, they have their beginnings elsewhere. They grew imposing at the same time as the coastal trade of the twelfth to the fifteenth centuries, and partly, no doubt, because of it; but their early history must be seen against a wider background.

How closely these Iron Age civilizations of the south were linked to an earlier and wider African background is not yet clear, though this whole question is less obscure than it was even a dozen years ago. The tricky nature of the problem rests in the fact that although the states and civilizations of this immense hinterland belong to different cultural patterns and periods, most of them show evidence of common origins. At the present state of knowledge one can neither treat them apart from one another, nor lump them together. To see this complex and intriguing picture as it now begins to emerge, perhaps the best beginning is to return through time to Axum and early Ethiopia, and to those "Azanians," in early East Africa, whom Greco-Roman traders knew of faintly from their ancient travels down the coast.

eight

After Axum

When I had established peace in the lands subject to me I came to Adulis to sacrifice on behalf of those who voyage on the sea.

Inscription of a king of Axum

The Azanians have left behind them numberless traces in the shape of buildings and earthworks of various kinds.

G. W. B. Huntingford in 1933

1 The Greatness of Ethiopia

CHRISTOVÃO DA GAMA, THE FOURTH SON OF his great father, led a Portuguese expedition into Ethiopia in 1541.

He was dressed "in hose and vest of red satin and gold brocade with many plaits, and a French cape of fine black cloth all quilted with gold, and a black cap with a very rich medal"; and must have suffered a good deal from the heat. He had with him some four hundred fifty Portuguese soldiers, as well as captains and fidalgos. Invited by the emperor of Ethiopia, their bold objective was to save Ethiopia for Christendom by helping to evict Muslim invaders from Somaliland. They succeeded in doing this, though not easily or at once and at the sad cost of Dom Christovão's life, largely because they had more matchlocks than the Muslims; for the matchlock then was lord of battles. A member of the expeditionary force, Castanhosa, afterwards wrote an account of what he had seen. It is a very useful account.

Not the earliest nor the longest description of Ethiopia after the Middle Ages, Castanhosa's is perhaps the most interesting. Through Castanhosa one may grasp the basic theme of Ethiopian history: the survival of a mountain people through the stubborn conquest and reconquest of its neighbors and invaders. Castanhosa speaks the wonder of a man who saw how this remote African country, converted to Christianity twelve hundred years before, had somehow managed to conserve its religion and identity amid a sea of enemies.

It is a theme of astonishing continuity. The very name of Negus, emperor, occurs as early as the third or fourth century A.D., when a Himyarite inscription of southern Arabia mentions an alliance with Gadarat, king of the Habashan, whose titles include that of *Nagashi* and "king of Habashat and Axum." * The Habashan themselves — they who would found Axum after centuries of Sabaean and other Arabian infiltration and invasion — appear in early inscriptions of the eighteenth dynasty (1580-1350 B.C.) which tell of trade with the land of Punt. And although the legend that takes the rise of the Lion of Judah back to Solomon and his love for the Queen of Sheba is of course a pious forgery, there is more than a little truth in its symbolic essence: northwestern Ethiopia, the land of Habashat, was part of the world of "Punt and frankincense" in that venerable time when the ships of Hiram, king of Tyre, plied up and down the Red Sea and brought the wealth of Ophir into Israel.

Yet this astonishing continuity was for the most part a continuity in isolation. Although the survival and growth of Ethiopia and its distinctive civilization add a splendid chapter to African history, it is a chapter which remains curiously on its own. Like Kush before it, Axum would briefly alter the balance of world power; yet Axum, unlike Kush, which it defeated, would count for little in the rest of Africa.

This can be said, of course, only with due reservation for present ignorance, which is large. Until the Persian conquest of southern Arabia, in 575 B.C., the Axumite kingdom must have played its part in the harbors of the "far side coast" — the African and Arabian terminals of the ocean trade. Undoubtedly it continued to play some part there until the rise of Islam closed the Red Sea straits to all but Muslim vessels. Thereafter it declined. From the sixth to the fourteenth century Christian Ethiopia disappears from recorded history in a welter of war — war against the Muslims of the north, war against the pagans of the south — and

* The southern Arabian inscriptions call the country that lay on the southern flank of the Red Sea strait Habashat, and the people Habashan.

when it emerges once again, it is still engaged in these wars although at last with hope of respite. But Axum by now has long since gone: it is the Amharic people of the central mountains and the Tigre who dominate the scene, just as they do today.

Yet it would be as silly to dogmatize about this part of African history as about any other. In Ethiopia the archeological record is only now beginning to be written, although the last few years, thanks largely to the enlightened attitude of the present emperor, have brought new evidence to light. And in spite of lack of clarity and detail in the evidence so far available, it may be that many primary influences did in fact irradiate from here.

It may be that Axum and the Amharic people and their neighbors were the channel through which knowledge and practice of hillside terracing spread down through Africa until it reached the far south. It may be that the skill in dry-stone building which distinguished the early medieval civilizations of east-central Africa — and culminated at Great Zimbabwe — was evolved and passed on from here. It may be that the practice of building temples or strong places in ellipse came from southern Arabia through Axum into southern Africa. Perhaps the habit of distinguishing men by carving a phallic ornament on the foreheads of their funerary statues, practiced still in southern Ethiopia, goes back to a common source with comparable practices in West Africa. Perhaps the tall stone phalli of the Sidama, also in southern Ethiopia, are related to the menhirs of West Africa, the phallic gravestones of East Africa, and the phallic trinkets of what is now Rhodesia.

All these things, and others like them, are possible; some of them seem probable. None is certain. In considering them, one is once again led back into a remote past.

Semitic people from southern Arabia invaded Ethiopia many hundred years before the Christian era, and produced, in the course of time, an Ethiopian civilization which reflected that of their homeland. Their earliest known inscription is at Yeha, not far from Axum. Attributed to the fourth century B.C., or thereabouts, it dedicates an altar to the pagan goddesses Naurau and Ashtar — that same Ashtoreth to whose worship old Solomon in his dotage was led astray by "foreign wives." But the Habashan, as Egyptian inscriptions of a much earlier date have shown, were already in the land. Not Semites themselves, these early Abyssinians survived Semitic invasion, took much from it, and gradually built their own strange and strangely distinguished civilization of Axum. Here was one more example of an invaded people surviving the invaders, absorbing their culture, and producing another culture of their own.

Axum flourished on the Red Sea trade. Its port of Adulis was big enough by the seventh century A.D. — when a visiting Greek described it — as to have long had commercial interests as far as India and Ceylon. From Adulis inland, caravan trails had continued this foreign trade down the river Atbara to the middle Nile and Meroë, and given, no doubt, the sharp edge of commercial rivalry to kingly quarrels between Kush and Axum. Wars of Kush against the Habashan, founders of Axum, are mentioned in Meroitic inscriptions (wherein proper names, at least, can be understood) as early as the Kushite monarch Harsiotef (397-362 B.C.) and Nastasen (328-308 B.C.); but it was Axum, as we have seen, that prevailed in the end. Sometime after A.D. 300, Axum at last vanquished Kush; and Aizanas, Axumite monarch of that conquest (or perhaps the successor of the actual Axumite conqueror) celebrated victory over a whole galaxy of enemies. His early money, fine coins in gold, carry a new moon and two stars, symbolic of his pagan faith; but his later coins are discreetly Christian, and portray a cross. Byzantine priests from the eastern Roman Empire had meanwhile converted him.

This conversion to Christianity was important in more than a religious sense. It helped the Axumite kingdom and its Amharic successor to acquire the consciousness of an identity and a distinction from their neighbors which gave great staying power. But it also meant that the wars they fought were wars of religion. Reinforced in their capacity for survival, they were also thrust into isolation among surrounding peoples who were nearly always Muslim or pagan.*

Thus it was that the culture and civilization of the Amharic people — those who dominate Ethiopia today — would become radically different from the pagan cultures of the south of their country or the Muslim cultures to the north and east. There would be cultural and political obstruction to the passage of ideas and techniques.

Yet at least three material aspects of Ethiopian life may be mentioned as possibly important to the record of what happened, or would happen, further south. They are hillside terracing, the habit of building forts and strong places on the top of steep hills, and phallic symbolism. They occur and recur; and perhaps they were developed independently in places far apart. But their presence in Ethiopia is far too interesting to be passed over.

Terraced hillside cultivation and irrigation were to be an integral and imposing aspect of early civilizations in east and southeast Africa. They had long existed in southern Arabia where the whole of that gleaming fabric of urbanity had depended on making a little water go a long way, and on conserving the soil of steep hillsides. Hillside terracing may still be seen, with evidence of great antiquity though continued on a very small scale even today, as far to the west as western Darfur. Surveyors in 1958 found it, long abandoned for the most part, over an area of some twelve thousand square miles from the sub-Saharan hills of the Jebel Marra and Jebel Si to the borders of Wadai; and carried, with painstak-

* The Christian kingdoms of the middle Nile survived until the fourteenth century; but Islamic onslaught had weakened them long before that.

ing care, right up to the rim of Jebel Marra's dead volcano, where no one lives or cultivates today.*

In Ethiopia this hillside terracing was developed with the same intricate determination. Visiting the Tigre in 1893, Bent could write of the landscape of Yeha that "all the surrounding hills have been terraced for cultivation . . . Nowhere in Greece or Asia Minor have I seen such an enormous extent of terraced mountains as in this Abyssinian valley. Hundreds of thousands of acres must have been under the most careful cultivation, right up almost to the top of the mountains, and now nothing is left but the regular lines of the sustaining walls." Nor was this terraced cultivation restricted to northern — Sabaean, Axumite, and then Christian — Ethiopia. Some of the most successful terracing of all may still be found in use and construction, for example, among the pagan Konso, a Negro people of southwestern Ethiopia; here too the hills are contoured with an infinite number of meandering lines.

This terracing had seemed unique to northern Africa; and yet it would prove to be nothing of the kind. Vanished peoples are now known to have practiced it right down to the Transvaal, and extensively in Kenya, Tanganyika, Rhodesia, and Mozambique.

The art of building in dry stone — of building without mortar — is another ancient skill of Ethiopia and the Horn of Africa. The Konso still use it today, just as they continue to build hillside terraces. To the east of them, beyond the high peaks and green valleys of southern Ethiopia, the plains of Somaliland conceal many ruins of medieval cities built in stone and brick whose precise identity and origins and history are not yet surely settled. Here in 1934 — making another contribution to the riddle of in-

---

* I am indebted for this information to the efficiency and kindness of the management and staff of Hunting Aerial Surveys, who obtained it during their work in 1957-1958 for the government of the Republic of the Sudan.

terwoven cultures in Africa — Curle saw triangular niches in tumbled thorn-grown brickwork of a kind which may be seen, to this day, in the brick buildings of Darfur and in other buildings of greater age as far west as Kumbi Saleh, probable site of one of the capitals of ancient Ghana. Once again one is faced with the evidence of an interplay and exchange of ideas between countries which now appear so completely severed from each other as never to have known any kind of common history. Once again the present appearances are evidently false. But once again one cannot yet tell which way the influences went, nor when, nor how.

To this the phallic symbolism of many monuments of old Ethiopia adds another characteristic note. Southwards from Addis Ababa, in abrupt valleys of the Sidama and Borama that lead down slowly into the choking plains of northern Kenya, one may come upon many stone monoliths that are carved to represent a phallus. Sometimes these stones, ten or twelve feet high, bear engraving in lines and unexplained symbols; more often they bear nothing at all. They do not seem to have been burial stones. No one knows when they were built; the present populations can say nothing about them.

Alongside these tall granite monoliths, at other sites, are other kinds of standing stones, sometimes engraved, sometimes not; perhaps contemporary, perhaps earlier. Often enough these are engraved with swords or daggers; but the daggers seem to be of a comparatively recent type, and there is nothing to suggest that this dagger-engraving on monoliths has any close parentage, for example, with the almost certainly much more ancient dagger-engravings of Bronze Age Europe at Stonehenge or Carnac, though the visible results are oddly reminiscent of each other.

"We are wholly ignorant of the age of these stones," commented Huntingford of Ethiopia in 1950. "It seems probable, however, that they are not all of the same age, and that some, like the banded menhirs of Axum, and perhaps some of the sword stones, may go back to Axumite times . . . while others, including the phallic stones, may be relatively modern."

Yet their influence, or something like it, would seem to occur again and again. Gravestones which are obviously phallic are found on the Bagiuni Islands off the Somali coast and on the mainland as far south as Bagamoyo in Tanganyika; some of the mosque minarets of the northern region of this coast are just as obviously phallic in shape, and add another native accent to this specifically East African Islamic culture. Some writers have suggested Indonesian origins for this architectural celebration of the male genital organ; most have preferred to suggest nothing at all. Many ancient societies appear to have had phallic rituals at one time or another, in one way or another; and traces of such rituals may be found in parts of Africa. Yet Ethiopia adds a curious chapter on its own.

The presence of summit forts and dwellings is puzzling and persistent in the same way. They occur in Southern Rhodesia and Angola; and as far away as Basutoland in South Africa. Perhaps they were simply the obvious best defense in a country that is often rich in flat-topped hills with steep sides; perhaps they too denote a line of "cultural drift" and therefore of migration. Consider two astonishingly similar descriptions: one from Ethiopia but the other from the northern Transvaal, two thousand miles away and more.

Christovão da Gama, coming to the aid of the Ethiopian royal family in 1541, found the Queen Mother living on the flat top of the precipitous mountain of Debra Damo. (The building of such places of security was in fact a matter of common form in old Ethiopia; sometimes they were used as convenient places of rustication — prisons, indeed — for potential rivals to the throne.) Part of the ascent to the summit of Debra Damo, says Castanhosa, who was there at the time, was by a winding narrow path which ascended from the foot of the hill; but from this point — about two-thirds of a height of "eighty fathoms," or about five hundred feet — the rock turned outwards and overhung the place beneath, and they could only reach the top in a basket, which was let down from above through a hole made in the rock.

At the close of 1932, in the wilderness of the northern Transvaal at the other end of Africa, a farmer and prospector called van Graan stumbled on a site that seemed worth investigation. On a flat-topped hill that rose from broken ground on the south bank of the Limpopo, it was said, treasure might be found. For a long time van Graan and his son could find no one to show them how to climb this strange hill, for it seemed unclimbable. Then at last they managed to induce one of the local people to point out what was evidently a secret way to the top. This was a narrow cleft or chimney in the rock, entirely hidden by trees in 1932. They cut their way to the foot of it and found, to their surprise, that those who had used it had drilled small holes on opposite sides of the cleft, into which crossbars could be slotted. Van Graan managed to climb the chimney to the top; and in this way, at last, the golden treasures of Mapungubwe were opened to the world.

Now there is nothing to say that any current of ideas ever linked Debra Damo with Mapungubwe, or need have linked them. One can only record that the building of hilltop forts and dwellings, if decided upon quite independently in different places at different times, produced — once again — remarkably similar results. Yet these results, together with great skill in dry-stone building, in terraced cultivation, in an occasionally emphatic use of phallic symbolism, do undoubtedly suggest the interchange and interplay of ideas across great distances and over a long period. Against a background of north-south migration trends in ancient

Africa, this evidence — take it as cautiously as one may — engenders a great uneasiness with any neat or obvious conclusion.

One appears to be strangely in the presence of a community of ideas which cannot be explained, of men and cultures whose lines of movement and whose limits of awareness of one another seem much wider and more immediate than the material finds will allow. This uneasiness becomes greater as one moves southward from Ethiopia and meets the terraced ruins of Kenya and Tanganyika and Rhodesia, the walls and towers of Zimbabwe, the dwellings of Niekerk and Inyanga, and the golden burials of Mapungubwe.

Yet this uneasiness with any neat or obvious conclusion — like an earlier and related uneasiness on the part of Europeans when they were asked to believe that Africans could never have built these walls and towers and terraces — need not discourage or dismay. To borrow a luminous passage from Caton-Thompson, it should rather enhance the interest of all these ruins and remains and their fragmentary pathways into the African past: "it enriches, not impoverishes, our wonderment at their remarkable achievement [and] it cannot detract from their inherent majesty"; for its mystery "is the mystery which lies in the still pulsating heart of native Africa."

2 Engaruka

A "LARGE RUINED CITY" AMID THE HILLS OF THE KENYA-TANGANyika border, some three hundred miles from the coast, was reported by a Tanganyika district officer in 1935. It lay on the steep escarpment of the Rift Valley southwest of Lake Natron, and was apparently hard to come at and well concealed, for the escarpment was littered with rocks and slithering scree, and spiked with thorn.

These were large ruins, he said; so far as was known, nobody before had reported their existence.

His report reached Dr. L. S. B. Leakey, then working on early stone age evidence in Kenya, and aroused his interest. Leakey decided to have a look at Engaruka, as the place was called. He knew that many years earlier, in 1913 under the German domination, Dr. Hans Reck of the University of Berlin had reported stone burial cairns in this vicinity; but stone cairns — indeed, all manner of stone huts and cairns and terraces — were scattered in abundance throughout East Africa; and Engaruka might be nothing out of the usual run of them.

But Engaruka was. What Leakey found was much more than a familiar scattering of dry stone fragments, solitary graves, and the blurred line of ancient terracing, although all these were present. He really found the ruins of a city. "I estimate," he wrote, "that there are about six thousand three hundred houses in the main city of the scree slopes . . . and that there are about five hundred houses in the valley ruins, where burials are far commoner than houses"; and the population figure, he thought, "was probably between thirty and forty thousand, and I think this may be an under-estimate."

As he toiled and persevered among the gray-brown stones and thorn, Leakey saw that this had been a long occupation, deliberately established and maintained. "The houses of the main city are all built upon very well made stone walls. The terraces include pathway terraces and house terraces . . . [and] there is a vast mesh of stone walls and terraces in the valley ruins which I take to be connected in some way with cultivation and irrigation, but this is not proved." Unfortunately he could recover no skeletal material — the common disappointment in African archeology and one of the reasons why Mapungubwe, as we shall see, would prove of cardinal importance — "apparently because the nature of the soil is not such as to preserve bone"; and he found no inscriptions. He did find stone engravings which consisted usually of irregular lines and round "cup marks"; these, he thought, were clan marks.

Leakey believes that Engaruka was built not more than three hundred years ago and perhaps a good deal less, and probably by the ancestors of the Mbulu people who still inhabit the neighborhood; and that it was ravaged and depopulated during or soon after Masai invasions from the north. In 1938 Fosbrooke pointed out that there was a striking similarity between these ruins at Engaruka and other stone structures to be found in Sonjo villages some fifty miles away, and said that Masai tradition links the inhabitants of Engaruka with those of Sonjo.

And that is the sum total of what may be said of Engaruka at the present time. Yet this city of Engaruka, among the most striking discoveries of East African archeology for recent times, belongs most probably to a wide tradition. Whether or not Engaruka is as recent as Leakey suggests, there can be little doubt that it belongs by descent to what Huntingford, writing in 1933, first called "the Azanian civilization of Kenya." What Engaruka does, forcefully and dramatically, is to offer a means of grasping what manner of Iron Age civilizations grew and flowered, through pre-medieval and medieval centuries, in the Kenya-Tanganyika hinterland behind the trading coast.

Was there an organic link between the civilizations of the coast and this "Azanian civilization" of the hinterland? Did the first help to promote the second with its demand for ivory and iron? Was it from cities like Engaruka that merchants took these goods to early Malindi and Mombasa, and to Kilwa?

The answers are dubious, for research has barely skimmed the surface. There is little or no evidence, so far, of coastal goods (or Eastern goods) having reached the distant hinterland; the great Iron Age earthworks of Uganda, for example, have yet to yield a single object from the coast. The "Azanian civilization," in this respect, is much less rich in evidence of trading contact than the more developed civilizations of Zimbabwe and its like, far to the south in the country that was to become Rhodesia.

Yet the coastal cities must always have had their suppliers in the interior. Trading narratives from the *Periplus* onward suggest that coastal settlements and cities were in more or less constant trade with mainland kingdoms in their neighborhood. Pottery types have occurred on the Kenya coast, at levels dating to the fourteenth century or earlier, which resemble those of Zimbabwe and Mapungubwe. Medieval Kilwa, greatest of these coastal markets and entrepôts, lay during the height of its prosperity — milking buyers and sellers alike of fat customs dues and tariffs — opposite the ocean terminal of an ancient caravan road that went inland to the region of the Great Lakes, and perhaps beyond.

The plain fact is that archeology has barely as yet begun to consider in any detail the question of interrelated development between coast and hinterland. Meanwhile, throughout this great belt of territory that lies behind the coast from Somaliland to Mozambique, there is monumental evidence of long-settled urbanity by peoples who were uncommonly skilled in the use of stone, whether for hillside terracing to irrigate and conserve their soil or for the building of huts; who mined for iron and other minerals and worked these for their own use as well as for export; who raised cattle and grew large crops of grain; and who were most probably of those peoples of the Zanj whose southern ruler, the Waqlimi, was so well described by El Mas'udi a thousand years ago.

Faint and blurred in many places, especially in Kenya, the ramifications of this "Azanian civilization" may be found to range — more or less closely related in their social structure and techniques such as mining, pot-making, ironworking — from the southern valleys of Ethiopia to the high walls of Zimbabwe and the goldstocked graves of Mapungubwe.

3 The Old Roads of Kenya

THESE TRACES OF MEDIEVAL CIVILIZATION IN EAST AFRICA ARE VANishing fast beneath the pressure of growing population and more intensive cultivation. Few writers have attempted to describe in any detail what remains — or remained until a handful of years ago. Yet Wilson, writing in 1932, could still report three main areas of hillside terracing in Tanganyika: around lakes Natron and Eyasi in the north, near the Kenya border; to the east, between Kilasa and Kisaki; and near Iringa at the head of Lake Nyasa, in the south. He remarked — as one may still remark, for example, in Darfur and Ethiopia — that the art of terracing was still practiced among some of the peoples who lived in these areas then.

"The average width of the top of the terraces," he wrote of Tanganyika, "is about a foot. They were probably about three feet originally, and the depth between terraces three feet." Many roads existed. These roads were graded, and "as a rule about ten or twelve feet wide," while "the strata of the hillside are exposed and have been worked with a tool." The longest of these "Azanian" roads, Wilson suggests, may have linked the head of Lake Nyasa, towards Abercorn in what is now Northern Rhodesia, with Arusha and Nairobi in the "white highlands" of Kenya; it may have run, that is, for some five or six hundred miles from north to south at a distance from the coast that varied between two and three hundred miles by crow's flight. Brief fragments of ancient roadway, or what look like ancient roadway, are also reported by Worsley and Rumberger between Iringa and the head of Lake Nyasa. One of these fragments is about nine feet wide, "apparently banked up to make it level, and with a line of small rocks along the outside edge."

"The points where these roads have been located," Wilson commented, "would suggest a system of communication running from north to south on the east side of the Great Lakes, and in no case does coastal communication appear obvious." But coastal communication presumably existed; north-south roads and roads to the coast could help to explain the similarity of pottery types at old Malindi and old Zimbabwe. Nothing like a full archeological survey has yet been made of this area, although the Tanganyika government has lately begun to show a useful understanding of the importance of the subject.

In Kenya, according to Huntingford, ruins are most numerous and most developed precisely in those highland regions that are now inhabited by European settlers. Here in the green splendors of Trans-Nzoia, Uasin Gishu, Kericho, and Laikipia, there had evidently dwelt a large population living in stone-built settlements of various types. Huntingford divides these stone-built structures into five categories: stone enclosures, hut circles, tumuli or cairns, linear earthworks, and irrigation works.

The stone enclosures consist of roughly circular dry-stone walls that ranged from quite modest affairs to double enclosures some sixty feet in diameter. Coursing and bonding, he found, had been sometimes attempted in building the hut circles. "Under the term linear earthworks," he continues, "are included artificial works which are beyond doubt roads; [and] works which appear to be ditches rather than roads. Undoubted roads, which in some places are graded, and in others pass through hillsides in cuttings not unlike railway cuttings, and cross swampy ground over carefully made embankments, occur in Kenya and Tanganyika." On one such ancient road in Uasin Gishu, in the Kenya highlands, he noticed a fourteen-foot cutting at one place, and a seven-and-a-half-foot embankment at another, for a road which had once been about fifteen feet wide.

"Irrigation works include canals, terraces, and walls. So far, ancient canals have been seen in Kenya in Nandi only: the best example I know is five feet deep and three feet wide in the last one hundred yards of its course. Irrigation by means of such canals, often of some length, is still practiced by the Suk of Maraket . . . on the west escarpment of the Rift Valley. They are too barbarous," he comments, "to have learnt it themselves, and it is probably an Azanian legacy."

One could multiply such evidence, which still remains to be systematically collected and collated and examined. Watson pointed out as long ago as 1928 that many wells, "bored through from sixteen to forty feet of limestone rock," were still used in the northern province of Kenya. Such wells, there and elsewhere, are still being bored by pastoral peoples in Africa today; but they seem to go back into a remote past, and to have formed another aspect of "Azanian" technology.

Watson's report is worth noting for the light it throws on another aspect of evolution — the evolution of European attitudes towards these traces of an ancient African civilization. "Among the officials," says Watson, "there are two schools of thought. The first attributes the cairns and wells to volcanic origin and the rain-pools to natural hollowing out of the ground by tropical deluges. The opposition believes in an ancient civilization . . ."

It is the opposition which has won. "There is," Fosbrooke would write of Tanganyika a quarter of a century later, "a considerable body of archeological evidence coming to light that at some time in the past there were sedentary, agricultural, iron-age folk living on the plains." These were the people who bored the wells, and who built and traveled on the old roads of East Africa.

4 Azanian History

THESE "SEDENTARY, AGRICULTURAL IRON-AGE FOLK" — THESE AZANI-ans, as Huntingford called them, restoring a classical Greek usage — have left behind them all this quantity of evidence: ruins of stone settlements and cities, terracing, irrigation channels, roads, mine workings and smithies, cairns and rock paintings. It is vast, but it is also vague. There is little or nothing else by which to identify or know them closer.

Were they the early suppliers of the coast? It is possible and even probable; but ancient records of the coastal trade are few and far between, and reach us almost always through the obscuring veil of coastal monopoly. When Europeans first came up and down this coast they found the coastal peoples, and notably the Swahili, well seized of the value of maintaining their monopoly of trade with the interior, and therefore of knowledge of the interior; and the practice, as the *Periplus* suggests, must have been an old one.

That little or nothing is known of the peoples of the interior during the great centuries of the ocean trade does not mean that there was nothing to be known. These centuries were the period of growth of eastern and southeastern Africa's Iron Age, and the "Azanian civilization," vague and mysterious though it is, was contemporary with the foundation and early growth of Zimbabwe; and, as the pottery suggests, may have had trading links with it. Yet the coastal peoples have interposed their veil; and it is only in the south, where the Iron Age civilizations of the hinterland were more powerful and perhaps more advanced, that the veil is broken here and there, and a good deal of the truth can be seen beyond it.

Huntingford has suggested an early dating limit of about A.D. 700, or somewhat earlier, for the beginning of this stone-building metal-using agricultural civilization of Kenya and Tanganyika. The date must obviously be imprecise, not only for lack of evidence, but also because the founding and building of this extensive culture in East Africa was certainly a process, and not a single event or brief series of events. Probably this process was linked with movement from the north; and the origins of these modes and manners of life are perhaps to be looked for in southern Ethiopia — where the Konso and Kaffa, for example, still retain some of the characteristics that mark the Azanian achievement.

"We may surmise," says Huntingford, "that a civilization which flourished in the Horn of Africa at some time during the first seven hundred years A.D." — a civilization, no doubt, which had taken much from the Sabaeans* and the Axumites, as from Meroë and the Middle Nile — "was destroyed by Islam; that its makers retreated southwards through Kenya (where Islam never penetrated); and that it finally came to an end somewhere about the fourteenth to fifteenth centuries, possibly earlier."

Tribal history does not quarrel with this. While tribal legend in West Africa refers frequently to eastern origins, tribal legend in East Africa as frequently refers to northern origins. Not, of course, that tribal legend in either case will indicate more than a slender portion of the truth. There would have been no mechanical transfer of cultures from one place to another; if many formative ideas reached the "Azanians" from the north, they in turn would have changed and modified them, in applying them, into something essentially their own. Engaruka may have had some parentage of technique with Ethiopia; the one, we may safely assume, was as distinctive to its own place as the other. Something of the same adaptation and transformation would have taken place, here in East Africa, as occurred when Northern Europe borrowed the

* Hillside terracing had been a feature of southern Arabian civilization. "In one district," reported Haig of the Yemen in 1887, "the whole mountain side was terraced from top to bottom. Everywhere, above, below, and all around, endless flights of terraced walls . . ." Quoted in Hall, 1909.

ideas and techniques of Iron Age civilization from the Mediterranean. The one was related to the other; but it was not a simple copy.

5 *Who Were the Azanians?*

THE PERIOD BETWEEN A.D. 500 AND 1500 WAS THE MILLENNIUM OF maximum commerce between East Africa and the maritime countries of the Indian Ocean. It was also the millennium of maximum growth and development of Iron Age culture in eastern and Southern Africa.

Four great stimuli to social and economic growth may be detected from about A.D. 500 onwards: the southward spread of iron-using techniques with their consequent impulse to a more advanced agriculture; the emergence of larger and stronger tribal societies and the beginnings of urban settlement; the strengthening demand from the coast for ivory and iron and gold and other goods; and the expanding capacity of these settled peoples of the interior to supply this demand and to buy, in turn, imports from the coast.

Engaruka, coming at the end of this long, civilizing growth, shows something of its endurance and achievement. Supposing Leakey's population figure of "between thirty and forty thousand" — medieval Florence, to make a purely numerical comparison, achieved about sixty thousand — Fosbrooke has shown that the population of Engaruka could not have had less than eight thousand acres under cultivation of grain. Even in the somewhat better rainfall conditions of the past, no such population could ever have considered living where it did without a skilled knowledge of irrigation; and the presence of this knowledge at Engaruka is amply proven.

A full description of Engaruka must await further research. Yet enough is known to indicate that it sheltered a civilization which was well evolved for its time and type. Its agriculture was evidently capable of producing a regular food surplus, for the city was not only densely populated but had as well an important division of labor. There were numerous craftsmen. It was not a solitary affair; people had long traveled on well-established roads to north and south. Many of the village sites of old Tanganyika had as many as a hundred houses. Their grain growing is proved by grindstones and other tools. Their metal culture is shown by slag and broken tuyères. No iron implements have yet been found in these villages — they would, Fosbrooke considers, have long since oxidized away; but their pottery is plentiful and of relatively high standard.

Who were these people, and why did their growth come so roundly to an end? On the second of these questions, at least, we arrive on somewhat firmer ground. From about the fourteenth century East Africa began to suffer a long series of migratory invasions from the northward, mainly by pastoral nomads from the Horn of Africa — Galla, Somali, Masai, and others. They appear to have overwhelmed, subjected and finally dispersed these "Azanians" — although the supposed lateness of Engaruka shows that the process was a long one.

The more civilized, as on many occasions before and since, were ruined by the less. Nomads triumphed once again over peoples who were "soft and settled." "Whenever the two sides are equal in number and in strength," Ibn Khaldun would write at about this time, though not of East Africa, "those more used to nomad life will win." What proved true in Asia and Europe proved true in East Africa as well: technically more primitive, the nomads of the north were militarily stronger, both by the manner of their life and the method of their organization.

Thus the "Azanians," we may suppose, were organized whether

for peace or war on the "extended family" of Negro tradition, Bantu tradition; while the nomads were organized to move and fight in larger and more cohesive groups. Discussing how the pastoral (and nomadic) Bahima who invaded Uganda in or around the fourteenth century overwhelmed the agricultural (and settled) Bairu whom they found in possession of the land, Oberg has pointed out that the "unilateral *ekyika* or lineage" of the cattle-keeping Bahima "offered wider political and military co-operation than the relatively smaller Bairu *oruguanda* or extended family." Superiority of weapons apart, "nationalized" Europeans would later show the same kind of organizational superiority (however different in degree) over "tribalized" Africans. And Crazzolara, in his work on Lwoo migrations, has described how the southward migrations of this cattle-keeping people caused them, as they passed through the trials and dangers of leaving the upper Nile and entering unknown country, to broaden their clan groups until these vied in outnumbering one another, and to become so little exclusive that they could and did absorb many whom they conquered in their path.

All this helps to answer the first question, as to who the Azanians really were; though it does not help very much. They were not recent immigrants from the north. On the contrary, they were overwhelmed by such immigrants — by relatively barbarian Hamites like the Bahima, Lwoo, and Masai — and this over a period of several centuries, for the Bahima had reached the height of their power in Uganda by about 1600, while the Masai were not at the height of theirs, in Kenya and Tanganyika, until 1800-1850.

Whom did these barbarian nomads find as they swept southward? Along the coast the inhabitants were probably Swahili and their Bantu-speaking neighbors — those whom the Swahili would later bundle together under the generic term of Wa-Nyika and who would give a name, much later, to Tanganyika. In the hinterland the Azanians were probably Bantu-speaking peoples as well; although this does not settle their racial type. This racial type may have been Bushmanoid or Negroid; or, as seems more likely, it may already have shown a mixture and mingling of several African stocks. The only certainty is that the Azanians were a purely African people.

Their greater material culture, compared with that of the barbarians who overwhelmed them, is proved by many things, though by nothing more than by the cessation of their social and political growth. Engaruka grew and flourished; but it also fell into ruin.

Thus the settled, agricultural peoples of Africa have almost invariably treated their blacksmiths as an honored and "socially equal" caste, and often as a socially privileged caste. The Bantu-speaking kings of Congo whom the Portuguese found at the end of the fifteenth century were traditionally members of the blacksmiths' "mystery." Krige has pointed out that "in some parts of Zululand the profession of smith was not only secret, but ranked amongst the highest known, and was confined to one family." Among the Dogon of West Africa, says Griaule, "iron working is one of the most important crafts": ironworkers, as among other peoples of the Western Sudan, were an honored group apart. "In theory, these craftsmen own no land, nor do they receive any direct payment for the agricultural implements which they make or repair. At harvest time they are given a portion which constitutes their recompense." And it must have been much the same with the Azanians, and at Engaruka.

But the nomadic barbarians who overwhelmed the Azanians had no use for the settled civilization they found except to profit from its power of labor and production. They used the blacksmiths, of course, just as they used the growers of grain and doubtless the makers of pottery; but they set them in a subject posture.

Having conquered the settled Bairu, the Bahima in western Uganda established in their Kitwara empire at least seven "tradesman categories" among their new subjects; and among these the blacksmiths, the *abahesi*, were prominent. All these craftsmen paid tribute to their craftless "protectors," to whom, indeed, they stood in much the same semi-serf relationship as in early European feudalism. The parallels are often surprisingly close. Of the Batutsi ruling caste among the Banyarwanda of modern Ruanda — a bold and handsome people occupying something of the same position of dominant caste as the earlier Bahima had occupied among the Bairu — Maquet says that "they do no manual work and have leisure to cultivate eloquence, poetry, refined manners, and the subtle art of being witty and drinking hydromel with friends." Was the position of chivalry and of the troubadours so very different in medieval France?

The parallels would continue. On his Bairu *omutoizha*, the Bahima conqueror of the fourteenth or fifteenth century imposed a strict prohibition of intermarriage, though sometimes permitting himself a Bairu concubine. He refused to allow the Bairu to possess productive cows, and barred to the Bairu all positions of high official influence. The Bairu, says Oberg, "had no political status"; they paid "tribute in food and labour, and for this purpose the Bahima endeavoured to keep them in subjection." Would the attitude of European settlers in East Africa prove so very different?

This caste system gradually broke down among Bahima and Bairu, though it still exists nearby. The point is that it was imposed by a stronger but technically more primitive society on a weaker but technically more advanced society. The Somali, another group of Hamitic invaders further north, would behave in the same way; for them the Tumal blacksmiths whom they found would be useful but socially inferior. Craftsmen among the Hamitic Galla are held to be effeminate. In eastern Kenya, also subject to nomadic invasion from the north, blacksmiths are "serfs" — members of a "submerged class," says Huntingford; with the Suk people they are found only among poor agricultural peasants.

In this way, by barbarian invasion from the north, the Azanians were overwhelmed and their civilizing growth stultified and brought to an end. Had the fabric of their civilization been older and stronger, perhaps it might have absorbed and transformed its barbarian conquerors — just as Greece and Rome, in their day and their degree, had absorbed and transformed the barbarians who assaulted them. But the fabric in East Africa was new and fragile and relatively crude and simple. These rude shocks from the north, together with the cutting of the ocean trade by European intervention after 1500, closed the story of its growth and muffled, for many centuries, even the very fact of its existence.

Its traditions have survived here and there. The German missionary Rebmann, who was the first European to go among the Chagga people of Kilimanjaro, wrote in 1848 of their great care for "irrigation channels and entrenchments," and of their powerfully centralized social life. The nature of European occupation, after 1890, would destroy much valuable evidence; but here and there the records of thoughtful administrators bring a little of it to light. The Matengo people of southwestern Tanganyika, wrote Pike in 1938, "can cultivate incredibly steep hillsides and yet erosion is almost non-existent . . . The underlying principle of the system is that if a large volume of water can be broken into sufficiently small parts, it is controllable; and, accordingly as the rate of flow of each of these parts is reduced, erosion is eliminated." This principle which the Matengo had inherited or discovered so as to cultivate steep hillsides without erosion, Europeans would later apply in Africa as an invention of their own.

Trade with the coast also continued, though on a small scale. As late as 1824, at Mombasa, Reitz would tell of an annual fair that was held at Kwa Jomvu on the nearby mainland, noting that iron, ivory and cattle were the main objects of trade, and that Arab purchasers preferred the iron they could buy at this fair "to that of Sweden" — a remarkable echo of that earlier "iron of Sofala" whose virtues Edrisi had celebrated seven hundred years before.*

Yet it is only to the southward, in Rhodesia and Mozambique and the Transvaal, that the nature of this Azanian civilization — modified and changed once more by further migration and development in new circumstances — can be traced in any detail. And it is one of the ironies of history that this greatest flowering of the African Iron Age should have occurred, judging by its remains and monuments, not in the lands that fringed the Sahara and the sources of the Nile, but far into the southern distance.

There, on the high veld of southern Africa between the Zambezi and Limpopo, several thousand miles from Nile or Niger, Africa produced a contribution to the story of human growth that is unique and memorable, no matter from what point of view one may consider it.

* Sir John Gray has told the story in his valuable book, *The British in Mombasa 1824-26*. He adds, in a letter to the present writer, that he thinks the iron of the Kwa Jomvu fair was in fact antimony.

nine

The Builders of the South

There has been as much labour expended here as on the building of the Pyramids.

David Randall-MacIver:
overheard at Niekerk Ruins
in 1905

We have got 25 ounces of Gold and the manufacture of jewellery is even finer than the other lot . . . Old George dropped on to two of their hiding places and got about 6 lbs. weight in one and 3 lbs in the other . . .

Report to the
Ancient Ruins Company in 1895

1 "An Exceeding Great Country"

Beyond this country towards the interior," wrote Barbosa of the coast of Mozambique in 1517, "lies the great kingdom of Benametapa pertaining to the heathen whom the Moors call Kaffirs: they are black men and go naked save from the waist down." Later on, the Portuguese would make bold efforts to reach this inland kingdom as well as others of which they heard; meanwhile they were obliged to content themselves with coastal gossip.

They could also meet emissaries from the far interior, often wearing skins but eager for the purchase of cottons, camlets and silks that were found in the shops of Sofala, and "some, the most noble," tail-tasseled skins which trailed on the ground as token of state and dignity, and carrying "swords thrust into wooden scabbards, bound with much gold and other metals, worn on the left side, as with us . . ."

"They also carry assegais in their hands, and others carry bows and arrows of middle size . . . The iron arrowheads are long and finely pointed. They are warlike men, and some too are great traders."

Coastal gossip spoke of several kingdoms in the interior, but of that of Benametapa as the most powerful of all. "Fifteen or twenty days' journey inland is a great town called Zimbaoche, in which are many houses of wood and of straw. It pertains to the heathen, and the king of Benametapa often stays there; it is six days' journey thence to Benametapa. The road thereto goes inland from Sofala towards the Cape of Good Hope.

"In this town of Benametapa is the king's most usual abode, in a very large building, and thence the traders carry the inland gold to Sofala and give it unweighed to the Moors for coloured cloths and beads, which are greatly esteemed among them."

Now the great stone ruins of Zimbabwe in southeastern Rhodesia, since famous throughout the world, lie some two hundred fifty miles by crow's flight from the ancient port of Sofala. It is not impossible that "warlike men and traders" could have reached them in twenty-six days' journey from the coast. Barbosa, it is true, does not speak of great stone ruins; but other Portuguese would do so a few years later.

"In the middle of this country," says de Goes (who was born the same year, 1501, that Barbosa sailed the Indian Ocean for the first time), "is a fortress built of large and heavy stones inside and out . . . a very curious and well-constructed building, as according to report no lime to join the stones can be seen . . . In other districts of the said plain there are other fortresses built in the same manner, in all of which the king has captains . . . The king of Benametapa keeps great state, and is served on bended knees with great reverence." De Barros, writing at about the same time and doubtless using much the same coastal sources of information, speaks of a wall "more than twenty-five spans in width."

There is in fact nothing to show that Portuguese or other Europeans ever reached Great Zimbabwe; if they did, the records are lost or are still to be published. They knew in any case that there were many Zimbabwes. Speaking of the forts of the interior, de Barros points out that "the natives of the country call all these edifices Symbaoe, which according to their language signifies court, for every place where Benametapa may be is so called; and they say that being royal property all the king's other dwellings have this name . . ."

All this today is a good deal clearer. Many stone ruins exist in southern Africa; and several are of great size and skillful construction.

Many square miles are covered by hillside terracing no less extensive than anything the "Azanians" of East Africa could show.

Thousands of ancient mine workings are recorded — perhaps as many as sixty or seventy thousand.

Most of these ruins and remains are found within a wide segment of the south-central hinterland including Rhodesia, the southern fringe of the Belgian Congo, the western fringe of Mozambique, and the northern Transvaal. With more research this region of ancient building and mining may be seen to have been wider still. The king of Benametapa, Barbosa had told his sixteenth-century audience, "is the lord of an exceeding great country"; and it was little of an exaggeration.

Not that all these ruins and remains are the fragments of "one exceeding great country." The king of Benametapa — the Monomotapa — may have exercised direct and indirect power over much of what are now Mozambique and Rhodesia at one time or another. Whether he did or not, the various and widely scattered ruins of this "Zimbabwe Culture" are only the petrified record of a long and complex social and political experience. That experience comprises the history of Iron Age civilization in southern Africa. It covers a "building period" of many centuries.

In this long time of slow and yet successful material and social growth among peoples remotely isolated from the outside world, the ruins of Great Zimbabwe as they exist today may have had their beginnings much more than a thousand years ago, though as simpler structures long since vanished; and these simpler structures may in turn have had their foundations upon the debris of still older buildings of wood and straw and mud; and these earliest dwellings may have taken their rise as long ago as the fifth or sixth centuries A.D. But the last of the ruins of Zimbabwe — perhaps including the great walls that lift toward blue sky above the puzzled visitor's head — were probably completed as late as 1700-1750. Thus the walls of Great Zimbabwe, and the "occupational debris" on which they rest, may be taken to represent a more or less continuous Iron Age occupation through at least twelve centuries.

The exact chronology of all this building, majestic in its culmination, is still unknown, and may prove unknowable. But a few broad probabilities seem established. Great Zimbabwe itself, as a feudal-tribal capital of more or less dominant importance in this southern land, evidently flourished in the period between about A.D. 1250 and 1750. Mapungubwe, another important site-complex still further south, lying on the south bank of the Limpopo River in the Transvaal of today, was undoubtedly settled some time — and probably a long time — before A.D. 900, and not deserted until the eighteenth century; although more than one kind of people succeeded each another there. Large and finely wrought structures in the western part of Southern Rhodesia — notably at Dhlo Dhlo, Khami, Naletali — are probably of seventeenth or even eighteenth century date. Most of the hillside terracing and stone-founded dwellings of the eastern part of Southern Rhodesia (and the western border of Mozambique) — Niekerk, Inyanga, Penhalonga — are of the same or somewhat earlier date; though all of these, of course, may rest on previous settlements, and several of them certainly do.

Blurred at the edges though it is, such is the outline. Yet it is possible to look a little closer than this, and to clothe this outline with some of the detailed reality of human experience.

2 *Zimbabwe*

GREAT ZIMBABWE IS A GROUP OF STONE RUINS LYING ABOUT SEVenteen miles southeast of Fort Victoria and a few miles from the main road which now links Salisbury, capital of Southern Rhodesia, with Johannesburg in South Africa. These ruins have their fame and reputation, among many ruins in Rhodesia, for their skillful putting together and their large conception, their tall girdling walls and towers, their rounded gateways, their evidence of power and unity and ordered settlement.

Two of its buildings stand out among the rest. Known as the "Acropolis," the first of these was a strong defensive structure on a hilltop. The second, known variously as "the temple" or "the elliptical building," rests on the plain beneath. All are made of local granite, of flat bricklike stones chopped skillfully from wide "leaves" of exfoliated rock which nature has slipped away from the parent hillsides. And the whole complex of buildings, whether in the valley or perched on the bouldered *kopje* overhead, has a dignity and strength of purpose in this lonely place that is irresistibly impressive.

At first glimpse these walls and terraced battlements will seem, as they seemed to stray explorers seventy and eighty years ago, the image of ancient structures in Mediterranean Europe. The impression of power and skill remains on being looked at closer, but the exotic image disappears. The more one ponders on these buildings the more they appear to have sprung from the native craftsmanship and ingenuity of peoples who worked here without any outside architectural influences to guide or help them. Everywhere these structures are marked with an originality which seems to owe nothing to the rest of the world.

It is not only that the walls abut on one another without bonding; this had been a common feature of Azanian stonework, for example, and may be seen as far north as the walls of Jebel Uri in Darfur. It is rather that the fortress buildings seem to have grown naturally from the defensive convenience of huge boulders; and that the dwellings, where foundations remain, seem to have grown just as naturally from an attempt to build in stone what formerly had been built in mud and straw.

All around, after all, would have lain — as they still lie — great "leaves" of naturally split granite; it would have required little effort or invention, once the need and the incentive for strong and conspicuous buildings were present, to break these into good stone "bricks," or to split away more "leaves" by building fires on the bare rock. Iron Age concentrations of power in this country, beginning here in the first millennium A.D. at much the same time as they began in the Western Sudan, would infallibly provide both need and incentive — both the need for defense against rivals and the incentive for display of wealth and power. Here again there would occur the same general processes of power concentration — with the coming of metal technology and the social stresses, ambitions, and ideologies this would help to promote — as in other parts of the world.

With the passage of time, the simple piling of stone upon stone was elaborated into rounded gateways, timber-linteled doors, stepped recesses, closed passageways, platforms offering the slim silhouette of single-standing monoliths, and other features peculiar to Zimbabwe. And at last the girdling walls grew taller and stronger until they achieved the compelling power that may still be seen; the whole "elliptical building" being some three hundred feet long and two hundred twenty feet broad, with girdling walls reaching to a height of thirty feet and a thickness of twenty feet.

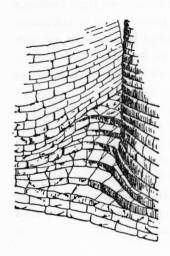

Steps at Great Zimbabwe

These girdling walls surrounded the dwelling of the ruler of a powerful state. They were topped with a chevron decoration copied from coastal examples, seen by the traders and travelers and king's messengers who went back and forth across the plains and mountains to the ports of the Indian Ocean, or possibly invented on the spot. They guarded the mysteries of those who smelted gold and other minerals. Other walls nearby enclosed tall soapstone bird-gods and the temple homes of divine rulers whose powers of government had also grown with the years, but whose peoples had "chosen them to govern with equity." They towered above clay and stone settlements, clustered near, which became more numerous as the artisan and trading population multiplied. They imposed their reputation on coastal visitors whose strange reports would travel as far as maritime Europe, and suggest to learned gentlemen in libraries that the throne and seat of Prester John himself, legendary lord of inland Africa, was found at last.

The reports were embroidered; and yet, on reflection, by little enough. Though not the Prester John of a lost Christendom, the Monomotapa was a religious figure of no mean order. He was scarcely the lord of inland Africa; but he was certainly the lord of a state power, of a tribal-feudal organization, whose authority would have reached at its apogee across a land that was not much smaller than the Mali which his near-contemporary, Kankan Musa, had inherited. His court would not have glittered like the courts of the Holy Roman Empire, nor even like those of Plantagenet England; and his servants were illiterate. But it could have seemed neither poor nor unimposing to most of the men of his day, at least in Africa and Europe.

No Europeans reached it, so far as the record goes. None came here from the outside world but licensed traders and travelers from the coast, Africans and Arabs, who left no words of their own; and the manners of this inland civilization, its gods and customs, thoughts, beliefs and social growth, revolved only within their own native orbit. There was great development, but never a revolutionary break with tradition; no outside cultures intruded here and crossed their influence fruitfully with what they found. Yet the true greatness of achievement of these builders of the south may best be measured, no doubt, by this very isolation in which they dwelt.

3 *King Solomon's Mines?*

Europeans who first saw Zimbabwe could not believe that the forbears of the Africans they knew — the "natives" whose land they were inspecting and preparing to invade — had built these stone walls and massive places.

Prospectors, hunters, pioneers, they took Zimbabwe and its many companion ruins, casually reported up and down the land, for a strange marvel, erected by an unaccountable but obviously remote history in a country where the men they knew built solely in mud and straw. Only Selous, wisest of them, would afterwards insist that Africans even at the end of the nineteenth century still continued, if in lowlier form, this art of building in stone.

But all the others followed Renders, a wandering hunter who had seen Zimbabwe in 1868 and thought little or nothing more about it; or else they followed Mauch, a German geologist who reached Zimbabwe in 1872 and declared upon returning that this was obviously the work of a civilized people in high antiquity — pioneering in this forgotten land as Europeans were pioneering now.

This fortress on a hill, said Mauch, was no doubt a copy of King Solomon's temple on Mount Moriah, while the great building in the valley — the "elliptical building" — was no less surely a copy of the palace which the Queen of Sheba had inhabited while staying in Jerusalem in the tenth century B.C.

Little was added to this traveler's tale until 1890 when an invading British column from Bechuanaland camped within seventeen miles of Great Zimbabwe and became aware of its gray challenge in the solitude of the veld. Driving into a Mashona people whom they believed entirely savage, these pioneers — or those few of them who bothered with more than the job in hand — had no difficulty in believing Mauch's version of Zimbabwe origins. "Today then," wrote one of them in 1891, the year when an imperial Britain took effective possession of Mashonaland and Matabeleland (Southern Rhodesia of the near future), "the Englishman is in the land of Ophir — opening afresh the treasure house of antiquity." Before many years were out, he went on, "we may expect to see the image of Queen Victoria stamped on the gold with which King Solomon overlaid his ivory throne, and wreathed the cedar pillars of his temple." An agreeable vision, if somewhat wide of the facts; and it long persisted. Indeed, it still persists.

There was some excuse for it. The Portuguese, borrowing legend from the Arabs, had linked the gold of Sofala with the gold of Ophir; and the version had become so current in Europe as to give Milton one of the kingdoms that the fallen angel, in *Paradise Lost*, shows to Adam. The pioneers of 1890, of course, hoped to find gold; and Ophir must be somewhere in this world. Moreover, they and their kind could not believe — the difficulty remains with them today — that these ruins were in any way related to a native population whom they despised as primitive and savage.

This attitude would be strengthened by wars of conquest against the Matabele and Mashona. "The theory of shooting a nigger on sight," declared a correspondent of the *Matabele Times*, arguing for an end to the policy of shoot-on-sight, "is too suggestive of the rule of Donnybrook Fair to be other than a diversion rather than a satisfactory principle. We have been doing it up to now, burning kraals because they were native kraals, and firing upon fleeing natives simply because they were black." It was a little much to expect these pioneers to consider that such trash — or any of its neighbors — could have built Zimbabwe, the most imposing monument to a vanished glory that many of them could ever have seen; and the "legend of Ophir," naturally enough, came to firm establishment.

To later archeology this "legend of Ophir" would bring sad disaster. For if Mashonaland had given Solomon his gold, it might reasonably be expected to continue giving it to others who should come and seek. By 1900 some one hundred fourteen thousand gold claims were officially registered in Mashonaland and Matabeleland; more than half of these, it is said, were pegged on the obvious sites of ancient workings. This destroyed much of the gold-working evidence, so far as implements and smelting methods were concerned; but it was nothing to the ravage that fell on the ruins themselves.

An explorer called Posselt began the ransacking of the ruins as early as 1888. Though with little success in finding gold, he discovered some of the large soapstone "birds" for which Zimbabwe would later become famous, and noted, in so doing, that his bearers regarded the ruins with awe, for they "sat down and solemnly saluted by clapping their hands."

The main gate at Zimbabwe, Posselt found, was in a state of decay, a portion having fallen in. "We climbed on to the wall and walked along this until we reached the conical tower. The interior was covered with dense bush: tall trees towered above the undergrowth, and suspended from them were masses of 'monkey rope,' by means of which we lowered ourselves and entered the ruins. I could not find any trace of human remains or of any implements, nor was the hope of discovering any treasure rewarded with success. Profound silence brooded over the scene."

Others eagerly followed. In 1895 a prospector called Neal, together with two hopeful investors of Johannesburg, the Honorable Maurice Gifford and Mr. Jefferson Clark, formed an enterprise they called The Ancient Ruins Company Limited, securing for it a concession from the British South Africa Company to "exploit all the ancient ruins south of the Zambesi." The company was wound up in 1900, evidently by order of Cecil Rhodes; and in 1902 the newly formed Legislative Council of Southern Rhodesia passed an ordinance for the protection of ancient ruins. "But the damage done," comments Schofield, "was immense, for everything except the gold was treated in a most reckless manner."

Neal said in 1902 that he had personally explored forty-three ruins out of a total of one hundred forty that he knew to exist; others had doubtless done the same, or much the same. And although in five years the company recovered no more than five hundred ounces of gold — a tidy weight, however, in museum objects — nobody will ever know how many pieces of worked gold were found by others as well as by Neal, melted down, and lost forever; or how much other damage was done. Only the treasures of Mapungubwe, found by scientists in the northern Transvaal some forty years later and carefully preserved, would show the full splendor of what these "explorers of Ophir" discovered and destroyed.

Against this background — and with archeology a less developed, experienced, and systematic discipline than it has since become — it was hard to know what to think of the origin of the buildings themselves; and the difficulty was increased because it was known that the Matabele, at any rate, were invading newcomers to this land. Two schools of thought emerged: the "Phoenician" and the "medieval."

Zimbabwe, thought the first school, had "a minimum age of three millenniums": there were two main periods of building, the earlier being Sabaean of from 2000 to 1000 B.C., and the later being Phoenician "somewhat anterior to 1100 B.C. down to some time before the Christian era." This school of thought reflected the "land of Ophir" pioneers and was resolutely sure that no "natives" had ever taken a hand in this building of a civilization. It evolved many variations; and there is scarcely a people of high antiquity whose influence was thought to have been absent here at one time or another.

"To the glory of the Motherland beyond the seas," writes in 1950 Mr. B. G. Paver, latest representative of this imaginative school of thought, "aliens in Africa are building a new dominion." He means the white settler communities of British Central Africa, hoping for "Dominion status" in the years ahead. "As they build and mine, and dream and die, can it be that history is using them to repeat itself? Did an ancient Motherland beyond the seas provide sons who, as aliens in Africa, mined and built and were overwhelmed? Is this the path that we should follow beyond the vale of time?"

Come off it, replies — and replied — the other school, you ignore the evidence under your very noses. These ruins are the ruins of a native African civilization. They were built by the lineal ancestors of African peoples over whom you rule, and from an earliest date that is not so remote in the past — not more remote, perhaps, than times when Saxon England faced invasion by Norsemen and Normans.

4 Verdict from the Evidence

THIS OTHER SCHOOL OF THOUGHT — THE ARCHEOLOGICAL AND SCIENtific school — first made itself heard through David Randall-MacIver, an Egyptologist who examined the stone ruins of Southern Rhodesia in 1905 on behalf of the British Association. He concluded that those at Great Zimbabwe and others of their kind were African in origin and medieval or post-medieval in date, basing this on an investigation of seven sites from which no object, as he said, had been obtained by himself or others "which can be shown to be more ancient than the fourteenth or fifteenth centuries."

In the architecture, "whether military or domestic, there is not a trace of Oriental or European style of any period whatever"; while "the character of the dwellings contained within the stone ruins, and forming an integral part of them, is unmistakably African," and "the arts and manufactures exemplified by objects found within the dwellings are typically African, except when the objects are imports of well-known medieval or post-medieval date."

This verdict, returned by the first qualified archeologist to examine the ruins (the first, moreover, to have shown respect for stratigraphical levels), was met with a good deal of anger and denial by the "Phoenician" school. Such was the controversy that raged — and so explosive the political and racialist implications it concealed — that the British Association decided a quarter of a century afterwards on a second expedition. This was entrusted to the skillful hands of Dr. Gertrude Caton-Thompson, whose eventual report, *The Zimbabwe Culture*, confirmed with gemlike clarity and wit, as well as great archeological insight, what MacIver had said before her. It is indeed the classic of sub-continental archeology for periods relatively recent and remains, if not the last word on Zimbabwe and its towers, the indispensable guide to all who wish to understand the subject in its details.

"Examination of all the existing evidence gathered from every quarter," Caton-Thompson concluded, "still can produce not one single item that is not in accordance with the claim of Bantu origin and medieval date." Discussing this elsewhere in her book, she adds: "I am . . . definitely unable to fall in with the oft-repeated and compromising suggestion that Zimbabwe and its allied structures were built by native workmen under the direction of a 'superior' alien race or supervisor." There might be foreign influence: the conical tower might reflect a wish to imitate coastal minarets, while the chevron-work along the girdling walls had many Arab or other Islamic forerunners;* but the builders were African, and the polity they belonged to was African no less.

This explanation of Zimbabwe has withstood all serious questioning since Caton-Thompson reached it. In the light of later evidence, it appears subject to revision only in two respects: radiocarbon dating has recently pushed back the probable early limit of "building settlement" to a point that is somewhat before the beginning of the European medieval period; while the type of people who first built here — on skeletal evidence from Mapungubwe that may be inferential for early Zimbabwe as well — may have differed from the Bantu-speaking peoples who built the later structures, and whose lineal descendants are well known today. If they did so differ, as at Mapungubwe, they differed in the sense of being a more emphatic mingling of Hottentot and Negro than the Bantu-speaking peoples of a later time; they were not the less native to Africa.

The broad conclusions reached by Caton-Thompson thirty years ago — as by Randall-MacIver before her and other workers in this field, like Summers, after her — rest on tangible evidence from many sides: on datable Chinese porcelain, on beads from India and Indonesia which are also, to some extent, datable, and on other objects of foreign importation. They rest on the probable course of evolution of indigenous stone-building which advanced slowly from the conception of a mud and straw hut to its imitation in stone, and thence onward to the tall structures of Zimbabwe. They agree with what is known of Bantu custom and religion. They draw, usefully though less certainly, on the little

---

* I have myself seen such ornamentation as far afield as the girdling walls of the tenth century ruined city of Karakhoja in Chinese Turkestan.

that the Portuguese could learn from African and Arab coastal travelers.

"In the midst of this country," de Barros had recorded in 1552, writing from hearsay, "there is a square fortress, of masonry within and without, built of stones of marvelous size, and there appears to be no mortar joining them. The wall is twenty-five spans in width, and the height is not so great considering the width. Above the door of this edifice is an inscription, which some Moorish merchants, learned men, who went thither, could not read, neither could they tell what the character might be. This edifice is almost surrounded by hills, upon which are others resembling it in the fashioning of the stone and the absence of mortar, and one of them is a tower more than twelve fathoms high." A fanciful description, perhaps, and full of errors; and yet unquestionably a description of the Zimbabwe which survives today, although the walls were almost certainly rebuilt in a later time. The *square* shape of the fortress is embroidery, of course, for there is no evidence that any such ever existed in Rhodesia; while the inscription that is mentioned here was nothing more, perhaps, than decoration such as the chevron frieze which topped the later walls.

The evidence, it will be noticed, is much stronger than any yet discovered in the hinterland of Kenya and Tanganyika, or in Uganda; and this is precisely because it includes much evidence from the coastal trade. The commerce which channeled Chinese porcelain and other Indian Ocean goods into southern Africa appears not to have succeeded further north; if it did, its traces have yet to be found there. But here in the south the evidence is stronger, just as the buildings of this southern iron age are more impressive, technically advanced, and suggestive of greater social power and unity than the stone ruins of East Africa.

There is surely more than an accidental link between this much more extensive trade and these much more extensive ruins. "The trade connexion with India," remarked Caton-Thompson, "is undoubtedly strong — indeed, I believe it to be the primary stimulus which led to the development of the indigenous Zimbabwe culture." These men of war and great traders from the interior, as Barbosa called them, must have grown powerful in their Iron Age civilization not only because they understood the use of iron, but also because they had many trading links with the outside world. They flourished and advanced, that is, under the same kind of stimulus as the ocean trade gave to the coast — or the trans-Saharan trade gave to the old Sudan.

One may ask why this greater elaboration and concentration should have occurred here in the hinterland of south-central Africa, and not in the north that was geographically nearer to India and Arabia. The full answer, no doubt, will be complex when archeologists and historians have worked it out; but almost certainly this answer will base itself on one great difference between the two regions — copper and gold were plentiful in the southern region, but almost nonexistent in the northern. Yet gold and copper were what the early traders prized from Africa, as the early records repeatedly show. They would always have reached far inland for it. In so doing, these traders exercised on the south-central hinterland an influence for change and growth that was absent, or much weaker, in the north. This Iron Age civilization of south-central Africa was above all, one may think, a mining civilization; and its course and development were linked with the fortunes of the coastal trade.

Just how far the myriad mine workings of the ancient hinterland were dug and controlled by the builders and ruling peoples of these forts and palaces and stone-built settlements remains an open question. This relation between mines and buildings is indeed the great central question of the Rhodesian Iron Age still to be resolved, and may hold the key, if it can be resolved, to a detailed chronology for the sixth to sixteenth centuries A.D. There are many difficulties. Thus Wagner showed in 1929 how the limits of ancient mine workings — whether for gold, copper, tin, or iron — are more extensive than the known limits of the ancient ruins; and it happens that Great Zimbabwe itself is linked with no mine workings, though it has yielded plenty of evidence of smelting and working in metals. (See map on page 276.)

But the importance of these old mine workings, spread in their thousands across the southern hinterland from the fringe of the Belgian Congo (the Katanga copper belt of today) to Natal and Bechuanaland, remains central for the whole growth and flowering of the Zimbabwe culture. The hammer of its iron-shod picks and the glow of its charcoal-fired ovens are as much the essential background to medieval Rhodesia as were railways to the growth of nineteenth-century Europe. By the eighteenth century, if not a good deal earlier, copper bars and H-shaped ingots were familiar currency here; these peoples lived and moved, within the possible limits of their time and place, fully in an age of metals.

Who were these peoples? If an exact chronology still eludes them, there is now a broad agreement among most authorities not only on the sequence of events but also on the kind of peoples who experienced them.

5 *Medieval Rhodesia*

THE FOUNDATIONS OF ZIMBABWE, CATON-THOMPSON THOUGHT, "BE-long to some period between about the ninth century and some time during or after the thirteenth century when . . . the porcelain shows the place to have been in full occupation." But the first building, she thought, might possibly be a century or two older than the earlier date. The early growth of the Zimbabwe culture, therefore, belongs to the same period when El Mas'udi, writing of the coastal kingdoms of the Zanj, described "the land of Sofala which produces gold in abundance and other marvels."

To this opinion a series of radio-carbon tests has now brought confirmation and a slight modification. Carried out in Chicago in 1952 and again in London in 1954, these tests were made on two fragments of drainage timber recovered from the base of one of the walls of the "elliptical building" and have yielded dates between A.D. 591 (plus or minus one hundred twenty years) and A.D. 702 (plus or minus ninety-two years). This dating is not quite so neat and satisfactory as it may sound, however, partly because its limits are disconcertingly wide — between the fifth and late eighth centuries at their widest — and partly because the wood in question is of tambootie, a tree of great longevity. The builders may have used it a good deal later than its actual period of growth; or they may have used it in association with stone walls after others had already used it for earlier structures which have disappeared.

Excavations at Zimbabwe accordingly continue. In 1958 Summers and Robinson were digging into the foundations of the "Acropolis" and the "elliptical building" in order to discover, if they could, whether the "ash stratum" or "occupation soil" which is known to underlie these buildings, or some of them, betokens another and distinctive occupation. Caton-Thompson had left this question open, though inclining to the view that the "ash stratum" had been created by the stone-builders themselves, perhaps in the eighth or ninth centuries when they were putting up their first structures; but work in 1958 seemed after all to indicate an earlier occupation by another people.

There is thus a fair assurance that Iron Age people of one kind or another were living on the site of Great Zimbabwe in the sixth or seventh centuries and perhaps earlier. They may have appeared there a good deal earlier, of course, because we know from Clark's work at the Kalambo Falls that this southern plateau had entered its Iron Age early in the first millennium A.D. The

THE RUINS OF THE OLD SOUTH

Kalambo site would not have been the only Iron Age settlement
of early times; and although there are no known ironworkings
near Zimbabwe itself, the processes of growth and migration
which iron technology helped to set in motion would almost
certainly have carried people into occupation of new lands. Another hypothesis would be that the earliest — pre-stone building —
occupation of Zimbabwe was by Hottentot or other southern
African people who had yet to learn the use of metals.

A little is known of the movement of peoples across south-
central Africa in medieval and post-medieval times. How does this

slender historical knowledge fit together with the archeological evidence? Not very well, so far. But most authorities seem now agreed that three main periods of occupation at Zimbabwe can be detected: the pre-Monomotapa period, the Monomotapa period (first Shona), and the Mambo period (second Shona).

The first of these periods comes to an end in the twelfth century; but it goes back into a vague beginning — with the fourth century generally regarded, at the moment, as the earliest possible date. This is the period of what Summers has called the Rhodesian Iron Age A.1 people, who introduced the use and working of iron — techniques that came, probably like themselves, from the north — and settled in the places where they or their successors would build in stone.

These peoples were perhaps the first Bantu-speaking inhabitants of the Rhodesian plateau — the Batonga, as the Sotho people of today call their ancestors; and there is some reason to believe that they represented an early southward-thrusting wave in that great movement and multiplication of peoples which, with the coming of iron among other things, gave the forerunners of its present populations to most of continental Africa. How early they appeared, what exactly were their racial types, how closely they resembled the early Iron Age dwellers at the Kalambo Falls — whether, for example, they drove off the people who made the "ash stratum" at Zimbabwe or made it themselves — these questions are unanswered, and perhaps unanswerable.

But the movement of migration, predominantly from the north or northwest, continued through the centuries. Around the twelfth century a people of Shona stock, whose ruler had the title of Monomotapa, came southward from the Zambesi and occupied Zimbabwe. Archeologists know them as the Rhodesian Iron Age B.1 people; and their dominance of Zimbabwe appears to have lasted until about 1450, when they are thought to have deserted the site. About half a century later the "Acropolis" at Zimbabwe

is thought to have been reoccupied by Shona people; and somewhere around 1600 the Rozwi and Venda, also peoples of Shona
stock, undoubtedly built imposing forts and stone settlements at
Naletali, Dhlo Dhlo, Regina, Khami and elsewhere. Further to
the south, beyond the Limpopo, they probably occupied Mapungubwe and its many nearby sites.

These Rozwi grew strong. By 1700 their Mambo, or ruler,
whose name was Changamire, invaded the state of the Monomotapa and destroyed it. And soon after 1725 these successful invaders refashioned the buildings at Great Zimbabwe, probably enlarged them, and left them much as they may be seen today. Then
Nguni invaders from the south, a century later, destroyed this
state, completing the destruction of this southern civilization in
much the same way as barbarian Hamites had already destroyed
the earlier and technically simpler civilization of the Azanians in
East Africa.

This brief tale of invasion and reinvasion will mislead if taken
too literally. What is known of its social background — and
Mapungubwe has thrown on that a flood of light — shows that
this was nothing like a mechanical succession of one whole people
after another. It was little more than the succession, perhaps, of
one strong ruling group after another. Each ruling group and its
armies, invading and conquering and settling, no doubt took
wives from the conquered and rapidly merged with the conquered
people.

Though ruled by different immigrants, these settlements of the
southern plateau (of Rhodesia and its neighboring lands) may be
thought to have had great continuity of social life. Perhaps all
that happened, in anthropological terms, is that peoples of an
emphatically Hottentot type were gradually displaced by peoples
of an emphatically Negroid type. In social terms these slowly
evolving peoples of the Rhodesian Iron Age passed through
steady processes of growth whose physical embodiment remains,

for our inspection, in the advance of their architecture. In economic terms their progress was related to the steady enlargement of trade with the coast; and the principal form this took was an export of metals and ivory against an import of cotton goods and luxuries. Far from remaining "unmoved, in primitive savagery," while "all the pageant of history swept by," these peoples undoubtedly embarked on active and successful development.

This is where the matter largely rested when the hill of Mapungubwe was climbed at last.

6 The Golden Burials
of Mapungubwe

THE FINDS AT MAPUNGUBWE ARE IMPORTANT FOR TWO REASONS: they were rich in skeletal material and in gold and other objects, and since no Ancient Ruins Company had plundered here, nearly all were undisturbed and could be examined where they lay.

A small "table mountain" of rough sandstone precipitous on every side, the hill of Mapungubwe is only one of many such hills amid the blue and ocherous solitudes of the northern Transvaal. It lies just south of the Limpopo River, which divides the modern states of South Africa and Southern Rhodesia, near a ford through this slow river that may be used without difficulty for ten months of the year. It faces to the northward where the ruins of Great Zimbabwe, rather less than two hundred miles to the northeast by north, stand beyond the broad horizons of the veld.

Even today this is wild and barely settled country. When the surprising finds of Mapungubwe came to light over a quarter of a century ago, most of it was scarcely prospected. Elephant and lion roamed and foraged here, and many of the "farms" were used only for a few weeks' shooting every year. White men of this uncharted country, mostly of Boer stock, had long heard tales of a "sacred hill" where unknown forerunners of the Venda people of the country were said to have buried their treasures. One of these white men, gone native forty years before, was even said to have found and climbed the sacred hill.

In 1932 a farmer-prospector called van Graan decided to find and climb it if he could. He knew this would be difficult, for the people of the country had always thought of the hill of Mapungubwe as taboo. For them it was "a place of fear": even after whites had found it — as Fouché would record — Africans "would not so much as point to it, and when it was discussed with them they kept their backs carefully turned to it. To climb it meant certain death. It was sacred to the Great Ones among their ancestors, who had buried secret treasures there."

Van Graan, who had with him his son and three other men, at last found an African who gave away the long-kept secret. He pointed out the hill — a hill about a hundred feet high and a thousand feet long — and also a concealed way to climb it, a narrow "chimney" in the cliffside that was masked by trees. The explorers chopped a path through thorn and scrub to the foot of this chimney, and saw when they came to it that vanished dwellers on Mapungubwe had cut small holes inside it, facing one another, as though for the crossbars of a ladder. They went up this cleft as well as they could and climbed out to the summit of the hill; and here they found themselves faced by a low breastwork of stones as well as by large boulders balanced on smaller ones, as though ready to be thrust over on intruders who should try to come that way.

They wandered over the hill and saw that its flat and rather narrow summit was littered with broken pottery. When they scuffled in its loose sandy soil they turned up beads and bits of iron and copper. But they were lucky, and so was history. Only a few weeks earlier a cloudburst had washed out a layer of topsoil here and there. In one of these newly eroded places the elder van Graan saw something that glittered yellow. He picked it up and said that it was gold.

Fouché has told the story. "An excited search now started, and soon the members of the party were finding gold beads, bangles and bits of thin gold plating. The next day" — the first day of 1933 — "the party continued their search, scratching over the loose soil with their knives. They found large pieces of plate gold, some of them shaped. These were the remains of little rhinoceroses which had consisted of thin plate gold tacked by means of little gold tacks on to some core of wood or other substance which had perished. Solid gold tails and ears, beautifully made, had likewise been tacked on to these figures. Presently they came upon the remains of a skeleton, which was dug out carefully; but the skull and most of the bones crumbled to dust on being exposed to the air."

Tempted by all this — and the gold they recovered from this burial, in plate and beads and ornaments, weighed as much as seventy-five ounces — the five explorers at first decided to keep it and say nothing. "This," as Fouché says, "was a most critical moment in the history of Mapungubwe." Happily the van Graans were troubled, and young van Graan, who had studied at Pretoria as Fouché's pupil, soon decided to tell his old master about the finds and send him some of them.

Fouché in turn sent these specimens to Pearson, deputy master of the Royal Mint at Pretoria, who reported them as gold of great purity. What was much more, they were the first wrought gold objects ever to be found in South Africa: and their archeological importance, both for South Africa and for the whole problem of Zimbabwe, was manifestly great. Professor van Riet Lowe at once went out and gave the site a preliminary inspection, and inquiries were set in train to find the other three men who had been with the van Graans. These inquiries were successful; all of the gold and other objects they had taken were safely recovered.

Meanwhile van Riet Lowe reported that the summit of the hill could not have less than some ten thousand tons of soil, "most of which has every appearance of having been artificially transported from the surrounding countryside." Here was a site of obviously major importance; and it was practically intact. Thereupon the Union government of the time acted with commendable promptitude and acquired from its absentee owner the "farm" of Greefswald on which Mapungubwe was located. The University of Pretoria was entrusted with responsibility for investigations at Mapungubwe, and these investigations were declared to be of national importance. Later Union governments would show less interest in the matter.

All this was the kind of rare and illuminating luck that archeologists need from time to time; and the first find of a skeleton was to be, in fact, only a small beginning. Working on his own in 1934, one of the excavators, van Tonder, uncovered an extensive grave area and was able to hand to scientific judgment a large quantity of gold and other metal objects as well as the fragments of twenty-three skeletons — the first fully authenticated and more or less fully preserved "royal burial ground" of pre-European times in southern Africa. One of these skeletons was associated with another seventy ounces of gold in various forms, and a third had its legs "wreathed in over a hundred bangles constructed of coiled wire. Several pieces of beautifully worked gold plating were also found, as well as about twelve thousand gold beads."

The results of work on this site — and twenty other occupation sites were noted to east and west of Mapungubwe along the south bank of the Limpopo — were published in a handsome volume in 1937. Thereafter, or at any rate until 1955, a strange silence appears to have fallen upon the whole question of Mapungubwe, site of black achievement in a land that is ruled by whites. And yet much remained to be done. Summing up at the end of his report and those of his colleagues, Fouché said that "up to June 1935 some two thousand tons of midden had been examined; but on and around the hill there are probably one hundred thousand tons of midden which have not been touched." And after noting the disparity of evidence between the skeletal material and the cultural material of pots and implements, he went on: "One conclusion at least emerges . . . The investigations at Mapungubwe must continue! . . . A dozen experts should be set to the task, each on his own side of it, in order to sweep away uncertainties and establish the true story of the rise and fall of the empire of the Monomotapa."

In fact one expert, not a dozen, was set to the task; but he, G. A. Gardner, continued stubbornly working on Mapungubwe and nearby until 1940, and with interesting results. Publication of these results then had to wait another fifteen years before anything could be generally known of them. In 1955 a brief article of Gardner's appeared in the *South African Archaeological Bulletin*. "It is naturally impossible here," Gardner commented, "to do more than give the barest outline of what we found and the conclusions derived therefrom, although details will eventually be given in the second volume of *Mapungubwe* — if it is ever published." This, it seems, may at last become possible in the near future: meanwhile Gardner has summarized his findings in a presidential address to the South African Archaeological Society.*

Yet for all this delay in securing publication of the evidence as well as difficulty in assessing the evidence itself — and this difficulty, as will be seen, is unexpectedly great — Mapungubwe has already proved of capital importance to a deeper understanding of

* Since I was unfortunately unable to read this before completing these pages, Captain Gardner has been kind enough to outline his conclusions in letters to me. This does not make him, of course, responsible for what I have written.

the nature and vicissitudes of Iron Age civilization in southern Africa. Here on this remote hilltop, whether in retirement or retreat, whether as victors or vanquished, whether as "lords of the southern frontier" of the old imperial state-system of the Monomotapa or as pioneering chieftains of another state with a separate history of its own, medieval rulers lived and were buried with pomp and veneration.

Their precise links with the Zimbabwe culture remain to be shown. Such links undoubtedly existed. Mapungubwe pottery types occur at many places across the plains to the northward, and some are akin to those of early Zimbabwe. Much more than a coincidental connection seems indicated by the quantity of gold interred with "royal corpses" on Mapungubwe being the same, or so nearly the same, as with one of those "gold burials" onto which "old George" had dropped in looting for the Ancient Ruins Company at Dhlo Dhlo to the northwest.

What in any case is certain is that men at Mapungubwe had evolved a complex Iron Age culture no different in its essence from similar phases of civilization elsewhere. Defended by their strong system of fortified *kopjes* to east and west, with the river on one side of them and the ranges of the Zoutpansberg on the other, these lords of Mapungubwe in their solitary splendor throw down a curious challenge to posterity.

7 *In the Old Transvaal*

W<small>HO EXACTLY WERE THESE PEOPLE WHO LIVED AND FLOURISHED</small> and suffered their disasters at Mapungubwe and nearby? It was in trying to answer this that Fouché and his colleagues found their troubles really began. Hitherto it had been generally assumed that all the mining and stone-building cultures of the southern plateau were the work of Bantu-speaking peoples whose physical origins and appearance had been pretty much the same as those of their descendants living today — Shona and Sotho, that is, of one branch or another. And the material evidence of pottery and objects in metal at Mapungubwe seemed to confirm this.

But Mapungubwe also produced much skeletal material; and the evidence of this skeletal material was roundly declared by the anthropologists to be in conflict with this simple view of the matter. These skeletons — and eleven out of the twenty-four recovered on the summit were found to be capable of investigation — showed a people with "great scarcity of Negro features" who represented, in Galloway's words, "a homogeneous Boskop-Bush [that is, Hottentot or near-Hottentot] population physically akin to the post-Boskop inhabitants of the coastal caves" of South Africa. They showed some Negro features, but far fewer than the skeletons of Bantu-speaking inhabitants of Rhodesia and South Africa today.

How to reconcile these conflicting judgments? It was rather as though the skeletons of William the Conqueror and his Norman knights had been taken from their tombs, and found to be skeletons of people of Saxon stock.

The controversy was not resolved. Either solution seemed impossible. To assume that the "royal burials" of Mapungubwe had been Bantu was to assume that physical types alter almost out of recognition within a few hundred years, which they undoubtedly do not. Moreover, the "royal burials" were made in a flexed position which Bantu-speaking peoples are not known to have used. Yet to take the other view and assume these burials to be Hottentot seemed no better; for this was to assume that Hottentots had enjoyed a metal-using culture at a much earlier date (and a much higher level of skill) than they were otherwise known to have done.

Even now, after Gardner's painstaking additions and correc-

Institut Français de L'Afrique Noire: Thomassey

Probable Site of the Last Capital of Ghana: An Excavated
House in the Ruins of the Muslim City at Kumbi Saleh

IFE
Brass Head (Height, 14½ inches)

BENIN
Ivory Pendant (Height, 6½
inches)

CENTRAL CONGO
Helmet Mask in Wood, Probably
Baluba

olden Death Mask of King Kofi
of Ashanti

Bushongo

CENTRAL CONGO: Wooden Goblets

*Musée Royal du
Congo Belge, Tervuren*

Ba-Kuba

Ba-Kuba

DAHOMEY
Shrine Figure Said to Have Been Made for the Cult of
Gu, God of Iron and War. It Is the Largest Piece of
Wrought-Iron Sculpture Known from Africa, Being 5
Feet 5 Inches High

Mr. Eliot Elisofon,
Musée de L'Homme, Paris

ETHIOPIA
The Tallest "Obelisk" at Axum

National Library of Ethiopia,
Archaeological Section

LWA ISLAND: The Old Castle

nganyika Government

KILWA ISLAND
Gateway to the Old Castle

Kilwa Island, "City of the Zanj": The Small Domed Mosque, with Pillar; and the Old Castle in the Background

KENYA: The Ruins of a House and Street at Gedi, Perhaps the Site of Old Malindi

KENYA: Great Mosque at Gedi, Built c. 1450

TANGANYIKA
An Ancient Well Still in Use

SONGO MNARA
The Old Palace: "a Mass of Chinese Porcelain . . ."

GREAT ZIMBABWE: The "Elliptical Building" and Nearby Ruins

GREAT ZIMBABWE: Outer Wall of the "Elliptical Building"

GREAT ZIMBABWE
The "Acropolis"

GREAT ZIMBABWE:
Soapstone Bird Figure

RUINS AT NALETALI
A Decorated Wall

Spearheads of the Zimbabwe Culture

Dr. Gertrude Caton-Thompson

Soapstone Bowl of the Zimbabwe Culture

NORTHERN RHODESIA
Iron Ingot of Old Africa

tions, solutions remain tentative. All that can be said with certainty is that the purely African origins of everything at Mapungubwe is established beyond doubt, while many direct links with the Zimbabwe culture of Southern Rhodesia are probable if not entirely certain.

Briefly, the picture is as follows: Stone Age peoples lived on Mapungubwe in Magosian times — a period in South Africa "shortly" before the discovery of agriculture but much earlier, of course, than the general period we are considering here. Others followed them. At a nearby site which he has named K.2 (Fouché called it Bambandyanalo), Gardner has established the prolonged occupation of a pastoral Stone Age people who were Hottentots or something like them, and who were perhaps beginning to know the use of copper though not of iron.* Much skeletal material found here has enabled Galloway to establish these K.2 people as "pre-Negro." They buried cattle in a ceremonial way as well as their own dead; and charcoal from the sixth of these "beast burials" of K.2 — considered by Gardner as relics of an old Hamitic cult and comparable with the beast burials of a neolithic culture of ancient Egypt† — has lately given a radio-carbon age of about a thousand years. The settlement at K.2 would therefore date to about A.D. 900, and perhaps a good deal earlier.

These Stone Age Hottentots, living in pastoral simplicity, were invaded by peoples from the north who knew both agriculture and the use of iron. This new population — intermarried, no doubt, with women of the K.2 people — moved their settlement for greater security to the top of Mapungubwe. Here one finds the evidence of a food-growing people for the first time. Holes were cut in the rock for pounding up meat and grain: hut platforms were built that were sometimes strengthened by stone revetment.

---

* This point is difficult: Hottentots smelted copper by ironworking technique, which they, including these people of K.2, presumably learned from their northern neighbors.

† Badarian, in Gardner's view.

People began carrying up soil from the neighboring countryside.

Now the great questions are who were these newcomers, and when did they come? On the first point it is generally agreed that they were successive offshoots of migration from the peoples who built and occupied Zimbabwe and its like: Sotho and Shona and Venda — all of them Bantu-speaking peoples whose descendants are numerous today (and include, for instance, the Basuto of Basutoland, the Mashona of Southern Rhodesia, and the Bavenda of the Transvaal*). Of these the last were the Bavenda, who were succeeded in the eighteenth century, it would seem, by another Hottentot population (these last being finally dispersed by the northward-driving Matabele in 1825).

In Gardner's view these last Hottentot invaders took over some of the cultural fabric of Venda life; they seized from the Venda the excellent gold ornaments that were later found by Fouché and his colleagues, and used these for ceremonial burials after their own fashion. Hence the skeletons were Hottentot all right, as was also the manner of burial; but the gold was Bantu.

Though founded on much care and labor, this particular solution of the anthropological riddle of Mapungubwe has yet to win acceptance; but there, in any case, the riddle must be left until fuller publication of Gardner's material or until further discoveries are made along the Limpopo between Mapungubwe and the sea.

Whatever ultimate conclusion may be reached, there is now substantial agreement that this metal-using culture of Mapungubwe, evolving through many centuries, was a southward extension of the central-southern African Iron Age — leaving for the future, perhaps, a final answer on the exact nature of the peoples who introduced and first developed an early civilization here; the exact nature, that is, of the African people of what archeologists

* The prefix Ba- is merely a plural — thus muntu, a man, and bantu, people; Muvenda, one Venda; Bavenda, many Venda.

have agreed to call the Rhodesian Iron Age A.1. But when did this southward extension begin?

Some have argued — basing themselves on calculation from tribal legend — that the first southward-moving Bantu migrations did not cross the Limpopo until late medieval times, perhaps later than the twelfth century, and have dated the beginnings of the Iron Age on the Limpopo from that time. Then the Sotho are thought to have gone south over the river into what is now the Transvaal in the middle of the fifteenth century, or thereabouts, and the Shona a little later. Afterwards there came the Rozwi-Venda dominion over the Zimbabwe culture, and these people in their turn also sent their migrants southward.

The later migrations may have occurred like that; the earlier ones almost certainly did not. There is something wrong with an explanation which supposes that Iron Age culture failed to reach the Limpopo until the twelfth century when it is known, beyond reasonable doubt, that it was well established a few hundred miles northward, over easily traveled plains, at least six or seven hundred years earlier. Moreover there is the evidence of the coastal settlements. Only four hundred miles of river separate Mapungubwe from the mouth of the Limpopo as it flows into the sea; and we know from Edrisi, writing in 1154, that in his day there were coastal settlements not far from the mouth of the Limpopo that were not only working iron but actually exporting it, and in considerable quantities. These coastal settlements would undoubtedly have had links with the hinterland behind them.

Excavations at Mapungubwe and its nearby sites, to sum up, have enriched and modified an earlier picture of Iron Age civilization in southern Africa without essentially changing it. One sees again that the Bantu-speaking peoples of Africa today are the product of migration, intermarriage, and multiplication over many centuries, remotely into the past; and it is this as much as anything else that is confirmed by the evidence from all these sites.

The only useful conclusions to be drawn, so far as the origins of most of the present Africans of southern Africa are concerned, are that their ancestors evolved from a mingling of indigenous pre-Negroid stocks with successive waves of Negroid migration from the north; that these migrations became important at least fifteen hundred years ago; and that they were numerous and powerful, along the banks of the Limpopo, from the beginning of our own millennium and probably a good deal earlier.

The peoples of southern Africa whom Europeans of the nineteenth century would describe had become dominant there, by all the evidence, some three or four hundred years before. But other African peoples, non-Negroid or Negroid, had preceded them; and these others, or some of them, had played a major part in the growth and development of early civilization. The crucial advances in technology — agriculture and the use of iron — had come slowly southward during the first millennium A.D. Those who brought them were possibly the lineal ancestors of the Bantu populations of today, or possibly they were men of a different stock, but through the years the Bantu established their supremacy. They took women from the peoples whom they found. They mingled and settled and fused. They fathered the men who would raise Zimbabwe and its towers. They buried their chiefs and heroes on the hill of Mapungubwe.

8 *Niekerk and Inyanga:*
Forts and Terraces

B EFORE DISCUSSING WHAT MANNER OF CULTURE AND CIVILIZATION this southern African Iron Age supported, there remains to be considered one other wide region of ancient ruins. These include the petrified remains of states and settlements on inland hills which rise from the coastal plain and climb to the great central plateau of Rhodesia, and which are no less interesting in their fashion than Zimbabwe or Mapungubwe.

Although the Portuguese were never at Zimbabwe or Mapungubwe, they undoubtedly had contact with inland states of the southeastern escarpment on the present Mozambique-Rhodesian border; it was from these, apparently, that successive Portuguese captains of Sofala had the greater part of their income. Something of the importance of these inland states, as initial producers or as intermediaries for trade with the far interior, can be measured from the amount of wealth that Sofala, the port of entry, could return — even though the getting of this wealth might fail to endure for long.

Thus the secretary of Philip II in 1607, Luiz de Figueiredo Falcão, who drew up an accountancy of Portuguese imperial wealth a century after trade with Sofala had become regular, says that the captaincy of Sofala was the most lucrative of all those established on the coasts of the Indian Ocean. It yielded even more than that of Ormuz on the Persian Gulf. The three-year captaincy of Sofala was reckoned as being worth two hundred thousand cruzados; while Ormuz was reckoned at one hundred eighty thousand, and even the captaincy of Malacca, drawing on the trade and loot of southeast Asia, at no more than one hundred thirty thousand. Writing in 1918, Dames gives the cruzado "at not more than 60 gr., that is 9s. 9d. of English money." This would make the Sofala captaincy worth about two hundred eighty thousand dollars in the sterling of 1918 — perhaps eight hundred forty thousand dollars or more today — a tidy income in taxfree wealth for three years' work. But the captain of Sofala could only take a cut (though a fat one) in the profits of the trade; the total profits must have been enormous. Here was fresh witness to the truth of earlier Arab reports on the wealth of southeast Africa in medieval times.

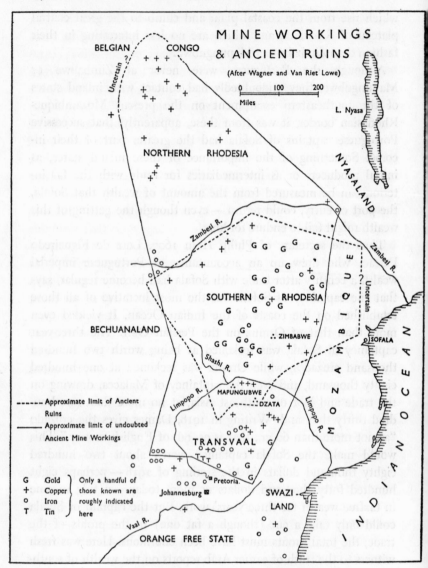

MINE WORKINGS
& ANCIENT RUINS

(After Wagner and Van Riet Lowe)

0   100   200

Miles

THE LAND OF MONOMOTAPA

The states through which this wealth was filtered, and by which it was partially created, lay in a broad band running from north to south — from the region of Sena on the lower Zambezi southward towards modern Swaziland and Natal. It would be natural to expect they had left something behind them; and the hope is not disapointed. (See map on page 261.)

Rumors of extensive ruins in these inland hills, lying on the western frontiers of Mozambique, began to filter back into South Africa soon after British occupation of Mashonaland in 1891; but it was not until 1905 that Randall-MacIver wrote the first detailed description of them. Northward from Penhalonga — where alluvial gold is still worked by the Manyika people (the Manhiqua of early Portuguese report) — MacIver found ruins that were different in style from those of Zimbabwe and other stone settlements further west, but were no less imposing. These many forts and dwellings, storepits, and terraced hillsides of eastern Rhodesia and western Mozambique are now known to extend across an area of two or three thousand square miles, and a proper inspection of Mozambique may yet reveal them as still more extensive. When MacIver saw them, just over fifty years ago, they had "never been reported upon, and seldom visited save by an occasional hunter."

On the hillsides of Niekerk and Inyanga, running for many miles north and south along this steep escarpment, he found what one is tempted to call a "southern Azanian" culture. Here again were the traces of a people who had known how to use stone and water for the conservation and irrigation of soil on steep hillsides, who had raised cattle and grown grain, understood the mining and smelting of several minerals, and traded much with the eastern countries of the Indian Ocean.

At Niekerk, for example, MacIver describes some fifty square miles of intensive terracing — he took the terrace walls for defensive structures, but later agreed with others who held that their purpose had been cultivation — that closely resembles, in its technique and intention, the terracing of Ethiopia and the Sudan. Here too the hills were terraced, with astonishing care, to within a few feet of their summits. Here too "there are few places within this large area where it is possible to walk ten yards without stumbling on a wall, a building, or an artificial heap of stones." And here too the craftsmanship in dry-stone building was admirably conceived.

At Inyanga, somewhat to the south of Niekerk and still in wild mountain country similarly terraced and built upon, he describes how a stream had been tapped at a point near its source, "and part of the water deflected by a stone dam." This, he says, gave the inhabitants "a high-level conduit, by which the water could be carried along the side of a hill and allowed to descend more gradually than the parent stream. There are very many such conduits in the Inyanga region, and they often run for several miles. The gradients are admirably calculated, with a skill which is not always equaled by modern engineers with their elaborate instruments. The dams are well and strongly built of unworked stones without mortar; the conduits themselves are simple trenches about one metre in depth . . ."

The "Azanian" echoes seem clear enough. These people of Inyanga had also had the custom — like those of Engaruka on the present Tanganyika-Kenya border — of building their huts or houses upon stone platforms banked against the hillside, yet with peculiarities of their own. Thus they had a common practice of making pits within these stone embankments; these pits they linked to the outside world with a low tunnel, about four feet high, building their dwellings on the tops of the embankments, around but above their pits. Early European judgments considered them "slave pits"; today the generally accepted view is that they were either for storing grain or for penning small livestock.

Partial excavation and reconsideration of earlier work, undertaken in 1951, has offered several keys to the dating of this vast meshwork of terrace cultivation and dry-stone fortress and dwelling place. Beneath these sites Summers has now reported traces of two cultures of the early Rhodesian Iron Age — of that Iron Age A.1 which saw the initial occupation of Zimbabwe by iron-using people soon after (or conceivably a little before) A.D. 500. These he has named Ziwa 1 and Ziwa 2, after one of the sites; and they make another contribution to the emergent picture whose beginnings can be traced, so far, most clearly at the Kalambo Falls.

Most of the ruins are much more recent. Thus at Niekerk "very little dating evidence was found in the ruins; but from a few beads from some four different sites it seemed probable that an eighteenth-century date is not unreasonable." Beads from ruins near Inyanga have suggested a somewhat earlier date; probably one is on safe ground in saying that the greater part of the surviving ruins was built and occupied over a period of two or three centuries before 1750 or thereabouts. There is evidence, as would be expected, of at least a trading link between these Niekerk-Inyanga ruins and those of Zimbabwe and others to the westward; and there is equal evidence of trading links with the coast, whether from objects found in the ruins or from early Portuguese documents.

The probability, in sum, is that most of these ruins belong to the same period which saw the rise, further westward, of the Mambo or "second Shona" state, and were built at much the same time as the tall and often elegant structures of Dhlo Dhlo and Naletali; while their markedly defensive character suggests that their peoples lived to see a period of bitter rivalry and internecine warfare. The relative peacefulness of the earlier period of the Rhodesian Iron Age, in other words, was over; concentrations of power had brought their characteristic wars of raid and conquest.

The problem of how far these various stone-building cultures of eastern and southern Africa were linked together, like the problem of their varying intensity of trade with the Indian Ocean seaboard, is difficult and complex. Here, perhaps, one should only emphasize that these southeastern cultures, like others to the north and west, were the product of strongly organized peoples who possessed a wide range of skill in the use of stone and metal, who were pastoral as well as agricultural, and whose development must be measured in centuries of steady growth.

This development was large, and some of its material aspects can be traced even today. Re-examining the Niekerk ruins in 1951, Summers could match MacIver's admiration for those who had built them. "The walling of the terraces and of the buildings connected with them," he says, "looks at first sight rough and unfinished, but further acquaintance with it reveals its finer points, and leaves one in no doubt about the skill of builders who, with the greatest economy of labour, regularly used boulders weighing anything up to a ton for their building." From foundations laid by their humbler predecessors of Ziwa 1 and 2, these Inyanga builders had contrived an important growth of material technique. Their ideologies and social organizations, if only we could know them, would no doubt show the same change and expansion.

Many questions about them remain unsettled or unanswered. Why exactly did they feel so unsafe? They built many forts. Their grain stores appear to have had a military guard; in any case they were placed in situations that were easy to defend. How many were they? At first sight it must seem that only dense populations could have lifted and piled all those myriad stones; yet Summers concluded in 1951 that the hillsides had in fact been terraced little by little according to the needs of a shifting agriculture, and by a relatively small population.

Carbonized grains show that their crops were millets, sorghums, and pulses, for which the decomposed doleritic stone of these hillsides would have provided good drainage as well as good soil. Yet these narrow hillside fields may have been incapable of intensive cultivation every year. "So that what one sees today are the imperishable remains of a century or more of continuous work, only a very small proportion of the whole thing being cultivated at a time. The sparseness of occupational debris is itself evidence of constant removal to new fields, whilst the very ubiquity of terracing in this district shows how thoroughly the past inhabitants sought out every scrap of available land." This conclusion seems confirmed by what is believed of earlier populations: that although they were not much more numerous than the populations of today, they were much more strongly and centrally organized, and possessed, with their independence, a social and economic dynamism which would afterwards be lost.

Like Zimbabwe and Mapungubwe, Dhlo Dhlo, Khami, and many others, these ruins of the Rhodesian-Mozambique border are therefore not a "riddle" to be answered by calling up some more or less mythical people "from outside." They are not miraculous nor even mysterious. In their bare reality, they are more impressive than that. For these are the material remains of people who pioneered a civilization — a rough and simple civilization, no doubt, but recognizably deserving the title — in a land where none had existed before — painfully, with toil and ingenuity, pushing out of barbarism with no one from the outside world to guide them.

What became of their achievement will be seen in the sequel; meanwhile, one may note that here again there entered the "factor of mobility" which Europe was so largely spared after the Norse and Magyar invasions of early medieval times. Whatever the precise reasons for their insecurity, there is no doubt that these southeastern peoples were often at war with one another. This is shown not only by their hilltop forts and grain stores and cattle-pens entrenched within tough stone walls; the Portuguese records, beginning for this region in the sixteenth century, illustrate as well the habit of their rivalry. More than this, though, they faced another danger: they were never safe from new invasions of less developed and less settled peoples, and their achievement was still too new and fragile — as with the "Azanians" when they faced the nomads of the north — to absorb and tame and civilize those who would attack and overwhelm them.

Their monuments remain. "There has been as much labour expended here," someone said of Niekerk to MacIver, who quotes the observation with approval, "as on the building of the Pyramids, or even more." It may or may not be so. What is certain is that Niekerk and Inyanga, like Zimbabwe and Khami and their like, mark a high point of indigenous growth in the mastery of nature, and the maturing of society, that may take its place alongside other medieval and post-medieval achievements in continental Africa.

Various and contrasting though they were, the foundations of Zimbabwe go back to much the same period as the foundations of Ghana. The initial raising of the walls of the "Acropolis" and the "elliptical building" was not much later than the time when Mali grew strong, and Timbuktu and Djenné saw their transformation into seats of thought and learning. The miles of careful terracing and the hilltop forts and store-pits and stone dwellings of Niekerk and Inyanga were made while Mohammed Askia and his successors ruled the Western Sudan.

Little by little, as one considers these various growing points of civilization in continental Africa, whether in west or east or south, one begins to understand how the history of their times, splayed out across these plains and hills and forests, reflects itself in stubborn and continuous development. Even today, lacking much information that the next few years may yield, one can see how pioneering peoples, thrusting this way or that, brought new ideas and forged new means of livelihood and subsistence — now advancing, now falling back, and yet moving always toward the same objectives and against the same obstacles and discouragements that emergent civilization would meet elsewhere in the world. The solutions were peculiar to Africa; the driving motives, and essentially the driving forces, were common to all mankind.

ten

The Reality Behind
the Ruins

Thus, from every point of view, Western Europe, from the ninth century onwards, appears in the light of an essentially rural society, in which exchange and the movement of goods had sunk to the lowest possible ebb. . . .

Henri Pirenne

1 Some Points of Comparison

But "civilization"? isn't that, after all, saying too much?

Modern anthropology has undermined the old certitudes of human progression. Savage, barbarous, civilized — what do they really mean in terms of historical experience? Is African sculpture "primitive"? On the contrary, says William Fagg, it has "come to be regarded very highly among the world's great art traditions. Most of our art schools come constantly to the museums where tribal art is to be found and have learned as much from it about the nature of sculpture as from the art of Egypt and the Etruscans, Greece and the Renaissance, the Orient, and modern art itself."

Is African religion "primitive"? On the contrary; many African peoples, it transpires, have systems of belief about themselves and the universe that are subtle and developed. Confronted with this fact of African philosophy, writes Father Tempels, "the false image of primitive man, of the savage, of the manlike creature deprived of a full growth of the intelligence, irremediably disappears." We have thought ourselves to be educating children, he says of Belgian colonial attitudes in the Congo, "and that seemed simple enough. And now quite suddenly it appears that we are dealing with an adult humanity, conscious of its own wisdom, conditioned by its own universal philosophy."

Very often, though, the opposition between "primitive" and "nonprimitive" is thought of in purely technological terms. Is it true, even in these terms, that Iron Age culture in medieval southern Africa was "primitive," uncivilized?

The early Portuguese, one may remark, had no contempt for

these African states they found and traded with. The lord of Monomotapa, Barbosa had explained in 1517, "is the lord of an exceeding great country. It runs far inland. It extends to the Cape of Good Hope and to Mozambique." And the claim was easily accepted, for the little that was known in Europe of the lands beyond the southeastern coast of Africa seemed to confirm it. These people might have no firearms (though they soon obtained some); but then the firearms of Europe were rare enough, and if Vasco da Gama's flagship could boast of twenty small cannon of cast-iron and brass, to those who served them the fighting with swords and spears could have seemed neither primitive nor "uncivilized." Europe itself, for the most part, still fought in no other way. These inland kings and chiefs had powerful armies, as the Portuguese well knew. What more natural than that they should rule the land? Moreover, the African coastal cities were as civilized as most of the maritime cities of Europe; more civilized than some of them. What more natural than that the cities of the interior should be the same?

The Portuguese, it may be answered, were mistaken in much of this; besides, were they not the natives of a rather backward European country without the glitter and sophistication of the great commercial cities of Germany and the Netherlands? Yet the Dutch, pressing hard on the heels of the Portuguese, thought no differently of the coastal cities they saw. Thus the trading island of Kilwa, standing to southeast Africa in the fifteenth century in something of the same relationship as Venice to the Mediterranean of that time, could still be described by the sober van Linschoten, who saw it as late as 1583, with frank admiration. Its inhabitants, he said, "are all most white-apparelled in silk and clothes of cotton wool: their women weare bracelets of gold and precious stones about their neckes and armes: they have great quantitie of silver workes, and are not so browne as the men, and well membered: their houses are commonly made of stone, chalke and wood, with pleasant gardens of all kinds of fruit and sweet flowers." Not quite sixteenth century Amsterdam, perhaps, but not barbarous or savage either.

Van Linschoten's object was to uncover the trading secrets of the Portuguese. The wealth of Kilwa, he found, came on the one side from India and the Persian Gulf; on the other side it came from the interior of Africa. They had the gold, he heard, from "a certaine mine named Monomotapa"; and in this "mine of Monomotapa is great store of gold, and withall a certaine kinde of gold, called by the Portingales *Botongoen onroempo* or sandie gold" — the earliest known reference to those Ba-Tonga who worked alluvial gold, or mined for gold, beyond the mountains of the coastal skyline — "for that is like very smal sand, but the finest gold that can be found."

This gold, he learned, the Portuguese got by trade, not by conquest. "In this fortresse of Sofala," he goes on, giving bankers and merchants of the Netherlands their earliest commercial intelligence of secrets guarded closely by the Portuguese for nearly a hundred years, "the Captaine of Mossambique hath a factor, and twice or thrice every year he sendeth certaine boats called *Pangaois*, which saile along the shore to fetch gold, and bring it to Mossambique. These *Pangaois* are made of light planks, and sowed together with cords, without any nails" — lineal descendants, no doubt, of the *rhapta* vessels of antiquity — "and they say that the mine of Angola on the other side of Africa is not farre from the saide mine of Sofala, not above three hundred miles one from the other, for often times there cometh certaine Moores from Angola to Sofala overlande."

A garbled story (though many Africans may have crossed Africa), and the Portuguese themselves had yet to learn much better. But it was a story in which mercantile Europe saw no improbability, and the map- and globe-makers built ingeniously upon it. At the museum in the Radziwill Palace near Warsaw, for example, one may still see a globe dated 1693 which awards the government of most of central Africa to "Monomotapa" and the government of southeastern Africa to "Mana Motapa" — just as though two such states had existed.

We can make a better picture of the polities and manners of the interior than could Linschoten and his contemporaries. We know now that in those years which saw the rise of mercantile Europe and its maritime discoveries, the use of printing in Europe and the gradual spread of literacy, Bantu-speaking peoples had established over much of south-central Africa a system of more or less strongly organized and unified states whose relations with each other, though always modified by custom and tradition, were not essentially different from those between the various states and empires of feudal Europe.

It would obviously be wrong to suppose an identity of class and custom between medieval northern Europe and medieval southern Africa. They seemed close to Europeans, soon after, because these Europeans looked through eyes that were conditioned by royal precedence and feudal subjection. Accustomed to absolute power residing in their kings, these venturers thought they had found the same in Africa. They fell into errors of judgment because they imagined that succession and inheritance must needfully be through the father, as with them, whereas often it was through the mother. They thought they had gained everything when they had carried the king's will, whereas in fact the king could seldom move without his counselors' agreement.

Yet the pattern of government was near enough to European experience, especially in Portugal, to excuse these errors. So many things appeared the same. Penetrating inland from the mouth of the Congo after 1484, the Portuguese came upon a system of government which subordinated weaker states to stronger states, bound states together by "royal" marriages, and governed all the countries they could reach or get report of. The king of Loango, they found, was obliged to marry a princess of Kakongo, a neighboring country, while the king of Kakongo had had to choose a wife, in earlier times, from among the princesses of Congo. And the case was typical enough.

In fact these rulers — like their fellow rulers across the continent as far as the Indian Ocean — had few absolute powers, and it may be more accurate to call them paramount chiefs rather than kings; only later would autocratic rulers emerge here. The "king" or *mani* of Congo had no more power than the Monomotapa to legislate outside the framework of tribal law and custom. If he tried to go outside it he would be likely to suffer the same fate as the Waqlimi, that tenth-century monarch of the southeast coast whose people, in El Mas'udi's words, had "chosen him to rule them with equity" and whom they would kill or set aside if he should fail in that. Medieval African kingship was still close to the tribal structure which had evolved and proved its worth while these migrating peoples thrust southward across the continent, fused with other peoples whom they found in the way, multiplied with their advancing technique in craft and cultivation, and made the country increasingly their own.

Comparisons with medieval Europe may quickly mislead. They will be likely to mislead much less, though, than no comparisons at all. Southern African Iron Age society was very different from the medieval society of northern Europe — neither Greece nor Rome, for one thing, was at its back, yet it was moving unmistakably in the same direction; and if the word civilization is applied to the material technique and social fabric of the one it will have to be applied to the other. Even in so general a matter as the gradual differentiation of classes the parallels are clear enough.

At Mapungubwe of the Bantu period, indeed, the evidence appears categorical. The chiefs and their immediate kinship would appear to have lived in stone forts or dwelling places, enjoyed fine pottery or china, possessed wealth in gold and copper ornament, bedecked themselves with the beads of India and Indonesia, and gone into their graves with ritual that was consciously and consistently different from the common folk.

Whether this common folk was of a different stock, or even of a different tribal loyalty, seems doubtful. So far, at Mapungubwe, there is evidence only to show that they lived in a humbler way. Did they pasture the cattle, till the fields, and perhaps mine or work the gold and copper and iron from which so largely came the trading and ritual and personal wealth of those who ruled? We cannot yet be sure, but presumably they did.

Was this the rule of Shona or Venda lords over Sotho serfs? Was it the same kind of class-and-caste rule that Bahima would exercise over Bairu in western Uganda somewhat later, or Normans over Saxons in England somewhat earlier? It seems probable from the evidence that this stratification of Mapungubwe people was primarily a social stratification.

Recent excavation at Khami Ruins, an extensive system of stone structures some thirteen miles west of Bulawayo in Southern Rhodesia, and dating probably from the Ba-Rozwi hegemony after about A.D. 1600, bears out this view of social stratification. "Only a small portion of the population," notes Robinson, "lived on the stone-walled platforms; many more dwelt in huts, mainly west of the Hill Ruin, where walling was absent or very slight." But "the material culture associated with these huts is identical with that of the main ruins."

Yet the people living on the stone-walled platforms had lived better than those in the huts. Imported china, ornamental gold, and ceremonial pottery were found in the walled ruins, but not elsewhere. "In short, the Hill Ruin probably represents the residence of a powerful chief, and the buildings in its vicinity may have been occupied by members of his family, or by various functionaries attached to his court: while the common people lived outside the walls." One culture, that is, but two ways of life: the first equipped for rule and comfort, the second humble and laborious. The rich man in his castle, the poor man at his gate . . .

2 A Period of Greatness

THE CONCLUSION, THEN, MUST BE THAT ALTHOUGH THESE IRON AGE polities of pre-industrial and pre-European southern Africa evolved neither the "oriental despotism" of Bronze Age antiquity nor the "feudal despotism" of Iron Age Europe, they did evolve a social stratification which was regular and accepted, and in which new-comers and natives were increasingly fused. By the coming of the Portuguese, that is, they had long emerged from savagery. Even in the nineteenth century terminology of human progression, they had taken essential steps which lead from barbarism to civ-ilization.

We have glimpsed this same stratification — this division of labor — among the "Azanians" of medieval East Africa, just as we have seen it in full flower among the city states and kingdoms of the coast, "where they are great barterers, and deal in cloth, gold, ivory, and divers other wares." These polities of inland southern Africa show it most clearly in their working of metals.

If their finer products north of the Limpopo were lost to his-tory when "old George" and his friends dropped on chiefly burials at Dhlo Dhlo and elsewhere, Mapungubwe has done something to make good the loss. Among its gold objects there was found a "scepter" of plated gold — the same kind of "spokesman's staff," perhaps, as may still be seen in glittering magnificence during chiefly durbars in West Africa. But the gold covering of this Mapungubwe "scepter" is thinner than five-thousandths of an inch. "To produce gold plate of remarkably uniform thickness, free from holes, and of considerable area," Pearson has commented, "necessitated much skill and time; and it would tax the capability of a modern gold beater to do this work with what were no doubt very primitive tools." Miners, smiths, and craftsmen in wrought metal — these, by all the evidence, were numerous and were men of closed "corporations" or "guilds" whose work was possible because others could provide a surplus of food for their support.

Elsewhere, in earlier times, this pattern of society had channeled wealth into the coffers and warehouses of kings and Pharaohs; and from such royal wealth as this had come the wealth of priests and temples — and then records and calculation, arithmetic, literacy. Though they were often believed to incarnate the stuff of divinity, African kings (and queens) never gathered wealth on any such scale. Perhaps the explanation lies in the difference between the intensive wealth-producing capacities of river-valley irrigation, and the bare subsistence of cattle raising and hillside cultivation. Perhaps it lies as well in the difference between the autocracy that proved so easily attainable and convenient in small river-valley settlements surrounded by sand or semidesert, and the tribal democracy or sense of community which inspired these migratory peoples — peoples who had spread across a continent that knew no natural frontiers, or none which could not easily be crossed.

Accumulation by chiefs or priests, in any case, never reached the point where written records could have become necessary; and we are on safe ground in saying that these early civilizations were illiterate except along the coast. The famous "inscription" at Zimbabwe — reported on hearsay by de Goes and de Barros in the sixteenth century — was either a fable or a mistaken report of the chevron ornamentation which undoubtedly topped the outer walls of the "elliptical building." These inland people had no means of writing; any more than a need of writing.

Without wishing to push the point too far, one may add that the medieval peoples of northern Europe were in not much better case. "There is no doubt," Marc Bloch has written of them, "that most of the small and middle lords, at least north of the Alps and Pyrenees . . . were illiterate in the full sense of the word: so much so that in the monasteries, where some of them took refuge at the end of their lives, the words *conversus* or late-comer to religious vocation — and *idiota*, the name for a monk incapable of reading Holy Writ — were regarded as synonymous." Even those who wrote used Latin: much as learned men and merchants of the coastal cities of East Africa would use Arabic (although they, ahead of early medieval Europe, also wrote their own language, Swahili).

Another objection to according the title of civilization to the polities of this southern African Iron Age, it is often held, is that they failed to invent or adopt the wheel. Pedantry apart, this objection seems to betray a remarkably narrow concept of human growth. The peoples of medieval northern Europe did not invent the wheel either, and they used it very little until the twelfth and thirteenth centuries. Was Scotland altogether barbarous in the sixteenth century? But Scottish annals for 1577 speak of the Regent going from Edinburgh's Tolbooth in "the second coach that came to Scotland, the first being brought by Alexander Lord Seaton, when Queen Mary came from France." One needs to keep a sense of historical perspective in these matters.

Extensive use and understanding of trade is a clear function of evolving civilization that was present in these southern polities. Sofala, notes de Barros in 1552, is famous "for the much gold that the Moors there obtain from the negroes of the land by way of commerce"; and this commerce, as we know from Arabic records, was already half a thousand years old. No doubt the growth of a native trading community in these inland states was slow and partial, and trade with the coast conducted through many intermediaries; yet we are a long way here from that "silent trade" which the barbarous or civilized peoples of North African antiquity had conducted by mute exchange with savage peoples to the south of them.

Much of the trade might be in barter, as in medieval Europe; but currencies of one kind or another were coming into use, and coins were being struck at Kilwa before the end of the thirteenth century. The complexity of this developing trade would have required them. Principal exports from the interior were gold and ivory and copper and iron, and at least by the seventeenth century, slaves as well; in return, these inland peoples wanted cotton cloth or luxury goods, while they valued highly the red beads of medieval India. When Alvares Cabral touched at Sofala on the way from India in 1501 — shortly, that is, before the trade was ruined — he was able to exchange "the cloth of Cambay and red beads, crimson silk, mirrors, caps, trappings for hawks, little bells from Flanders, small transparent glass beads," for "gold beads strung on threads to twelve or fifteen times the value."

As well as cotton cloth and beads, traders with the interior — or traders from the interior — also bought the occasional piece of china; though not often, judging by the great rarity of fragments so far recovered. Having come through many intermediaries, china must in any case have been vastly expensive. Kilwa's customs dues in the thirteenth century, not to mention all the others, were so high as to mulct every merchant of sixty per cent of his trading cottons. Yet imports of china continued on a small scale through several centuries. The fragments so far known from Southern Rhodesia and the Transvaal are all of Sung or Ming ware — china that was made between the eleventh and seventeenth centuries.

The oldest Rhodesian pieces so far recovered were found by Kenyon in 1929 when excavating the floor of a hut — "hard yellow cement resting on bare granite" — in the "east ruins" at Zimbabwe. This large hut, eighteen feet wide by twenty-three feet long, yielded a fairly large quantity of coarse black and brown pottery, one badly corroded bronze bangle, and two small fragments of celadon china.

These were later reported by the British Museum as probably of the Sung period, and became, in Caton-Thompson's words, "within the margins of uncertainty of the ascription, the oldest datable objects, with the exception of the imported beads, ever found in Rhodesia." The only complete piece of china — in fragments but reparable — was found at Dhlo Dhlo west of Bulawayo and is a bowl of Ming type dating to the end of the seventeenth century. It was disinterred together with a Dutch stone bottle of about the same date — odd leavings of early international trade in central Africa! At Mapungubwe, so far, Chinese porcelain is represented only by two small fragments of late Sung (A.D. 1127–1279).

All this agrees well with coastal evidence which gives the twelfth to fifteenth centuries as the best that Kilwa and its sister cities would ever know. The growing power and stability of centralized societies in the interior, that is to say, marched hand in hand with the expanding prosperity of the coast. The people of the Monomotapa raised their walls and towers while Kilwa's trade was at its zenith; and it was this large fact which enabled Caton-Thompson, in spite of the paucity of objects, to conclude that "the trade connexion with India" was "the primary stimulus which led to the development of the indigenous Zimbabwe culture." As with the Western Sudan and the East African seaboard, the stimulus of long-range trading had once again displayed its potency.

This civilizing growth in the interior was not, of course, a simple process. Some peoples, like groups of Bushmen who still survived on the central plateau, stayed outside it altogether, or retreated little by little into less accessible regions. Others, like the Hottentots of the extreme south, seem to have learned ironworking only from the Dutch, who settled at the Cape of Good Hope in 1652, although further north they had it from the Bantu. Material techniques apart, there must always have been a great variety and complexity in social relationships, offering in their manifold and often contrasted loyalties a whole world, or several worlds, that Europe had forgotten or never known.

It was the fusion of this tribal world, looking backward to a primitive communism, with material and social changes looking forward to civilization — to food surplus, division of labor, commerce and city settlement — that produced the unique symbiosis of these stone-building metal-using cultures of southern and central Africa. And to seize their nature in all its sensitive and self-regulating and yet inwardly mobile reality — primitive in appearance, pre-industrial, often overtly stagnant, and yet the consequence of great discoveries and revolutionary modes of thought — calls for an effort of the imagination. Spare in its tools, it was profuse in its ideology. Simple in its means, it was complex in its methods. Rigidly traditional in theory, it was daringly experimental in practice. Nothing so much astonished its European discoverers as the readiness of these peoples and their rulers to consider new ideas, adopt new faiths, try new methods.

However simple in achievement when laid beside the cathedrals of Norman Europe or the poetry of Dante, this Iron Age civilization was even so the product of pioneering triumph in the solving of problems never before solved in sub-continental Africa. For once these solutions are laid beside the barren reality from which they came, they can be seen in quite another light: law and order, technical progress, the gathering of wealth, the accumulation of knowledge, the growing mastery over nature — all these are seen to emerge from the void. This might not be a Golden Age of innocence and bliss, although the morals of its tribal loyalty could be firmer and more to be admired, often enough, than those a later world would know; it was none the less, in human terms, a period of greatness.

3 *The Bud and the Flower*

IT IS NATURAL TO ASK ONESELF WHETHER THESE GROWING POINTS of Iron Age civilization can be seen as branches, in different regions of Africa, from a single stem.

So immediately similar in their use of stone for dwellings, irrigation, soil conservation; in their mining and metal work; in their knowledge of a widely various pharmacopoeia; in their fusion of tribal law and custom with an intertribal and tribute-paying system of centralized power; in their trading habits; in their cultivation of new plants and fruits which had come from outside Africa; even in their indigenous pottery — were all these cultures of a common origin?

Did the builders of those southern hill-forts that perch above the gorges of the Pungwe River, and are veiled so often in mountain mist, look northward to the plains of Tanganyika and the highlands of Kenya — even to Ethiopia — for their beginnings? A few years ago the question might have been dismissed as rhetorical nonsense. Today it must be taken seriously. Archeology within these coming years may after all link Engaruka with Inyanga, and even with Mapungubwe; it may prove that the builders of Great Zimbabwe passed back their governing ideas to distant Uganda; it may show that all this was indeed within the heritage of that "Azanian civilization" which, in Huntingford's words of a quarter of a century ago, has left "traces over a large part of Africa."

Exponents of the "Phoenician school" have had no difficulty in answering such questions. For them, these early Iron Age cultures were the lonely triumph of pioneering columns from another continent. Maritime Phoenicians, southward-probing Sabaeans, early Arab captains and their slender bands, were those who built these inland cities and dwelt in them and disappeared — leaving the local savages to copy crudely what remained and continue a debased tradition which had not been African.

Patient research has denied this exotic description of the past; but in showing both the native quality of these cultures, and their great inner complexity, it has also tended to confirm their initial community of origin and to trace this origin mainly from the northward. If many of the governing ideas and techniques of Iron Age West Africa had come from North Africa and the Middle Nile, Iron Age southern Africa appears to have taken as much from the neighborhood of the Great Lakes, from the Horn of Africa, perhaps also from the Nile. Early migrants from the north would have brought into these southern solitudes many ideas that underwent transformation and adaptation as the centuries passed — until all that remained, often enough, was the faint and puzzling echo of a distant parentage. This was the northern echo that was heard so attentively by the "Phoenician school"; their misinterpretation of its meaning should not lead one, for all that, into denying its existence.

For it was the central achievement of the founders of Great Zimbabwe and its like that they adapted and invented pre-industrial solutions to new problems in a new land. The chiefs and courts and craftsmen, rulers and ruled, of Zimbabwe and so many other points of strength and settlement were not simply imitating what others further north had done before them; they were adapting what they knew and, in the process of adaptation, engendering new forms and structures, new ideas and motives, a new stability as well as a new spur to change and variation.

The objects they left behind them are convincing evidence of all this; even the relatively few objects that archeologists have managed to recover and preserve.

Old Posselt in 1888, after climbing the hill above the valley ruins at Zimbabwe, saw "four soapstones carved in the image of a bird and facing east." One of these — preserved now in Cape Town — he managed to uproot and take away with him, although the Shona guides who were with him greatly opposed the desecration.

Three years later Bent found six more such birds and took them away — four were large, and stood on pillars, while two were small. "From the position in which we found them," he wrote, they "would appear to have decorated the outer wall of the semi-circular temple on the hill." He considered they were stylized representations of hawks or vultures, probably of phallic meaning, and quickly fitted them into his "Phoenician theory."

The hawk, he argued, had served as an emblem of maternity to the ancient Egyptians, while a southern Arabian tribe of Himyarite times had used the vulture as a totem. There was little doubt, he thought, that these Zimbabwe birds were "closely akin to the Assyrian Astarte or Venus, and represent the female element in creation. Similar birds were sacred to Astarte amongst the Phoenicians and are often represented as perched on her shrine." If Bent could have known how widely the Egyptian cult of Amun had occurred in western Africa, he might well have argued that the spreading of this Arabian cult of Astarte into southern Africa was nothing so remarkable.

Yet he was saying both too much and too little: too much because this mechanical transference of ideas from southern Arabia to southern Rhodesia supposed a human vacuum in between; too little because further inquiry has shown that many peoples of the southern Bantu regard lightning as a giant bird, and set up effigies of giant birds in order to deceive the lightning and send it elsewhere.

The effigies vary, apart from any question of artistic style, because the "lightning birds" vary: the southern Sotho imagine the lightning bird as a hamerkop, the Venda imagine it as an eagle, the peoples of the northwestern Transvaal imagine it as a flamingo; but the cult is in any case widespread. Walton records from 1951 "a number of bird effigies carried on tall poles surrounding the *lelapa* of a witch-doctor in the Dilli Dilli valley of south Basutoland"; and other such effigies have occurred in Mozambique and the Transvaal. The peculiarity of Zimbabwe — a peculiarity, no doubt, of long-enduring settlement and steady technical growth — is that its birds were carved, uniquely, in stone. Perhaps the idea had come, remotely, from the far north; if so, it had changed in the course of time and migration into something entirely native to southern Africa.*

Other echoes of northern origin, remote and yet persistent, are more easily established. The people of Great Zimbabwe also carved soapstone into bowls which varied in size from thirteen and one-half to twenty-one inches in diameter, with pictures or geometrical patterns on their broad outer rims. Stone bowls of this kind are rare in Africa; and once again it would seem that the peculiarity of the Zimbabwe culture was to make in stone what others made in pottery or wood. Western Uganda, it is true, has yielded circular dishes up to four feet in diameter; but these are lost, and may have been of earthenware rather than stone.

Stone bowls from Zimbabwe are interesting because their decoration includes pictures of cattle with long "lyre-shaped" horns such as were common in northeastern Africa and are still reared in southern Ethiopia. This link by way of cattle, together with the finding at Zimbabwe and elsewhere of many small stone cylinders — often supposed to resemble a penis, and perhaps the objects of a phallic cult — have encouraged some writers to trace a more or less direct connection between southern Ethiopia, with its huge stones carved to resemble a penis, and the early settlements of

---

* Summers, however, says of these "birds" that "there can be little doubt they were memorials of departed chiefs."

Rhodesia. Wainwright has even felt able to argue that these last were founded by the Galla, a nomad people originally dwelling in Somaliland but now largely in southern Ethiopia. "The Waqlimi and his people," he says, recalling El Mas'udi's tenth-century description of the southeastern coast, "came from Gallaland and its neighbourhood, and were already installed in Southern Rhodesia before A.D. 900"; and, since that was the date of foundation of some of the greater buildings, it is natural — he goes on — to suppose that it was the Waqlimi and his followers who had built them.

This "Galla theory" is in fact not much better than the "Phoenician theory." There is nothing to suggest that the Waqlimi and his people were Galla and not Bantu (or proto-Bantu — a mingling of ancient stocks); nor that El Mas'udi had any knowledge of the southern interior beyond a few miles from the coast. On the contrary, there is a great deal in migration legend to suggest that the Waqlimi were not Galla. The word W*aq* occurs in the Galla language, true enough, and means god. But Cerulli says that it was also the old Kushitic term for heaven, and therefore used from ancient times by the Somali as well. May it not be that trading Arabs who sailed up and down that ancient seaboard knew the word from coastal Somali, and transferred it to the god-king of the land of Sofala? (For them, as well, the land beyond Sofala was the land of Waq Waq.) To build a whole Galla migration into southern Africa on such thin linguistic threads is making bricks, in any case, with little straw.

The "Phoenician school" had done the same thing, once again, with the cross-shaped and H-shaped ingot molds that were found in Southern Rhodesia. After digging up one of these in a cave on the "Acropolis" at Great Zimbabwe, Bent observed that it corresponded "almost exactly to an ingot of tin found in Falmouth harbor" whose manufacture was presumably Phoenician. Perhaps it did so correspond; but Bent went on to conclude that "the finding of two ingots in remote places where Phoenician influence has been proved to be so strong"— on the evidence in Southern Rhodesia of the soapstone birds and so forth — "is very good presumptive evidence to establish the fact that the gold workers of ancient Zimbabwe worked for the Phoenician market." And so back once more to that much-traveled lady, the Queen of Sheba.

The gold workers of Zimbabwe worked in truth not for the Phoenician market but for the Indian Ocean trade after about the ninth century A.D. However the notion of ingot molds in the form of a cross or an *H* may have reached them — and *some* Phoenicians had certainly traded down the east coast (and the west coast) in ancient times, and had even circumnavigated Africa, according to Herodotus, in the seventh century B.C. — these molds were indigenous to the metalworking region that lies between the head of Lake Nyasa and the northern Transvaal, and castings from them would be peculiar to the African metal trade for many hundreds of years.

They were evidently used at Zimbabwe for casting gold ingots, since the mold recovered by Bent was associated with a gold-smelting furnace, there being with the mold a number of small clay crucibles having specks of gold still fastened to their fire-hardened bowls. Perhaps they were also used for the iron export trade that Edrisi mentions in the twelfth century, and for the copper on which medieval Kilwa grew so rich. Currency bars of inland copper, as much as four feet long, were reaching Mozambique in the latter half of the eighteenth century, as were also large quantities of copper ingots in the St. Andrew's cross of *H* form, slung together at either end of a carrying pole. "Scrappy as the evidence is," says Walton, "it all points to the conclusion that the *handa* ingot" — the cross or *H* form— "reached Southern Rhodesia from north-east Africa at the beginning of the Monomotapa period" — that it was, in short, another aspect of metal age development which got into its stride, on the southern plateau, after the tenth and eleventh centuries A.D.

Not all these outside influences came from the northeast, though most of them probably did. Some types of iron gongs, common in chiefly ceremonies throughout central Africa, evidently came from the northwest; and further inquiry in the Congo and Angola, if and when it may be made, seems likely to reinforce this northwestern connection.

Architecture in unmortared stone was common to all these countries from Ethiopia to the Transvaal. Sometimes the forms seem remarkably alike; at other times remarkably different. Of the dwellings of the "Azanians" of the Kenya highlands in medieval times, Huntingford says that "the hut circle, in its simplest and commonest form, is a circular hollow dug out of a slope, with a nearly level floor and an entrance on the lower side protected by banks formed of the upcast from the excavation." Far to the south, and probably a long time afterward, people in the highlands of southeastern Rhodesia had much the same ideas in hut architecture, though with variations of their own. The center of each complex of dwellings, says York Mason of Penhalonga and Inyanga, "is a circular stone-lined stone-paved pit, surrounded by a platform of earth concentrically arranged and faced with stone. On the hillward side, the platform is barely raised above the ground level; on the opposite side, the height of the platform depends upon the slope of the ground . . ."

Did these people of the south develop their architecture by influence from the "Azanians" who had built before them in the north? "All the structures," says York Mason, "appear to be of the same period and to have emerged fully-fledged from some previous design." It is not too difficult to imagine that the people who built Inyanga had come from the north, or received immigrants from the north; and that the architectural links between the northern city of Engaruka and its southern contemporaries were more than accidental.

Yet the movement of ideas, apparently, was not simply from north to south. In Western Uganda, during these past few years, archeologists have reasserted the importance of huge systems of earthwork fortification — the largest in Africa, perhaps the largest in the world — which were thrown up and occupied, it would seem, during a period which corresponds to the later centuries of Zimbabwe's greatness. Traditionally associated with a semilegendary ruling caste called the Bachwezi, these earthworks have many echoes of Zimbabwe and its kind. Like the fortress of Mapungubwe, the fortress of Bigo was raised on the southward side of a river ford. Like the "temple" of Zimbabwe, the Bigo earthworks are elliptical in outline. Some of the pots seem to be like the pots of Zimbabwe, and so do some of the beads. Like Rhodesia, this was an area of extensive mining and smelting.

Little can be said of these great sites in Western Uganda, first reported by a district commissioner in 1909, since archeologists have yet to recover a single datable object; but a twelve-foot trench dug by Shinnie at Bigo in 1957 has proved a long-enduring occupation. The resemblances with Zimbabwe are so striking as to seem more than a coincidence; where the builders of Zimbabwe built in abundant local stone, those of Bigo, having no stone available, built in earth. Which way had the current of ideas flowed?

Whatever details may emerge from research in the future, the right answer was surely given by Wayland, who remarked in 1934 with a masterly insight which later discoveries would confirm, that "Bigo is far more primitive than Zimbabwe, though it is almost certainly younger: yet both are, so to say, growths from the self-same stem. Bigo was a late abortive bud and Zimbabwe an early flower, and both are Bantu . . . In the last analysis their cultures spring from a common root."

The same words have their application to many of these Iron Age cultures. Emerging under different suns, whether in the pleasant uplands of Kenya or Uganda, the steep gorges of Inyanga, or the rolling plains of Rhodesia, and growing over many centuries of pioneering migration and settlement, mingling with more primitive peoples, solving a whole wide range of contrasting problems, these early civilizations asserted once again a dominant African theme of unity in diversity, continuity in isolation. We cannot at present understand them clearly. Even when we glimpse them faintly their apparent meagerness of achievement and crudity of means can blur their success, diminish their greatness. Yet they pushed civilization into the empty lands.

4 *What Is Now Required*

IF AN OUTLINE OF THESE ACHIEVEMENTS IN EASTERN AND SOUTHERN regions now becomes possible, details are in poor supply and are likely to remain so for some time to come. Much more is known today than was known twenty years ago; but much less, one may reasonably think, than will be known twenty years hence.

Several broad lines of advance seem indicated by the present state of knowledge and research. Archeologically, they are the need first of all for a deeper and more systematic knowledge of the coast — covering the period, mainly, between about A.D. 500 and 1500 — and its links with the interior; secondly, for inspection of lands in the interior now lying more or less completely blank upon the archeological map; thirdly, for further work on some of the principal sites already listed and partially understood.

Apart from these tasks in archeology there is a great need for new and up-to-date translations and re-editions of some of the more important Arabic classics, as well as for research in lesser

Arabic works not generally known or available. The European documentation, moreover, has certainly a great deal more to yield; for the combing of the great libraries and archives of Europe has only just begun. Lastly, the work of collecting and sifting tribal legend is far from complete.

Happily for all this, the pre-European history and archeology of Africa have begun to attract serious attention in the academic world; the School of Oriental and African Studies of London University, for example, has already held two international conferences on these subjects. Africans themselves are beginning to study their own past. The first conference of independent African states, held in Ghana in the spring of 1958, made special mention, in its closing declaration, of the need for research into African history; and this, too, ought to result in new funds and opportunities.

Meanwhile, pioneering work along the east coast during the past ten years or so has added much new knowledge. Mathew and Freeman-Grenville, in completing a preliminary survey of coastal sites, have shown the limits of about a thousand years of continuous settlement from the early and as yet unidentified houses of Sanje ya Kati to the costly palaces of Kua and Kilwa. Kirkman has made the first full-scale excavation of a medieval site at the city of Gedi or old Malindi, and revealed, among other things, some possible links with Zimbabwe.

What seems now required is systematic excavation of the more promising of these sites and continuation of the survey southward into Mozambique. As far south as Cape Delgado the coast was undoubtedly known to Greco-Roman mariners, let alone to pre-Islamic Arabs; while the Arabs of the tenth century, if not the Himyarites long before them, just as surely knew the Mozambique coast for many hundreds of miles further on. South of the Kilwa Islands off the Tanganyika coast Freeman-Grenville has identified two sites, one at Lindi and the other at Mikindani, this last being some forty miles north of the Mozambique border. Beyond that little or nothing is known; and yet for many centuries it was from there — from Sofala and its sister ports — that the highroad to Zimbabwe and the far interior ran.

Investigation of links between these coastal cities or trading stations and the suppliers of their goods from the interior is at an even more primitive stage. Yet for medieval Rhodesia and its immediately neighboring lands the trading contact with the coast was strong and continuous, at any rate after the tenth century; and it is this more than anything else, perhaps, which may explain the difference between the "abortive bud" of Ugandan Bigo — having apparently no trading connections with the coast — and the "early flower" of Zimbabwe. If it is true, as it seems to be, that coastal demand for minerals and ivory was a vital stimulus to the growth of Iron Age civilization in the south, then a closer survey of the course and nature of the trade should be fruitful of results. This calls, first and foremost, for systematic archeological search in coastal and inland Mozambique, and in inland Tanganyika. Coins and imported durable goods, like china and beads, are likely to be helpful in both. (It calls as well for much more work on Indian and southeast Asian beads, the early dating of which remains vague and variable; and for still more systematic study of the Chinese records.)

Nyasaland, lying at the back of Tanganyika and Mozambique, is another archeological blank which may now provide its own surprises. Yet if Mozambique and Tanganyika — and perhaps Nyasaland — hold keys to an explanation of the growth and success of the civilizations of the central plateau, it is the lands of southwest and central-west Africa which seem to promise explanations of their more distant origin. Something of what Northern Rhodesia may yet offer was shown dramatically by Clark's discoveries at the Kalambo Falls in 1953. Five hundred years earlier, or nearly so, the Portuguese found Iron Age states in strong development near the mouth of the Congo. Beyond these in the inte-

rior, during later centuries, their marching columns came upon hilltop forts such as Pundo Andongo; yet the archeology of Angola,
whether Stone Age or Iron Age, remains more or less completely
unknown. But it is through this large region — of northwestern
Rhodesia, Angola, the western Kasai and Congo — that lines of influence and contact with pre-medieval and medieval West Africa
must be sought.

Northward, in western Uganda and the highlands of Kenya, the
earthworks of Bigo and its sister-sites and the stone-building of the
"Azanians" may both look back to origins in the eastern Congo,
the southern Sudan, and southern Ethiopia, as well as to influence
from Zimbabwe. Lanning has done preliminary work of great
value at Bigo and other Ugandan sites that are linked, or seem to
be linked, with Bigo; but much that may illuminate the origins of
the contemporary states of Uganda, and their links with medieval
or post-medieval neighbors, still remains to be done. A dating sequence in Uganda may ultimately depend upon a dating sequence
in the southern Sudan, and that in turn upon a dating sequence
at Meroë and in southern Kush — and here the lack of information
is almost total.

Several colonial governments, notably those of Rhodesia and
Tanganyika, are now awake to the value of archeological research,
and have given useful though small sums of money for its prosecu-
tion; but it is clear that much more will be required before this
southern and eastern patchwork can be changed into a coherent
picture. The central fact, the new fact, is that a coherent picture
is likely to be possible.

And yet if the past was rich, and could tell this story of growth
and change in relative isolation, why did southern Africa appear so
primitive and savage to those who traveled there a century ago
and less? If this fabric of emergent civilization had been so strong
and so resilient across the centuries, why did it rend and tear and
apparently disappear? Having gone so far along the road — solv-

ing, if in different terms, the same problems that other Iron Age civilizations would confront and solve elsewhere — why was this progress halted? They are reasonable questions; and there ought to be reasonable answers to them.

eleven

Decline and Fall

That vast empire [of Monomotapa] is in such decay that no one has dominion over it, because everyone has power there . . .

King of Portugal
to his Viceroy of India in 1719

1 The Fabric of Society

Marching down the unmapped Zambezi in 1856, walking from tribe to tribe on his long journey back to the east coast, David Livingstone would hear the last sad echoes of the Monomotapa. This obscure chief "of no great power," and subject to another who was equally obscure, the Portuguese had "formerly honoured . . . with a guard, to fire off numbers of guns on the occasion of any funeral, and he was also partially subsidised." But now, adds Livingstone in his journal, "the only evidence of greatness possessed by his successor is his having about a hundred wives," although "when he dies, a disputed succession and much fighting are expected."

The decline and fall of the empire of the Monomotapa, as of other states and feudal systems in southern Africa, did not necessarily mean — any more than it meant in western Africa — a disappearance of the culture on which it was based. Here one needs to review the evidence with a carefully measuring eye. To European pioneeers and prospectors in the nineteenth century these unknown lands might seem a desperate wilderness; to the public at home, schooled now by generations of contemptuous slaving clichés, they seemed much worse than that. But the facts were otherwise.

Some of these southern Iron Age cultures continued to grow and develop and expand for a long time after early contact with the Portuguese. The elaborate ruins of Dhlo Dhlo and Khami, of Niekerk and Inyanga and Penhalonga, even the last levels of Mapungubwe, all belong to the seventeenth and eighteenth centuries; while the Mambo line of Ba-Rozwi rulers which had established itself at Great Zimbabwe in the first years of the seventeenth century would continue into the first decades of the nineteenth.

And then European estimates, understandably enough, varied with the beholder. Vasco da Gama and his contemporaries might be deeply impressed by the civilization of the coastal cities they found and wrecked. By the eighteenth and nineteenth centuries the European estimate had changed, vastly changed; because Europe, with a couple of hundred years of industry and science behind it, had also changed, while Africa had not only failed to keep pace but here and there had fallen back. Slave trading on an altogether unprecedented scale had done its degrading work, by now, both on the slavers in Africa and the slavers in Europe. Many of the since familiar slogans of a "natural African inferiority" were stamped on European minds. Much of the fabric of African civilization, at least in coastal regions, was rent or ruined and seemed to justify contempt.

Yet intelligent European judgments about central Africa, even in the nineteenth century, remained at variance with this manifold mythology of "African savagery and chaos." They show, if fitfully and fleetingly, something of the nature of this slow-evolving concentration of power which had laid the groundwork and foundation of a mature Iron Age society in this southern isolation. There survives from 1831, for example, the account of an altogether agreeable encounter between a brave little Portuguese expedition, headed by Major Monteiro and Captain Gamitto, and the court of the ruler of Lunda in the southern Congo — that Muata Cazembe whose lineage went back by tradition into a remote past.

Gamitto's story — an admirably modest one considering how far this expedition had gone beyond the beaten track — is enlivened by a donkey. No such beast, it would appear, had yet been seen in those parts; but Gamitto rode one down a broad beaten highway into the Cazembe's capital. Clad in a uniform of white trousers and blue nankeen jacket, with scarlet cords and tassels and an otter-skin cap, he himself was also much applauded by the welcoming crowd; but the donkey carried off the day, for it panicked at the noise and ran away with him. This was apparently taken in good part, and added to his welcome.

"On the morning of November 29, they were summoned into the presence of Muata Cazembe, entering a spacious court already filled with an immense crowd . . .

"The soldiers stationed [here] were the garrisons of Lunda, consisting of about four or five thousand men, all armed with bows and arrows and spears: the nobles and officers wearing in a leather scabbard suspended under the left arm a large straight two-edged sword, called *pocué*, about eighteen inches long and four inches broad . . . and all standing apparently without any military discipline." At Sofala, more than three hundred years earlier, Barbosa had seen just such haughty nobles wearing swords slung on the left side.

Gamitto and his friends found the Muata throned in some state, and "clothed with an elegance and sumptuousness such as the Portuguese officers had never witnessed in any other native potentate." He was wearing a feathered "mitre" about a foot high, brilliantly red, and encircled with a diadem of stones of various sorts and colors. "At the back of his head, and rising from the nape of his neck, was a fan-shaped ruff of green cloth, fastened by two small ivory pins."

On his shoulders this monarch of the far interior wore an ornamental cape, badges of royalty that were bands of blue cloth trimmed with fur, light-blue beads on his forearms, and a yellow cloth from waist to knees, "wound abundantly about him and fastened with an ivory pin." Gamitto found the whole get-up of "great elegance and good taste."

Ranged in ceremonial ranks about him were officers of the court, soldiers, licensed fools, royal wives and lesser wives, and other chiefs and counselors. The manners of the Muata, who seemed to be about fifty, "were majestic and agreeable, and his state and style of living were, in their way, showy. Most certainly it was not to be imagined that so much etiquette, ceremony and ostentation would be met with in the sovereign of a region so remote from the sea-shore, and among a people so apparently savage and barbarous."

Such was the outward seeming of an obscure inland ruler of the nineteenth century; and what was true of the Muata Cazembe's court and all that it implied in terms of centralized order and established law was also true of others. The Bushongo people of the Sankuru river, also in the southern Congo, could still tell Torday in the first years of the twentieth century of their "golden age" when Shamba Bolongongo had abolished warfare with the throwing knife, and introduced raffia weaving and other arts of peace. If their history as a state is really shorter than the fifteen centuries suggested by their legends, their magnificent sculpture in wood is an unmistakable embodiment of long and fruitful social experience.

After his journeys through central Africa Livingstone repeatedly commented on the peace and security that reigned over great expanses of the interior, and Krapf in east Africa at about the same time would find the same thing. These people might not be anxious for Christian teaching, Livingstone said, but there was "no impediment in the way of instruction." On the contrary, "every headman would be proud of a European visitor or resident in his territory, and there is perfect security for life and property"— he was thinking, of course, of human dangers and not of animals and disease — "in the interior."

Missionaries cooking in the cannibal pot would become a standby of European humor. As it happens, only six missionaries of some three hundred who penetrated into east and central Africa before 1884 are known to have been killed by Africans; and none of these, it would appear, was killed by wanton murder. What looked like chaos, in short, was seldom anything of the kind; what seemed like great danger of life was nearly always a huge exaggeration. Life for the traveler in middle Africa was in fact a good deal safer — from wars and human killing — than it generally was in Europe; which may explain, of cour.., the gentler way in which Africans were accustomed to welcome strangers.

This safety for foreign travelers, reflecting both a respect for life as well as the general maintenance of law and order, seems all the more remarkable in that these stray Europeans could seldom manage to explain why they had come and what they might want. "Their behaviour," Margery Perham has commented, "was generally unaccountable, and often menacing and improper . . . Yet these men, utterly dependent and sometimes destitute, were allowed to pass chief after chief and tribe after tribe, at the cost here of some restraint upon their impatient purposes, and there of a persecution for presents nearly always stopping short of violence which was well within the power of these chiefs. They were, on the contrary, not infrequently assisted at the cost of their hosts."

Now all this reflects the presence and general recognition, within a pre-industrial society, of reasonable and self-confident modes of life and manners of thought, and suggests, for anyone who cares to ponder on it, how far these peoples of the interior had traveled in creative adaptation to their environment. Much else might be laid beside it. The arts of Africa, so often shocking to the Victorian eye, could have come only from societies which had found creative answers to the age-old problem of the one and the many, the individual and the collective. Their philosophies, their thoughts about man and the universe, echoed the same distinctive genius. Neither art nor religion was the crude and wretched thing that suburban Europe, traveling in "darkest Africa," would generally say it was; neither revealed the shallow growth of yesterday, nor the hopeless gibbering surrender to violence and magic, that

Europeans would so generally imagine. Here was much that might evoke surprise, and a good deal that would call for help — nothing, in the general structure and conception of society, that could allow a charge of natural inferiority.

In the middle of the twentieth century one may see all this more clearly. Barred as they often were from many currents and cross-currents of thought and action that had fertilized and deepened civilization elsewhere, African peoples had moved by their own dynamic of advance, found their own way forward, worked out their own solutions. Stubbornly, slowly, they had gone ahead across the lonely years. Only where the slave trade made its worst ravages were they altogether stopped and their achievements rendered sterile; and much of the far interior was spared that fearful curse.

The Lozi of northwestern Rhodesia, for example, were spared it; and Lozi law and order, Lozi conceptions of the judicial process, can be found to support none of the assumptions of paternalist trusteeship. On the contrary, the basis of Lozi legal judgments would emerge, on examination in the twentieth century, as mature and solid as in European or American courts. In both, Gluckman has contended, the judicial process was basically similar. "On the whole," he goes on, "it is true to say that the Lozi judicial process corresponds with, more than it differs from, the judicial process in Western society. Lozi judges draw on the same sources of law as Western judges — the regularities of environment, of the animal kingdom, of human beings; and custom, legislation, precedent, equity, the laws of nature and of nations, public policy, morality . . ."

The fabric of society, therefore, was strong and could survive. Yet it remains true that the states of southern Africa's Iron Age undoubtedly declined and fell. Their rulers were dispersed or diminished to a shadow of their former greatness. Their strong stone settlements and forts, built across the years, were abandoned to an empty solitude.

2 *Barbarians at the Gate*

Eˑᵁᴿᴼᴾᴱᴬᴺˢ ᴾᴿᴱˢˢᴵᴺᴳ ᴵᴺᵀᴼ ᴹᴬᵀᴬᴮᴱᴸᴱᴸᴬᴺᴰ ᴬᴺᴰ ᴹᴬˢᴴᴼᴺᴬᴸᴬᴺᴰ some seventy years ago could find little or nothing which seemed to link the ruins they found with the peoples who lived beside them. For this decline of a civilization, three primary reasons may be detected.

The first reason lay in the natural instability of a system of feudal or near-feudal states and kingdoms which grew in rivalry with one another; here, just as in medieval Europe, dynastic rivalries would repeatedly erupt in war. The second, grossly disturbing the balance of power and destroying the system of trade, lay in Portuguese intervention after the beginning of the sixteenth century. And the third, thrusting into a chaos that followed this Portuguese intervention, lay in the invasion of barbarian peoples from the south.

As to the first reason, there is some evidence for thinking that the Portuguese arrived at a time when the centralizing trends of Iron Age civilization in central and southern Africa were passing from one crucial phase to another. Small concentrations of clan power had long since grown into larger concentrations of tribal power, and these in turn into still larger concentrations of multi-tribal power; but now these last, it would seem, were faced with the consequent problems of social growth and conflict.

Thus the earliest Portuguese intelligence of the states of the Congo estuary, gathered in the last years of the fifteenth century, showed that dynastic wars had lately remodeled the frontiers of authority; and the king of Congo whom they found, Nzinga a Nkuwa, claimed to be only the fifth of his line. Over on the other side of the southern continent, inland from Sofala, much the same dynastic strife was reported to the king of Portugal as early as 1506. In the kingdom of the Monomotapa, Alcançova is writing in that year, there had been war for the thirteen years or more; and this, indeed, was the period of a break at Great Zimbabwe, between the first and second Shona occupations, that other evidence has since suggested.

Alcançova's interest in these distant wars lay simply in explaining to Lisbon, if he could, why the gold export to Sofala had dried up so alarmingly. But in the course of explaining this he gives a long and detailed description of internal wars which occurred, beyond the coastal skyline, just over a century after the English Wars of the Roses had ended; but which evidently signified, with one chief warring on another and one noble faction on its neighbor, much the same kind of struggle for power.

These wars of English feudalism had led to a strengthening of the king, the central power, over against the barons and fief-holders; and the unity of Tudor England, coming in their wake, was much more real and obvious than the unity of the Plantagenet kingdom which had preceded them. A growing concentration of power seems to have occurred in southern Africa as well. Far out on the central plateau, across those distant plains where Portuguese intrusion was never known, the sixteenth and seventeenth centuries saw the building of the largest of the stone forts and settlements and kingly dwellings; and the great walls of late Zimbabwe may have signified, between a Mambo ruler and his Monomotapan predecessor, much the same kind of difference as that which held between a Tudor and a Plantagenet. At least on the western plains, the states became more centralized and the rulers, if fewer, became wealthier. And then, in the course of years, there occurred a fearful termination.

So far as the state of the Monomotapa was concerned — and Ba-Rozwi victories had pushed it northeastward by the seventeenth century — the Portuguese undoubtedly ruined it. They broke its central power and delivered its peoples into anarchy. But the finishing blow, both to the state of the Monomotapa and its neighbors to the southwest, was delivered by Africa itself. Migrant regiments of Nguni people — militarized tribes whose homeland lay along the southeastern coast of what is now Natal — broke back into these plateau civilizations, and ravaged and destroyed them. Driven themselves by the age-old need for migration to new lands, but knowing already the extreme difficulty of pushing further south — now that rifle-bearing Europeans were pushing northward from the Cape — these Nguni fragments sought refuge in the settled lands at their back.

In 1834 Zwangendaba came over the Limpopo with his regiments and destroyed Khami. Tschangana bands from Mozambique rushed the forts of Inyanga and Penhalonga; and thereafter the terraced hillsides were left in solitude for archeologists to wonder at. In 1835 the last Mambo, or Ba-Rozwi king, who had inherited the state which his forefathers had taken from the Monomotapa, was flayed alive; and his royal residence, Thabas ka Mambo, ruined by the Swazi. And in 1838, with final ruin, there came northward the *impis* of Mzilikazi, Zulu prince who had broken from Chaka's autocratic hand, and carried all before him. This last Nguni fragment, the Ndebele, would become the Matabele of European times; and thereafter the story is another one.

These barbarian invasions might in any case have proved irresistible to the states of the southern plateau; for here was once again the old familiar tale of nomad strength and settled weakness. Yet there is little doubt that the Portuguese, by the manner of their intervention along the coast and for some distance into the interior, had already flung the gate wide open.

The Portuguese intervened in two ways, and both brought disaster. They sacked and conquered the coastal cities and cut the trading links which had long bound the east coast — and its inland customers and suppliers — with the Persian Gulf and India and the Far East. They pushed into the interior and used their firearms on this side or on that of dynastic wars and rivalries, so as to weaken the whole and deliver the power of government into their ultimate control. Being too weak to hold this power, they left chaos in their wake.

In all this they ruined the coastal cities and devitalized a whole series of African polities in the lands behind the coast. Much of the culture of these southern peoples might persist, and beyond reach of the Portuguese there might be further development. Much, and especially in the southeast, was altogether stultified and brought to an end.

3 *The Gate Flung Open*

GOLDEN DREAMS CHERISHED BY THE EARLIEST OF THE PORTUGUESE discoverers along the southeastern coast had not been long in fading. Already in 1513 Pedro Vaz de Soares, royal agent at Sofala, is writing in long complaint to Lisbon that the "Kaffirs and Moors" deliver gold from the interior only in very small beads and trinkets, and "very little in large melted pieces"; this being quite different, says Soares (who is reflecting sorely on his own disappointed income), from Portuguese experience at Elmina in West Africa where the gold arrives "in large bracelets and necklaces." Like other Europeans, Soares had of course grossly overestimated the reliance on gold of the coastal cities whose wealth had seemed so golden; iron and ivory had long been the staple exports to India and beyond, with gold a steady but always a lesser item.

The first care of the Portuguese had been to sack and subdue the wealthier of the coastal cities, and thanks to their guns, this had proved relatively easy. That done, they tried to carry on the African-Indian trade themselves; but here they would be defeated, despite their stubborn courage and refusal to admit defeat, by their ignorance and greed. As imperialists, they wanted too much and they wanted it too quickly — ambitions that have not been peculiar, of course, to the Portuguese.

They met at first with passive opposition and evasion. Merchants in Sofala even began to weave their own cotton cloth, since they could no longer buy it from India except through the Portuguese. Barbosa explains that since these merchants had no skill in dyeing, they used to unravel the blue cottons of Cambay and "make them up again, so that it becomes a new thing. With this thread and their own white they make much coloured cloth, and from it they gain much gold." This they did, comments the honest Barbosa, "as a remedy after they had perceived that our people were taking from them the trade of the *zambucos*" — the coastal ships from Kilwa and beyond which brought Indian goods to Sofala — "and that they could only obtain goods through the hands of the factors whom the King our Lord has there in his factories and forts."

The *zambucos* continued in any case to get through. "The Moors of Sofala, Mombasa, Malindi, and Kilwa," Barbosa recalls in 1518 of Portuguese experience on the coast, convey their gold, ivory, silk, cottons, and Cambay beads "in very small craft concealed from our ships, and in this wise they carry great store of provender, millet rice and flesh of divers kinds." Complaints of such "smuggling" were numerous. Writing to the king in 1515, Soares adds to his complaint of gold shortage another complaint that "Moorish traders" up and down the coast are getting away with the trade in spite of all attempts to stop them.

Wars in the interior dammed the flow of gold. But Portuguese aggressiveness and greed had also their part in this. Francisco de

Brito, next agent in Sofala after Soares, says that all trade with the interior is at a stop: goods are arriving from India in Portuguese ships, but cannot be sold. The mistake — as one or two of the wiser heads would understand when it was too late — had been to try and seize not only the maritime monopoly but also the overland monopoly. The African coastal cities had learned better than to try to dominate their inland neighbors; Alcançova, in 1506, says that the people of Sofala were free to go four leagues into the interior — beyond that "the Kaffirs rob and kill them." But the Portuguese were not content to buy their goods from inland traders and intermediaries as the coastal cities had used to do. They wanted to buy direct and sell direct, and have the greater profit either way. They pushed, accordingly, into the interior.

Their captains and commercial agents would do the same in India with the same destructive consequences. Thus the Indian beads that were needed in large quantity for the African trade were supposed to be bought only for the direct account of the king of Portugal; but this hardly suited the local commanders and agents, whose cut in the profits suffered thereby. "The captains of Bassein and Chaul," says Whiteway, "became rivals in the trade: both fitted out armed bands to go up country to make purchases"; so that trade through intermediaries soon degenerated into a barely disguised pillage. The Portuguese became as hateful on the coasts of India as on those of Africa.

Penetration of the African interior was more difficult. Yet within thirty or forty years of da Gama's voyages there were Portuguese settlers and traders in settlements on the lower Zambezi, at Sena and as far as Tete; and a certain Antonio Caido was actually living at one of the courts of the Monomotapa, in 1561, when a Portuguese priest called da Silveira got there. The location of this court is uncertain: it was certainly not Great Zimbabwe, however, and was evidently in the hills southwest of Tete on the Zambezi — the Manicaland of present Mozambique.

Ten years later Francisco Barreto led a military expedition inland from Sofala. Dying on the way, he was succeeded by Vasco Fernandes Homem, who returned to the coast after reaching the fringes of the gold-producing country; and no doubt the "mines" he saw were those of the region of the Inyanga-Penhalonga escarpment. His expedition had to fight its way through the coastal kingdom of Quiteve — trading intermediaries between the interior and Sofala — and in so doing they burned down the wood-and-straw "Simbaoe" of the king of Quiteve. Beyond that they were well received by the king of Tsikanga — in the hills of the escarpment — and continued to the "mines."

They traveled hopefully. "Our men, finding themselves in the country where report said that everything was golden, expected to find it in the streets and woods, and to come away laden with it." But they were saddened when they saw that gold was rare and hard to work, and returned to the coast with little to show for their pains.

The lesson was unpopular, and efforts to dominate the interior continued. In a report of Antonio Bocarro, of 1607, there survives another witness to this fatal lust for monopoly. This is a document which records the cession to the Portuguese of all the mines of the Monomotapa and is interesting not only for the light it sheds on Portuguese intentions but also because it precedes, by two hundred eighty-one years, that other cession "of the complete and exclusive charge over all metals and minerals" in Matabeland which the agents of Cecil Rhodes and the British South Africa Company would extract, in 1888, from a sorely troubled Matabele chief.

"I, the emperor Monomotapa"— his name is given as "Gasse Lucere"—"think fit and am pleased to give to His Majesty [of Portugal] all the mines of gold, copper, iron, lead, and pewter which may be in my empire, so long as the king of Portugal, to whom I give the said mines, shall maintain me in my position, that I may have power to order and dispose therein in the same manner as my predecessors . . . and shall give me forces with which to go and take possession of my court and destroy a rebellious robber named Matuzuanha, who has pillaged some of the lands in which there is gold, and prevents merchants trading with their goods."

To be maintained in this way, of course, meant to be controlled; and so it fell out for the Monomotapa. The Portuguese played him easily and brought him safely into the net in 1629, when he signed a treaty accepting Portuguese overlordship as well as the right of Christians to proselytize and build churches, and agreeing "to allow as many mines to be sought and opened as the Portuguese may desire, without ordering any to be closed." He would, moreover, "enquire throughout the kingdom where there is silver, and make it known to the captain of Masapa" — the innermost Portuguese garrison of that time — "that he may inform the governor." He would "within a year expel all the Moors from his kingdom [that is, the coastal traders who rivaled the Portuguese], and those who shall be found there afterwards shall be killed by the Portuguese." And he would allow Portuguese visitors to sit down in his presence.

Yet the fish had fought hard against the hook. The treaty was forced on the Monomotapan empire only after the Portuguese at Sena and Tete had picked a quarrel and followed this with invasion by a well-armed force of two hundred fifty men and "thirty thousand Kaffirs, their vassals." "Two great armies [of the Monomotapa] were destroyed" — in 1628 and 1629 — "and on the second day the greater part of the grandees of the empire were killed . . ." A new emperor, who accepted baptism, was chosen in the place of the resisting but defeated monarch; and thenceforward the Monomotapa was invariably a Christian in name and increasingly a puppet of the invaders.

The dismal story continues. By 1667, the date of Manuel Barreto's invaluable report on the condition of these southeast African "rivers of gold," the Portuguese were in firm possession of the interior as far as Tete and the surrounding countryside.

Secure in their firearms, they did as they pleased; and some of them, like the captains of Sofala and Mozambique, no doubt continued to grow rich on the profits of trade that was little different from loot. "The Portuguese and even the mocoques of Camberari and the rest of the Mokaranga" — the dominant power, that is, and the chiefs and "nobles" who were backing it against their traditional rulers — "possess vast lands, or provinces, which they have bought, and buy every day," from the Monomotapa. By now, adds Barreto, these chiefs and nobles were more powerful than the king. "While I was there," he says, they declared war on him and killed him. "Antonio Ruiz was at the head of this unjust rebellion, and of other great disorders in that conquest."

Having ruined the states they found, they ruined themselves. Much may be read behind Barreto's careful and indignant words. Explaining the failure in gold deliveries, he says that "the Kaffirs would not dig for it through fear of the Portuguese. It is true that the encozes [chiefs] do not wish gold to be dug in their lands, because upon the report of gold being found the Portuguese buy the land from the king" — their puppet — "as has frequently happened, and they, the encozes, being great lords . . . are despoiled of their lands, and become poor capreros, which signifies labourers."

Barreto lists three reasons for the want of gold; and all of them speak clearly for the ruin of this long and stupid intervention. "The repugnance of the encozes, who will allow no digging in their lands, that the Portuguese may not covet them," is the first reason. "The want of population" is the second. "But the principal cause of the want of population is the bad conduct of the Portuguese, from whose violence the Kaffirs flee from our lands to others"; as, indeed, other Africans would later flee and still do, in Angola and Mozambique, from other Portuguese.

"This last is the third case of the want of gold; for in Morando, if they should respond to our demand for it, there comes immediately some powerful man, or in his default some mocoque with his people and slaves, and commits such thefts and violence against the poor diggers that they think it better to hide the gold than to extract any more as a further incentive to our greed and their own misfortune."

And thus the Portuguese, having found peoples in southeastern Africa who were confident and prosperous, and strong in their own evolving civilization, dragged them gradually down to helot misery. By 1719 the Portuguese king is having to explain — when writing to his viceroy in India — that his "vast empire" of central Africa "is in such decay at the present day that no one has dominion over it, because everyone has power there; and although there is a ruling prince, a descendant of the ancient line of Monomotapa, this right and pre-eminence that he hath avail him little, because Changamire and an infinite number of other petty rulers nearly always put these kings to death as soon as they take up the sceptre."

Thanks to Portuguese intervention, in short, the barons had won these Wars of the Roses; and no central government could stand against their reiving and raiding. The ordered power of the interior falters and falls apart; the coastal cities disappear beneath the veiling bush; the Portuguese themselves, here and there a handful of men and women within a lonely fort, slumber and die or fall prisoner to stronger rivals from Europe.

Within sixty years of da Gama's passing of the Cape the conquering vigor of the Portuguese was largely spent; and all that would remain, apart from bold spurts of military endeavor and the ceaseless vigor of individual enterprise, were small colonies that foundered as the years went by, or else wrapped themselves in futile memories of a glory that was gone beyond recall. For this eclipse, needless to say, the fault lay not in any special wickedness they had. Other Europeans would pursue much the same ends by much the same methods; and the record of Portuguese denunciation of greed and loot is often a better one than anything that other invaders can show. Time and again their archives glow with good sense and honest indignation.

The fault lay in their own antiquated system of society. Lacking a strong mercantile class, they understood little but loot and conquest. They stood outside the stream of mercantile democracy; and their rigidly autocratic methods of government and trade proved ruinous for themselves as well as for all those whom they conquered. Their individual genius for enterprise and courage, adaptation and invention, was repeatedly stultified by the stupidity of their institutions; and one disaster, fatally, followed upon another.

Having seized the terminal ports of India and Africa and ruined these by royal order and aristocratic piracy, they blindly wrecked all that sensitive network of mercantile interest which centuries of trading had woven from one end of the Indian Ocean to the other. Their early letters back and forth are full of proofs that they never succeeded in restoring any regular system of international trade. The most that happened was that a little of the old trade went on in spite of them. But having destroyed this great system of exchange and found its restoration beyond their powers, they went off desperately in search of gold; and when gold eluded them they looked for silver; and when silver failed they went for anything they could get, and were finally content with slaves.

Brazil would give their connection with southeastern Africa something of a lasting significance. And yet this was the most sad thing of all, for Brazil wanted from Africa only one commodity, and that was slave labor. From the end of the seventeenth century it is slaving that dominates the Portuguese endeavor on these coasts. And with that, pushed by the wars and everlasting upheavals of the time, hurried by the collapse of central powers and the decay of human values, the domestic slavery of Africa slides easily and grimly into a wholesale traffic in human flesh for sale and export.

By the nineteenth century a few small settlements remained to the Portuguese in the hinterland of their coast of Mozambique. Except for one or two, these were swept away and utterly extinguished by the same barbarian invasions that overwhelmed the stone-built citadels of Khami and of Dhlo Dhlo and the hilltop forts of Inyanga and Penhalonga. And it stands witness to the hatred and dismay which flowed from this earliest European penetration that the mines were forcibly closed, and the miners scattered and killed, by these new conquerors. Thus as late as the 1860s the Zulu warrior-chief Mzila, in order, as Bryant would record, "to prevent the Manica gold mines — where Nxaba, in his passage, had already exterminated the Portuguese — from ever presenting a tempting bait to whiteskin adventurers, had all potential native labourers in that region summarily blotted out, and the country reduced to a wilderness."

It was into this wilderness that Europeans of the late nineteenth century would push their way, and would imagine, as well they might, that what they saw was not the work of yesterday but had endured, in simple desolation, since time began.

twelve

History Begins Anew

We shall encourage and strengthen studies of African culture and history and geography in the institutions of learning in the African states . . .

*Declaration of eight
independent African
States* at Accra in 1958

History Begins Anew

IF THE MIDDLE YEARS OF THIS CENTURY,
pitched between nuclear annihilation and
a dubious peace, may at times seem pessimistic for the future
of humanity, they also record a number of things on the side of
good. Among these last there is the beginning of African emanci-
pation, the joining of the peoples of Africa to the common family
and equality of man.

These curious years, it may after all be seen, will have witnessed
the gradual lifting of a racialist mythology that has blurred and
muddled the progress of humanity, at one time or another, in one
way or another, everywhere in the world; yet nowhere worse than
in Africa. These years restore or at any rate prepare to restore a
decisive responsibility for their own lives to some seventy or eighty
million "black" Africans of the British, French and Italian colonial
empires; while other Africans — as well, of course, as the "white"
Africans of the Arab north — have taken the same direction.
There is now not a single African land, however small, remote, or
barricaded from the outside world, where men and women do not
meet together and discuss a different future.

In this brief review of some aspects of African history before
the period of major colonial contact and conquest, many matters
have been left aside, many problems passed over in silence, many
controversies only hinted at. Even a longer book and a wiser writer
must have done the same. For it is the next fifty years that will see
the detailed writing of African history — the putting together of a
coherent picture that is still beyond ignorance and doubt, and
perhaps beyond prejudice as well. Meanwhile this small attempt

at saying what seems clear and reasonable to believe, in several large matters, may be useful if it has shown that these emergent states do not come out of the void of a motionless past.

They spring from contact with the outside world — often a painful contact, sometimes a creative one; but they also spring from the inner dynamism of their own beginnings. The pastoral states of the old Sudan were not brief interludes of foreign growth. The fertile cities of the eastern coast were not strange foreign jewels on a mournful silent shore. The walls and towers of Zimbabwe were neither a monument to Mediterranean enterprise nor the solitary triumph of unknown peoples who have disappeared.

They and the life they had were part of a continuous movement which might wonderfully wander back and forth upon the stones of time but would always, in the end, resume its line of march. They were part of a growth that was no way different, in its essence, from the growth of society anywhere else in the world. Whether in music or in thought, the arts of government or the arts of life, these peoples made, and make, their valid contribution to the common culture of humanity.

Their history begins anew. They reappear today in the sad evening of the world of nation-states; yet their own tradition, one may note, was seldom one of narrow nationality. Their genius was for integration — integration by conquest as the times prescribed, but also by an ever fruitful mingling and migration; they were never patient of exclusive frontiers. They grew in large units, not in small ones. Thus the old empire of Kanem, with Mali and Songhay the greatest of all the power-concentrations of the old Sudan, had its proto-federal structure: its governing council of twelve princes who ruled the territories of the far-spread state through many generations.

Nineteenth century imperialism cut through boundaries and peoples, and left for a later Africa the problem of redrawing frontiers on a rational plan. As independence widens across these coming years, will this plan stop short with the making of nation-states, aping European example? Will these peoples be content merely to copy — and this in a period when the nation-state has lost its power to stimulate and become so often an obstacle to further growth? Must Africa renew the proliferation of nations and of national quarrels?

It remains to be seen. One may note in this connection, though, that the diverse peoples of Nigeria were preparing in 1959 for independence within a federal structure; while around them on their land frontiers the many and varied peoples of French West and Equatorial Africa were doing the same — and with them the emphasis on federalism, on integration within large units, was still easier to see. An independent federation of the lands of French West Africa would eclipse the size of all the medieval empires of the Old Sudan. African peoples followed their own road in the past; there is nothing to say that they will not follow it, constructively, creatively, again.

Their failings have been common talk for years, for centuries. Now it may be time to speak of their achievements. And their achievements, while the fuller canvas of their history unrolls across these years, will increasingly be seen and understood. We are only at the beginning of that story.

Bibliography

The following is a list of the principal sources I have used, but is comprehensive in no other sense. As an excuse for depriving the interested reader of a fuller list, it may be mentioned that the bibliography for Zimbabwe alone, as compiled by Miss Patricia Stevens in 1950 (University of Cape Town), has three hundred fifty-eight entries; and others have accumulated since. Under *One* I have included a number of general books and books bearing on tribal history and migration legend, and to avoid duplication I have listed books only once although they may be referred to in several chapters.

A few abbreviations:

ESA   Ethnographical Survey of Africa (ed.) Daryll Forde, International African Institute. 1950 on.
IFAN   Institut Français de l'Afrique Noire.
PPAC   Proceedings of the Third Pan-African Congress on Prehistory, Livingstone, N. Rhodesia, 1955.
SNR   *Sudan Notes and Records.*
TNR   *Tanganyika Notes and Records.*
UJ   *Uganda Journal.*

In addition, "first London conference" means the conference on history and archeology in Africa held at London University (School of Oriental and African Studies) in 1953, while "second London conference" means its successor in 1957.

ONE

THE PEOPLING OF ANCIENT AFRICA

Alimen, H.   *The Prehistory of Africa,* 1957
Arkell, A. J.   "Archaeology South of Khartoum" (paper contributed to second London conference)

	Shaheinab, 1953
Baumann, H., and Westermann, D.	*Les Peuples et les Civilisations de l'Afrique*, Paris, 1948
Briggs, L. C.	"Review of Physical Anthropology of Sahara and Its Prehistoric Implications." *Man* 19, 1957
Busia, K. A.	"The Ashanti," 1954. See Forde.
Butt, A.	"Nilotes of the Anglo-Egyptian Sudan and Uganda," *ESA*, 1952
Childe, V. G.	*New Light on the Most Ancient East*, 1934
	Dawn of European Civilisation, 1939
	Prehistory of European Society, 1958
Childs, G. M.	*Umbundu Kinship and Character*, 1949
Cleene, N. de	"Le Clan Matrimonial dans la Société Indigène," *Inst. Roy. Col. Belge*, 1946
Cole, S.	*The Prehistory of East Africa*, 1954
Colson, E., and Gluckman, M.	*Seven Tribes of British Central Africa*, 1951
Cooke, H. B. S.	"The Problem of Quaternary Glacio-Pluvial Correlation in East and Southern Africa," *PPAC*, p. 51
Danquah, J. B.	*Akan Society*, 1949
Dart, R. A.	"Proto-Human Inhabitants of Southern Africa" (in broadcast series), Johannesburg, 1953
Delafosse, M.	*Les Noirs de l'Afrique*, reprinted 1941
Diop, A.	(ed.) *L'Art Négre*, 1951
Diop, Cheik Anta	*Nations Négres et Culture*, 1954
Douglas, M.	"The Lele of Kasai," 1954. See Forde.
Du Bois, W. E. B.	*The Souls of Black Folk*, 1903
	The World and Africa, 1947
Elisofon, E.	*The Sculpture of Africa*, 1958
Ellenberger, D. F.	*History of the Basuto*, 1912
Evans-Pritchard, E.E.	*Witchcraft, Oracles and Magic among the Azande*, 1937
	Political System of the Anuak of the Anglo-Egyptian Sudan, 1940

	Divine Kingship of the Shilluk of the Nilotic Sudan, 1948
	"A history of the Kingdom of Gbudwe," *Zaire,* Oct., 1956
	"Zande Warfare," *Anthropos* 52, p. 239, 1957
	"Zande Border Raids," *Africa,* p. 217, July 1957
	"Zande Kings and Princes," *Anthropol. Qtrly.,* p. 61, July 1957
Ewer, R. F.	"Faunal Evidence on the Dating of the Australopithecinae," *PPAC,* p. 135
Fage, J. D.	*An Atlas of African History,* 1958
Forde, Daryll	(ed.) *Ethnographical Survey of Africa,* 1950 onwards
	(ed.) *African Worlds,* 1954
	(ed.) *Efik Traders of Old Calabar,* 1956
Fortes, M., and Evans-Pritchard, E.E.	*African Political Systems,* 1940
Frobenius, L.	*Histoire de la Civilisation Africaine,* Paris, 1952
Gluckman, M.	*The Kingdom of the Zulu in S. Africa.* See Fortes.
	Custom and Conflict in Africa, 1956
	Judicial Process among the Barotse of N. Rhodesia, 1957
Griaule, M., and Dieterlen, G.	"The Dogon," 1954. See Forde.
Gulliver, P., and P. H.	"Central Nilo-Hamites," *ESA,* 1953
Hamilton, R. A.	(ed.) *History and Archaeology in Africa* (Report of the first London conference), published 1955
	Oral Tradition: Central Africa (paper contributed to first London conference)
Herskovits, M. J.	*Acculturation,* 1938
	Dahomey (2 vols.), 1938
	The Myth of the Negro Past, 1941
Huntingford, G.W.B.	"Northern Nilo-Hamites," *ESA,* 1953

	"Southern Nilo-Hamites," *ESA*, 1953
	"The Nandi of Kenya," *ESA*, 1955
Jaspan, M. A.	"Ila-Tonga Peoples of N.W. Rhodesia," *ESA*, 1953
Jones, D. H.	"Oral Tradition: West Africa, The Forest" (paper contributed to first London conference)
	"Oral Tradition: The Yoruba" (paper contributed to first London conference)
Julien, Ch.-A.	*Histoire de l'Afrique*, 1955
Kenyon, K.	*Digging up Jericho*, 1957
Krige, E. J.	*Social System of the Zulu*, 1936
	The Lovedu of the Transvaal (with J. D. Krige), 1954. See Forde.
Kuper, H.	"The Swazi," *ESA*, 1953
	"The Shona and Ndebele of S. Rhodesia" (with A. J. B. Hughes and J. van Velsen), *ESA*, 1955
Lane-Poole, E. H.	*Discovery of Africa: Maps of the Rhodes-Livingstone Institute*, 1950
Lawrence, A. W.	"Archaeological Situation in Nigeria and the Gold Coast, 1953" (paper contributed to first London conference)
Leakey, L. S. B.	*The Stone Age Races of Kenya*, 1935
Lewis, I. M.	"Population Movements in Somaliland" (paper contributed to second London conference)
Lilley, S.	*Men, Machines and History*, 1948
Lowe, C. J. van Riet	"The Kafuan Culture" *PPAC*, p. 207
Mason, J. A.	*The Ancient Civilizations of Peru*, 1957
McCulloch, M.	"Southern Lunda and Related Peoples," *ESA*, 1951-1953
	"Ovimbundu of Angola," *ESA*, 1952
Middleton, J.	"Central Tribes of the N.E. Bantu," *ESA*, 1953
Monod, T.	"Découverte de Nouveaux Instruments en Os dans l'Ouest Africain" (with R. Mauny), *PPAC*, p. 242
Nadel, S. F.	*A Black Byzantium*, 1942

Oakley, K. P. "Dating the Australopithecinae" *PPAC*, p. 155

Paulme, D. "A Propos des Kuduo Ashanti." See Diop, A.

Prins, A. H. J. "Coastal Tribes of the N.E. Bantu," *ESA*, 1952

Richards, A. I. "The Political System of the Bantu Tribes in N.E. Rhodesia," 1940. See Fortes.

Schapera, I. "The Tswana," *ESA*, 1953

Seligman, C. G. *The Races of Africa*, 1930

Sheddick, V. G. J. "The Southern Sotho," *ESA*, 1953

Tempels, P. *La Philosophie Bantou*, 1948

Thompson, F. C. "Early Metallurgy of Copper and Bronze," *Man* 1, 1958

Tobias, P. T. "Bushmen of the Kalahari," *Man* 36, 1957

Torday, E. *On the Trail of the Bushongo*, 1925

Underwood, L. "Bronze Age Technology in W. Asia and N. Europe," *Man* 13, 37, and 64, 1958

Vaillant, G. C. *The Aztecs of Mexico*, 1950

Vansina, J. *Les Tribus Ba-Kuba et les Peuplades Apparentées*, 1954

Westermann, D. *Geschichte Afrikas*, 1952

Wilson, M. *Good Company: A Study of Nyakusa Age-Villages*, 1951

TWO

THE MYSTERY OF MEROË

Arkell, A. J. "Archaeological Research in West Africa," *Antiquity* 71, 1941

"Darfur Antiquities," *SNR* 27, 1946, pp. 105, 201

"Gold Coast Copies of 5th-7th Century Bronze Lamps," *Antiquity* 38-40, 1950

"History of Darfur A.D. 1200-1700," *SNR*

	32, pp. 37, 207, 1951; 33, pp. 129, 244, 1952
	A History of the Sudan, 1955
Balfour-Paul, H. G.	"Darfur," *Kush* 2, p. 27, 1954
	History and Antiquities of Darfur, 1955
Breasted, J. H.	*Ancient Records of Egypt: Vols. 1-4,* 1906
	A History of Egypt (2nd ed.), 1921
Cambridge Ancient History	*Vol. X: The Augustine Empire*
Dows, Dunham	"Outline of the Ancient History of the Sudan, 1947," *SNR* 28: p. 1
Herodotus	The Histories (trans de Selincourt), 1954
Kirwan, L. P.	"A Survey of Nubian Origins," *SNR* 20, p. 47
Paul, A.	*History of the Beja Tribes of the Sudan,* 1954
Reisner, G. A.	"Outline of the Ancient history of the Sudan," *SNR* 1, p. 1
Shinnie, P.	*Medieval Nubia,* 1954
	"On Meroë," *Kush* 3, p. 82
Stock, H.	"Proposed Revision of Pharaonic Dating," *Antiquity,* Sept., 1954
Wainwright, G. A.	"Iron in the Napatan and Meroitic Ages," *SNR,* p. 5, 1945

THREE

KINGDOMS OF THE OLD SUDAN

Barth, H.	*Travels and Discoveries in North and Central Africa 1849-1855* (5 vols.), 1857
Battuta, Ibn (Mohammed ibn Abd Allah)	*Travels in Asia and Africa 1325-1354* (trans. H. A. R. Gibb), 1929
Bekri (El, Abd Allah ibn Abd al Aziz)	*Description de l'Afrique Septentrionale* (trans. de Slane), 1859
Bloch, M.	*La Société Féodale: La Formation des Liens de Dépendance,* 1939

	La Société Féodale: Les Classes et le Gouvernement des Hommes, 1949
Bovill, E. W.	*Caravans of the Old Sahara*, 1933
	Golden Trade of the Moors, 1958
Bruce, J.	*Travels to Discover the Source of the Nile* (5 vols.), 1790
Cadamosto	*Voyages* (ed.), G. R. Crone, Hakluyt Society, 1937
	Voyages. See Ramusio.
Crawford, O. G. S.	*The Fung Kingdom of Sennar*, 1951
Delafosse, M.	*Haut-Sénégal-Niger* (1st series, 3 vols.), 1912
Fage, J. D.	*An Introduction to the History of West Africa*, 1955
Hodgkin, T.	"Historic Ghana," *West Africa*, June 14, 1952
	"Koumbi Saleh and the Capital of Ghana," *West Africa*, March 28, 1953
Jeffreys, M. D. W.	"Pre-Columbian Negroes in America," *Scientia*, July-Aug., 1953
	"Pre-Columbian Maize in Africa," *Nature*, p. 965, Nov. 21, 1953
Kati, Mahmoud	*Tarikh el Fettach* (Trans. Houdas and Delafosse), 1913
Lantier, R.	"Les Bronzes Sao," 1953. See Lebeuf 1950, Appendix One.
Lebeuf, J. F., and Masson-Détourbet, A.	*La Civilisation du Tchad*, 1950
	"Récentes Récherches Archéologiques et Préhistoriques en AEF et en Cameroun" (paper contributed to second London conference)
Leo Africanus (Hassan ibn Mohammed el Wazzan el Zayyati)	*History and Description of Africa* (Trans. Pory, 1600), Hakluyt Society, 1896
Lhote, H.	"Le Cheval et le Chameau dans les Peintures et Gravures Rupestres du Sahara," *Bull. de l'IFAN*, July, 1953
	"Contribution à l'Histoire des Touaregs

Sudanais," *Bull. de l'IFAN* 3 and 4, p. 391, 1956

Peintures Préhistoriques du Sahara: Catalogue for Exhibition, 1958

A la Découverte des Fresques du Tassili, 1958

Mauny, R.   "Une Route Préhistorique à travers le Sahara Occidental," *Bull. de l'IFAN,* p. 341, 1947

"L'Afrique Occidentale d'après les Auteurs arabes anciens," *Notes de l'IFAN,* Oct. 1948

"Le Bélier Dieu," *Notes de l'IFAN,* Jan., 1949

"Notes d'Archéologie au Sujet de Gao," *Bull. de l'IFAN,* July-Sept., 1951

"Essai sur l'Histoire des métaux en Afrique Occidentale," *Bull. de l'IFAN,* p. 545, 1952

"Préhistoire et Protohistoire de la Région d'Akjoujit" (with J. Hallemans), *PPAC,* p. 248

"The Question of Ghana," *Africa* No. 3 of 24

"Campagne de Fouilles à Koumbi Saleh" (with R. Thomassey), *Bull. de l'IFAN,* p. 438, April, 1951; p. 117, April, 1956

"Etat Actuel de Nos Connaissances sur la Préhistoire et l'Archéologie de la Haute Volta," *Notes de l'IFAN,* Jan., 1957

Meek, J.   *A Sudanese Kingdom,* 1931

Meyerowitz, E. L. R.   *The Akan of Ghana,* 1958

Palmer, S. H. R.   *Sudanese Memoirs* (3 Vols.), 1923

History of the first twelve years of the Reign of Mai Idris Alooma of Bornu (trans.), 1926

The Bornu, Sahara and Sudan, 1936

Park, Mungo   *Travels,* Everyman, 1954

Pirenne, H.   *Economic and Social History of Medieval Europe*, 1937

Ramusio, G.-B.   *Delle Navigationi et Viaggi, Vol. 1*, 1563

Rouch, J.   *Les Songhay*, 1954

Sadi, Abderrahman-es   *Tarikh es Sudan* (trans. Houdas), 1898

Sauvaget, J.   "Les Epitaphes Royales de Gao," *Bull. de l'IFAN*, April, 1950

Sharwood Smith, B.E.   *Kano Survey*, 1950

Thomassey, R.   See Mauny, 1951 and 1956.

Urvoy, Y.   *Histoire des Populations du Soudan Centrale (Colonie du Niger)*, 1936

                          Histoire de L'Empire du Bornou, 1949

Wainwright, G. A.   "Egyptian Origin of a Ram-headed Breastplate from Lagos," *Man* 231, 1951

FOUR

BETWEEN THE NIGER AND THE CONGO

Adam, L.   *Primitive Art* (3rd edition), 1954

Bacon, R. H.   *Benin, the City of Blood*, 1897

Biobaku, S. O.   Lugard Lectures, Lagos 1955

Blake, J. W. (ed.)   *Europeans in West Africa 1450-1560* (2 vols.), Hakluyt Society, 1942

Creel, H. G.   *Studies in Early Chinese Culture*, 1938

Delgado, R.   *História de Angola, Vol. 3*, 1953

Dike, K. O.   *Trade and Politics in the Niger Delta 1830-1885*, 1956

Fagg, B. E. B.   "Cave Paintings and Rock Gongs of Birnin Kudu," *PPAC*, p. 306

                          "A Life-sized Terracotta Head from Nok," *Man* 95, 1956

                          "Archaeological Field Work since 1953" (paper contributed to second London conference)

Fagg, W.   "De l'Art des Yoruba." See Diop, A.

                          "The Seligman Ivory Mask from Benin," *Man* 143, 1957

                          The Sculpture of Africa, 1958

Goodwin, A. J. H.   "Benin Palace Excavations, 1957" (paper contributed to second London conference)

Ihle, A.   *Das Alte Königreich Kongo*, 1929

Pereira, Duarte Pacheco   *Esmeraldo de Situ Orbis* (c. 1506-1508) (trans. and ed. R. Mauny), Bissau 1956 (Centro d'Estudos da Guiné Portuguesa)

Pigafetta, F.   A *Report on the Kingdom of Congo, etc.* (drawn out of the writings and discourses of Duarte Lopez, trans. Hutchinson), London, 1881

Willett, F.   "Archaeological Investigations among the Yoruba" (paper contributed to second London conference)

FIVE

TO THE SOUTHWARD

Clark, J. D.   "The Newly Discovered Nachikufu Culture of N. Rhodesia," *S. Afr. Arch. Bull.*, p. 19, 1950
"Review of Prehistoric Research in N. Rhodesia and Nyasaland," *PPAC*, p. 412
"Archaeology and Ethnography" (paper contributed to second London conference)

SIX

TRADERS OF THE INDIAN OCEAN

Alberuni   *Alberuni's India* (2 Vols., trans. Sachau), 1910

Allen, J. W. T.   "Rhapta," *TNR* 27 of 1949

Baxter, H. C.   "Pangani: The Trade Centre of Ancient History," *TNR*, p. 15, 1944

Chao, Ju-kua   *Chu Fan Chi* (trans. and ed. F. Hirth and W. W. Rockhill), 1911

Duyvendak, J. J. L.   "The True Dates of the Chinese Maritime Expeditions in the Early Fifteenth Century," *T'oung Pao*, Vol. *34*, 1938
China's Discovery of Africa, 1949

Edrisi (El, Abu Abdallah Mohammed ben Mohammed)   *La Géographie d'Edrisi*, 2 vols. (trans. Jaubert), 1836

Fa, Hsien   *Travels 399-414* A.D. (trans. H. A. Giles), 1923

Hamdani (El, Hasan ibn Ahmad)   *Antiquities of South Arabia*, Vol. *3* (trans. Nabib Amin Faris), 1938

Hirth, F.   See Chao, Ju-kua.

Mas'udi (El, Abdul Hassan ibn Hussein ibn Ali)   *Meadows of Gold and Mines of Gems* (trans. Sprenger), 1841 [one volume only published]
Maçoudi, Les Prairies d'Or (trans. C. Barbier de Meynard et Pavet de Courteille), 1864 [mainly volumes 1 and 3]

Needham, J.   *Science and Civilisation in China*, Vol. *1*, 1954; Vol. 6 [to be published]

Pelliot, P.   "Les Grands Voyages Maritimes Chinois au début de la XV Siécle," *T'oung Pao*, Vol. *30*, 1933

Periplus of Erythraean Sea.   See Schoff.

Piggott, S.   *Prehistoric India*, 1950

Rockhill, W. W.   Notes on the Relations and Trade of China with the Eastern Archipelago and the Coast of the Indian Ocean during the Fourteenth Century: part 1: *T'oung Pao*, Vol. *15*, 1914

Schoff, W. H.   *Periplus of the Erythraean Sea* (trans.), 1912

Storbeck, F.   "Die berichte der Arabischen Geographen des Mittelalters über Ostafrika," (Mittheilungen des Seminars für Orientalischen Sprachen), p. 97, 1914

Taylor, E. G. R.   *The Haven-Finding Art*, 1956

Vincent, W. Commerce and Navigation of the Ancients in the Indian Ocean (2 vols.), 1807

Warmington, E. H. *The Commerce Between the Roman Empire and India,* 1928

Wheeler, Sir M. "Archaeology in East Africa," TNR 40, 1955

  Rome Beyond the Imperial Frontiers, reprinted 1955

SEVEN

FAIR CITIES OF STONE

Arkell, A. J. "Cambay and the Bead Trade," *Antiquity,* Sept., 1956

Barbosa, Duarte *The Book of Duarte Barbosa* (2 vols., ed. M. L. Dames), Hakluyt Society, 1918

Coupland, R. *East Africa and Its Invaders,* reprinted 1956

Dorman, M. H. "Kilwa Civilisation and the Kilwa Ruins," *TNR,* p. 61, 1938

Elliot, J. A. G. "A Visit to the Bajun Islands, *Jnl. Afr. Socy.* 1925-1926 [four articles numbers 97-100]

Freeman-Grenville, G. S. P. "The Tanganyika Coast" (paper contributed to second London conference)

Grottanelli, V. L. *Pescatori dell'Oceano Indiano,* 1955

Guillain, M *Documents sur l'Histoire, la Géographie at le Commerce de l'Afrique Orientale* (3 vols.), 1856

Harries, L. "Swahili Epic Literature," TNR 30, 1951

Kirkman, J. S. *The Arab City of Gedi,* 1954

Mathew, G. "Islamic Merchant Cities of East Africa," *The Times* 26, p. 6, 1951

  "Recent Discoveries in East African Archaeology," *Antiquity,* Dec., 1953

  "The Archaeological Situation in East

Africa" (paper contributed to first London conference)

"The Culture of the East African Coast in the Seventeenth and Eighteenth Centuries," *Man* 61, 1956

"Chinese Porcelain in East Africa and on the Coast of South Arabia," *Oriental Art*, No. 2, 1956

"The East Coast Cultures," *Africa South* 2, No. 2, p. 59, 1958

Ravenstein, E. G.   (ed.) *Roteiro* of First Voyage of Vasco da Gama, Hakluyt Society, 1898

Revington, T. M.   "Some Notes on the Mafia Island Group," *TNR*, p. 33, 1936

Stigand, C. H.   *The Land of Zinj*, 1913

EIGHT

AFTER AXUM

Abbadie, A.d'   *Douze Ans dans la Haute Ethiopie*, 1868

Azais, R. P., and Chambord, R.   *Cinq Années de Récherches Archéologiques en Ethiopie*, 1931

Bent, J. T.   *The Sacred City of the Ethiopians*, 1893

Burton, R. F.   *First Footsteps in East Africa*, 1856

Castanhosa   *Portuguese Expedition to Abyssinia in 1541-1543* (trans. Whiteway), Hakluyt Society, 1902

Cerulli, E.   *Storia della Letteratura Etiopica*, 1956
Somalia: Scritti Vari, 1957

Crazzolara, J. P.   "Part 1: Lwoo Migrations," *The Lwoo*, 1950

Doresse, J.   *L'Empire du Prêtre Jean* (2 vols.), 1957

Fosbrooke, H. A.   "Rift Valley Ruins," *TNR*, p. 58, 1938
"Early Iron Age Sites in Tanganyika, etc.," *PPAC*, p. 318

Gillman, C.   "Annotated List of Ancient and Modern indigenous stone structures in East Africa," *TNR*, p. 44, 1944

Gray, Sir John   *The British in Mombasa 1824-1826*, 1958
Huntingford, G.W.B.   "On Blacksmiths," *Man* 262, 1931
                          "Azanian Civilisation of Kenya," *Antiquity*, p. 153, 1933
                          "Azania," *Anthropos* 35, p. 209, 1940-1941
                          "Hagiolithic Cultures of East Africa," *Eastern Anthropologist* 3, p. 119, 1950
                          "Oral Tradition: The Sidama Peoples" (paper contributed to first London conference)

Jensen, E.   *Im Lande des Gada*, 1936

Jones, A. H. M., and   *A History of Ethiopia*, reprinted 1955
  Monroe, E.

Krapf, J. L.   *Reisen in Ost Afrika 1837-1855* [including Rebmann's travels] (2 vols.), 1858

Leakey, L. S. B.   "Preliminary Report on the Engaruka Ruins," *TNR*, p. 57, 1936

Neuville, H.   "Contribution à l'Etude des Mégaliths Abyssins," *Anthropologie*, pp. 255 and 523, 1928

Nowack, E.   *Land und Volk der Konso*, 1954

Oberg, K.   *The Kingdom of Ankole in Uganda*, 1940. See Fortes.

Pankhurst, S.   *Ethiopia: A Cultural History*, 1955

Pike, A. H.   "Soil Conservation among the Matengo Tribe," *TNR*, p. 79, 1938

Watson, C. B. G.   "Wells, Cairns, and Rainpools in Kenya Colony," *Man*, p. 50, 1927

Werner, A.   "Some Notes on the Wapokomo of the Tana Valley," *Jnl. Afr. Socy.*, 1912-1913
                          "The Galla of the East African Protectorate," *Jnl. Afr. Socy.*, 1914

Wilson, G. E. H.   "The Ancient Civilisation of the Rift Valley," *Man* 298, 1932

Worsley, P. M., and   "Remains of an Earlier People in
  Rumberger, J. P.   Uhehe," *TNR*, p. 27, 1949

NINE

THE BUILDERS OF THE SOUTH

Barros, J. de	*Da Asia* (24 vols.), 1777 [first three *decadas* only, 1552-1553]
Beck, H.	"Rhodesian Beads," See Caton-Thompson, *Zimbabwe Culture*, Appendix One.
Bryant, A. T.	*Olden Times in Zululand and Natal*, 1929
Caton-Thompson, G.	*The Zimbabwe Culture: Ruins and Reactions*, 1931
	Trade Beads in Medieval East and Central Africa (note contributed to second London conference)
Couto, D. de	See Barros. *Decadas* 4 to 7 incl.
Crawford, O. G. S.	"Inyanga," *Antiquity*, June, 1950
Falcão, Luiz de Figueiredo	Livro em que se contem Toda a Fazenda e real Patrimoniio dos reinos de Portugal, India e Ilhas Adjacentes, 1607 (published 1859)
Fouché, L.	*Mapungubwe: Ancient Bantu Civilization on the Limpopo*, Excavation Reports, 1937
Galloway, A.	"Skeletal Remains at Mapungubwe." See Fouché, p. 127
Gardner, G. A.	"Mapungubwe 1935-1940," *S. Afr. Arch. Bull.*, Sept., 1955 and June, 1956. See also Walton for comment.
Goodwin, A. J. H.	"Metal Working among the Early Hottentots," *S. Afr. Arch. Bull.*, p. 46, June, 1956
Hall, R. N.	*Ancient Ruins of Rhodesia*, 1904
	Great Zimbabwe, 1905
	Prehistoric Rhodesia, 1909
Huntingford, G.W.B.	"Archaeological Survey of South-East Africa" (paper contributed to first London conference)

354 Bibliography

Jones, N.
"Mapungubwe: the 1934 Expedition."
See Fouché, p. 9.
The Prehistory of S. Rhodesia, 1949

Juta, C.
"Beads and Pottery from Lourenço Marques," *S. Afr. Arch. Bull.*, p. 9, March, 1956

Lowe, C. J. van Riet
"Mapungubwe," *Antiquity*, p. 282, Sept., 1936

MacIver, D. R.
Mediaeval Rhodesia, 1906

Malan, B. D.
"Ten Years of Archaeology in South Africa," *S. Afr. Arch. Bull.*, June, 1956

Mason, A. York
"The Penhalonga Ruins," *S. Afr. Jnl. Sci.*, p. 559, 1933

Pearson, R.
"Gold from Mapungubwe." See Fouché, p. 116.

Pole-Evans, I. B.
"Mapungubwe: Report on Vegetable Remains." See Fouché, p. 31.

Potekhine, I. I.
Formation of National Community among the South African Bantu [in Russian], 1955

Robinson, K. R.
"Excavations at Khami Ruins, Matabeleland," *PPAC*, p. 357

Schofield, J. F.
"Mapungubwe: The Pottery." See Fouché, p. 32.
"Ancient Ruins Company Ltd.," *Man*, p. 19, 1935
"Survey of the Recent Prehistory of S. Rhodesia," *S. Afr. Jnl. Sci.*, p. 81, 1942

Selous, F. C.
Travel and Adventure in S.E. Africa, 1893
A Hunter's Wanderings in Africa, 1907

Stanley, G. H.
"Mapungubwe: Report on Slag." See Fouché, p. 30.
"Mapungubwe: Metallurgical Material." See Fouché, p. 117.

Summers, R. F. H.
"Iron Age Cultures in S. Rhodesia," *S. Afr. Jnl. Sci.*, Nov., 1950
"Inyanga: A Preliminary Report," *Antiquity* 102, 1952

	"Archaeology in Southern Rhodesia 1900-1955," *PPAC*, p. 396
	"Possible Influences of the Iron Age in Southern Rhodesia," *S. Afr. Jnl. Sci.*, p. 43, Sept., 1955
	"African History and Archaeology in Southern Africa 1950-1957" (paper contributed to second London conference)
	"Zimbabwe: Capital of an Ancient Rhodesian Kingdom," *Africa South* 2, No. 2, 1958
Theal, G. M.	*Records of South-Eastern Africa*, 1898 [Mainly vols. 1 to 4.]
Wainwright, G. A.	"The Founders of the Zimbabwe Civilisation," *Man* 80, 1949
Walton, J.	"Corbelled Stone Huts in Southern Africa," *Man* 82, 1951
	"Some Features of the Monomotapa Culture," *PPAC*, p. 336
	"Soapstone Birds of Zimbabwe," *S. Afr. Arch. Bull.*, Sept., 1955
	"Mapungubwe and Bambandyanalo" (Comment on Gardner. See above.) *S. Afr. Arch. Bull.*, March, 1956
Weber, M.	"Mapungubwe: Notes on Gold Ornaments." See Fouché, p. 114
Whitty, A.	"Origins of the Stone Architecture of Zimbabwe," *PPAC*, p. 366
Wieschoff, H. A.	*The Zimbabwe Monomotapa Culture in S.E. Africa*, 1941

TEN

THE REALITY BEHIND THE RUINS

Burton, R. F. (ed.)	*Lacerda's Journey to Cazembe* [including travels of Monteiro and Gamitto], 1873
Gamitto	See Burton.
Gray, J. M.	"The Riddle of Biggo," *UJ*, p. 226, 1935

Lanning, E. C.   "Ancient Earthworks in W. Uganda,"
                      UJ, p. 51, 1953
                      "Protohistoric Pottery in Uganda,"
                      PPAC, p. 313
                      "Masaka Hill: An Ancient Centre of
                      Worship," *UJ*, p. 24, 1954
                      "Notes on Certain Shafts in Buganda
                      and Toro," *UJ*, p. 187, 1954
                      "The Munsa Earthworks," *UJ*, p. 177,
                      1955
                      "The Cairns of Koki, Buganda," *UJ*, p.
                      176, 1957
                      "An Iron Mining Tool from Uganda,
                      with a Note on Rhodesian Parallels,"
                      Man 40, 1958
Maquet, J. J.   *The Kingdom of Ruanda*, 1954. See
                      Forde.
Oliver, R. A.   "A Question about the Bachwezi," *UJ*,
                      p. 135, 1953
                      "Oral Tradition: East Africa" (paper
                      contributed to first London conference)
                      "Traditional Histories of Buganda, Bun-
                      yoro and Nkole," *Jnl. Roy. Anthrop.
                      Inst.* 85, p. 111, 1955
Wayland, E. J.   "Notes on the Biggo bya Mugenyi," *UJ*,
                      p. 21, 1934
Wachsmann, K. P.   "Ancient Earthworks in W. Uganda:
                      Notes on Finds," *UJ*, p. 190, 1954

ELEVEN

DECLINE AND FALL

Axelson, E.   *South-East Africa*, 1940
                     "The Portuguese in Southeast Africa
                     1488-1700" (paper contributed to sec-
                     ond London conference)
Linschoten, J. H. van *Voyages to the East Indies* (2 vols.),
                     Hakluyt Society, 1885

Livingstone, D.   *Missionary Travels and Researches in Southern Africa,* 1857

Strandes, J.   *Die Portugiesenseit von deutsch- und englisch- Ostafrika,* 1899

Whiteway, R. S.   *The Rise of the Portuguese Power in India 1497-1550,* 1899

Index

Abderrahman es Sadi, 77
Abiri, 140
Abu Abdallah Mohammed, emperor of Songhay, 99
Abu Bakr, 84
Abu Isaq es Saheli, 92
Abulfeda, 74, 155
Adal, sultanate of, 109
Adlan, king of Sudan, 71
Adulis, port of Axum, 218
Agades, 90, 95
Agathacides of Alexandria, 172
Agriculture: Jordan valley, 26; Nile valley, 26; Azanian, 233-234
Ahmed Baba, 103
Ain Fara, Darfur, 113-115
Aizanas, king of Axum, 218
Akan people, 62-64, 127
Alcançova, 260, 322, 326
Ali Dinar, sultan of Darfur, 115
Allakoi Keita, founder of Mali, 89
Almeida, 198-199
Amanirenas, Queen, 39-40
Amanitere, Queen, 39-40
Amenemhat II, Pharaoh, 31
Amenophis III, Pharaoh, 61
Amharic people, 219
Ammar Pasha, Moorish invader, 166
Amratian culture of Egypt, 65
Amun: worshiped at Napata, 44, symbol of, 61
Angkor Vat, Cambodia, 184
Angola, 310
Animism, 137
Anzuru, state of, 120
Aoudaghast, tributary city of Ghana, 83
Arabia: established itself in Ethiopia, 45; trading contacts, disappearance

of its early civilizations, 171-172; prosperity, 172-173; its traders on the African coast, 177-180; trades in the Far East, 179; and colonization of E. African coast, 206-207; practice of hillside terracing, 219-220
Arabs, 14, 104, 166; and the slave trade, 130
Architecture, 305-306
Arkell, Dr. A. J., 12, 28, 32, 43, 45, 61, 106-108, 112-114
Arma, the (of Songhay), 119
Art: figurine cult in Nok, 57-59, 70, 140-141, 144; of Benin and Ife, 139-141; of the Sao and Dan-Ngere peoples, 143-144; of the Baoulé and the Bambara, 144
Askia the Great. See Mohammed Askia.
Askia Ishak, emperor of Songhay, 103
Asseear, 7
Assuan, 29
Assyrians: invade Lower Egypt, 44, 54, knowledge of iron, 47-48
Ausan, Arabian state of, 153, 173, 178
d'Aveiro, Affonso, 136
Axum, kingdom of, 45, 53, 104, 173, 216, 232; Castanhosa's account of, 215-216; continuity and isolation, 216-217; Habashan invasion of, 218; introduction of Christianity, 218; hillside terracing, 219-220; drystone building, 220-221; phallic symbolism, 221-222; mystery of its standing stones, 221-222; summit forts and dwellings, 222-223